The Whole Book

THE WHOLE BOOK

Cultural Perspectives on the

Medieval Miscellany

——————

Edited by

Stephen G. Nichols
and
Siegfried Wenzel

Ann Arbor

THE UNIVERSITY OF MICHIGAN PRESS

Copyright © by the University of Michigan 1996
All rights reserved
Published in the United States of America by
The University of Michigan Press
Manufactured in the United States of America
♾ Printed on acid-free paper

1999   1998   1997   1996   4   3   2   1

*A CIP catalog record for this book is available from the British
Library*

Library of Congress Cataloging-in-Publication Data

The Whole book : cultural perspectives on the medieval miscellany /
   edited by Stephen G. Nichols and Siegfried Wenzel.
      p.   cm. — (Recentiores)
   Includes index.
   ISBN 0-472-10696-1 (alk. paper)
      1. Literature, Medieval—Criticism, Textual. 2. Manuscripts,
Medieval—Editing. 3. Literature, Medieval—Editing. 4. Books—
History—400–1400. 5. Books—History—1400–1600. 6. Anthologies—
Editing.   I. Nichols, Stephen G.   II. Wenzel, Siegfried.
III. Series.
PN162.W47   1996
809′.02—dc20   96-22423
                                                                     CIP

ELIZABETH B. WENZEL
1927–1996
IN MEMORIAM

Contents

Introduction

Manuscripts have always been essential to medieval studies as the primary vehicles that furnish the information necessary for studying every aspect of medieval culture and civilization, from setting up a chronology to perceiving and analyzing the thought structures of philosophers and theologians. But in the last decade, manuscripts—or, perhaps better, individual manuscripts—have reentered the focus of medievalists and regained importance to an unprecedented and exciting degree. They continue, of course, to be valued repositories of the texts that medievalists collect, read, edit, and analyze. But in addition to their simply preserving the texts, often in multiple copies that show more or less variation, they furnish material contexts that in recent years have come to be more fully appreciated than ever before. Such features as the ink and script of a given text; the quality and size of the material on which it is written; the layout in which it presents itself to the eye; the makeup of each individual volume, with its gatherings, colophons, subscriptions, and binding; further, the company of other works in which a given text was first gathered and has been preserved; and finally, its particular textual variants, especially those that resulted from factors other than scribal misreading or carelessness—all these features yield information, over and above that implied in the texts themselves, about the text's audience, its purpose, and even the intention an individual scribe may have had in producing this particular copy. Beyond transmitting basic information about a given text, they speak to us about its social, commercial, and intellectual organization at the moment of its inscription. Such attention to the single manuscript as a historical artifact—*materialist philology*—has become an exciting and richly rewarding new enterprise in medieval studies, an enterprise peculiar to the study of a manuscript culture.

As a historical artifact, the individual manuscript came into being at the crossroads of a variety of social and professional expertises, demands, and intentions, whether it was produced in a monastic scriptorium, by commercial stationers, or in the isolated study of a parish priest or humanist scholar. As a result of all these factors, individual manuscripts come to us in an astonishing variety of types. Like texts themselves—literary, philosophical, theological, historical, and so forth—they can be classified into a variety of types or genres. But whereas literary and historical scholars have spent much ingenuity in devising and defining medieval textual types, manuscripts have been subjected to considerably less intellectual effort devoted to their typology, even though they have not been exempt from classification. This is perhaps not surprising, since the concern with genres has largely been linked to analysis of the texts contained in the manuscripts rather than study of the manuscripts themselves. Previous scholars have focused their attention on the texts because these are presumably what the manuscript was designed to preserve; as a result, texts, as a rule, have been readily detached from their manuscript context when copied for editing.

Materialist philology thus goes beyond traditional textual criticism. It continues to consider versions of a given work as variant forms that must be evaluated, placed in a hypothetical textual history of the work, and mined for clues that allow the textual critic to reconstruct what the author wrote. But in addition, it demands that one look closely at the relationship of the individual version to its historical context in a given manuscript. Arguing that the individual manuscript contextualizes the text(s) it contains in specific ways, materialist philology seeks to analyze the consequences of this relationship on the way these texts may be read and interpreted. More particularly, it postulates the possibility that a given manuscript, having been organized along certain principles, may well present its text(s) according to its own agenda, as worked out by the person who planned and supervised the production of the manuscript. Far from being a transparent or neutral vehicle, the codex can have a typological identity that affects the way we read and understand the texts it presents. The manuscript agency—manuscript kind or identity—can thus offer social or anthropological insights into the way its texts were or could have been read by the patron or public to which it was diffused.

So the question of manuscript agency arises not as a matter of simple classification but as a tool for better understanding the "performative" context of its content. Questions of classification obviously come in a variety of forms and complexities. They may be relatively unproblematic, as when a codex is comprised of the Bible, a service book, a dictionary, or nothing else but Augustine's *De Trinitate,* a *Summa de virtutibus,* or the *Liber de Petro Plowman.* This may also be the case where the codex holds a number of items that historical investigation has shown to come from the pen of one and the same author—such as Grosseteste's sermons or the carols by John Audelay. Yet even when the codex contains only a single work, where one would think that the classification of manuscript and text would not be an issue—as is the case, for example, with many manuscripts of the *Roman de la Rose* and MS Arsenal 3353 of Jean d'Arras's *Roman de Mélusine*—the codex presentation of the work can pose questions that require us to proceed with caution in making assertions about the noncontextual classification of the work in question.

How should the modern reader react when confronted by a manuscript into which many things, sometimes of quite diverse content, have been copied? Although the generic term used to define such a codex—*miscellany,* or volume that contains miscellaneous subject matter—lies ready to hand, the term does little to address the dynamics of individual examples of the genre. *Miscellany* does not even provide an accurate taxonomy for catalogers, editors, and historians of bookmaking, let alone literary scholars. It sheds little light on the relationship of the texts to their codicological context, and it may even be misleading, suggesting, as it does, an arbitrary principle of organization for manuscripts in which there may be a perfectly clear organizing principle.

Precisely because so many different kinds of manuscripts seem to fall within the purview of this inadequate and finally enigmatic (or at least vague) term, a colloquium devoted to exploring some ramifications of the problem seemed to us an intriguing idea. The University of Pennsylvania and Johns Hopkins University provided funds to enable a group of medievalists to meet at the University of Pennsylvania in March 1993 to address the nature and usefulness of the concept "miscellany." The scholars invited to the conference all had prior experience working directly with manuscripts of this kind and thus could recognize the questions the colloquium sought to confront.

The chapters collected in this book trace the debates and findings of the colloquium itself and the reflections of them in the intervening two years. This book, then, is itself a miscellany—a single volume in which two editors have gathered ten separate pieces wrought into a more or less consistent format. The pieces represent different authors and deal with diverse subjects, covering Latin as well as vernacular manuscripts, theological treatises and sermons as well as poetry, the Carolingian period as well as the early sixteenth century, and beautifully illuminated anthologies as well as scrappy notebooks. Yet they all deal with a common subject matter: the medieval miscellany. And they intend to present to a wider audience of medievalists some of the problems connected with the subject as well as various insights that emerged in dealing with them.

We gathered to share our experiences with such codices—as large a variety of them as the span of a two-day colloquium would allow—and to discuss our findings. Though the colloquium focused on the taxonomy of medieval miscellaneous manuscripts and its problems, we did not anticipate, or insist on, emerging from the discussions with a clear schema that would, once and for all, solve the problems by proposing a new and binding terminology. But we had hoped that the papers presented there and the ensuing discussions would direct attention to a number of issues and problems shared by the participants and would perhaps open some new windows.

In this hope we were not disappointed. The papers presented at the colloquium discussed medieval miscellanies in both Latin and vernacular languages, ranging from the ninth century through the succeeding ages to the northern Renaissance. They covered a wide range of intellectual areas: theology, sermons, philosophy, meditation, the study of the classics, and vernacular literature from both England and France. Another area represented at the colloquium was medieval medicine, with a paper by Linda E. Voigts, which was not made available for this volume. The chapters in this book thus deal with a number of very different kinds of books, all the way from the ad hoc notebooks compiled for a scholar's personal use and scorned by modern bibliophiles because of their derivative contents, through unpretentious volumes made for practical use, to sumptuously arranged and decorated tomes written by professional scribes at the request of noble patrons.

E. Ann Matter, who is preparing an edition of some of the theological writings by Alcuin for the Corpus Christianorum Continuatio Medievalis Series (published by Brepols in Turnhout, Belgium), examines the company of other Alcuinian works with which his *De fide* appears in early manuscripts. Based on his search for macaronic sermons in a large variety of sermon collections, Siegfried Wenzel discusses different shapes that such collections take and the problems these variations pose to attempts to order them into neat categories. From a somewhat different perspective, Georg N. Knauer reports some important findings concerning the literary activities of Johannes Reuchlin, a small part of Knauer's extensive searches for late-medieval and Renaissance translations and commentaries on the works of Homer, which he has undertaken for the Catalogus Translationum et Commentariorum (Washington, DC: Catholic University of America Press, 1960–).

Turning from Latin to vernacular manuscripts, Ralph Hanna III extends his earlier work with books for religious instruction to a manuscript at Winchester College in England and shows that such vernacular miscellanies evidently collected material in part because of the common subject matter of the individual pieces and in part for the simpler reason that such material, never very widespread, happened to be available to the scribe. The same point about accessibility emerges again in the essays by A. S. G. Edwards and Julia Boffey, who both write about the preservation of late Middle English poetry in large miscellanies. Edwards discusses a late fifteenth-century Scottish book that contains works by Chaucer and Henryson, characterizes its uniqueness, and places it into the development of poetic anthologies in the fifteenth and sixteenth centuries as well as the emerging Chaucer canon. Utilizing her previous study of the transmission of late Middle English lyrics, Boffey examines the preservation of Lydgate's shorter lyrics and their collection into two fifteenth-century manuscripts.

Similarly, Sylvia Huot extends her earlier work on medieval French lyrical anthologies and manuscripts of the *Roman de la Rose* to anthologies of vernacular meditative material that were compiled and written for royal patrons, showing in the process how material that originated elsewhere becomes unified in such collections by means of small personalizing details found in their dedications and illustrations. Stephen G. Nichols also turns from questions of text and illumination in French vernacular manuscripts to consider the problem of the lyric anthology. A miscellany not often viewed as a heterogeneous compilation, the troubadour *chansonnier* as designed in northern Italy in the thirteenth century offers an excellent example of the benefits gained from the kinds of questions posed at the colloquium. For the troubadour *chansonnier,* viewed as a coherent construction, reveals cultural and professional preoccupations on the part of its compiler that have much to tell us about the social role of poetry as it passed from one cultural milieu and period to another.

Some of these chapters thus deal with single codices that are here examined from the standpoint of their miscellaneity, while others examine groups of manuscripts containing a particular set of works or look at an entire genre, such as sermons, and the variety of book types that has preserved them. Barbara A. Shailor, who has cataloged the medieval manuscripts at the Beinecke Library at Yale University, discusses three individual codices and presents considerations about miscellanies from the cataloger's perspective. Finally, James J. O'Donnell reflects on themes and insights that emerged during the colloquium from the standpoint of the student of classical and early Christian authors.

Despite the wide diversity of subjects and manuscripts that these chapters examine, they consistently—and we should add, not by prior editorial arrangement—point to a number of features and issues that a student of medieval miscellanies must attend to. First in order of concreteness are codicological features, such as the physical makeup of a volume, especially whether it is composed of "booklets," or fascicles; its general appearance and layout, including the quality and variation of its script as well as the presence of decorative features; and the presence of an apparatus, shown by such details as a medieval foliation and numbering of quires and the addition of rubrics and indexes that would facilitate use of the volume. The next topic of concern for both the textual student and the taxonomer is the subject matter contained in the volume: how is it arranged, and does it have any sort of thematic unity? Finally comes the question of intentionality: can one find a unifying purpose for the material collected, and if so, what precisely is it? Does the resulting book serve as a tool for a discernible and definable reader or group of readers, or was it merely made for the compiler's amusement? These issues surface repeatedly in the chapters of this book, and they clearly set an agenda that is difficult to ignore for anyone interested in miscellaneous manuscripts and sensitive to their taxonomy and function.

These chapters, then, yield a certain and firm methodological or heuristic consensus, and they also show that particular insights about medieval miscellanies, rather than being academic abstractions, can have tangible (and eminently practical) consequences. For example, Knauer shows how patient search through normally scorned volumes seemingly composed of fifteenth- or sixteenth-century gleanings from older texts can lead to the discovery of a hitherto "lost" work that, in turn, offers insights into the working habits of sixteenth-century humanists. Matter's examination of early manuscripts that assemble works by Alcuin forces the modern editor to redistribute the long-established corpus of that theologian into groups and categories that reflect the intentions of his work and its reception by his contemporaries more accurately than does the work of seventeenth-century scholars. And catalogers of medieval manuscripts, here represented by Shailor, will want to work in tandem with codicologists and textual students to push their descriptors beyond such terms as *miscellany, sermonnaire,* or *Sammelhandschrift.*

It remains for us to thank our two universities warmly for making this conference possible and our speakers and contributors for giving their papers and revising them for publication. We would also like to thank Julia Holderness and Vittorio Trionfi, graduate students at Johns Hopkins, for their work at the various stages of preparing the manuscript for publication.

Sermon Collections and Their Taxonomy

Siegfried Wenzel

Previous studies on vernacular verses used by preachers and on linguistically mixed sermons have repeatedly drawn me into dividing, at least tentatively, the relevant manuscripts into types distinguished by their form and function.[1] The results may look very orderly on the printed page, but in both cases the enterprise proved ultimately unsatisfactory because it left me with some manuscripts that did not entirely fit into the categories I used, while for others I could find no better term than *miscellany*. In the following pages, I want to explore such taxonomic difficulties further as they pertain specifically to sermon collections.

Medieval sermons made after the early thirteenth century tend to be preserved in two essentially different forms: the sermon cycle and what I shall provisorily call the random sermon collection. A cycle contains sermons neatly arranged in the order of the church year. Thus, cycles *de tempore* include sermons for the Sundays and major feast days from the first Sunday in Advent to the last Sunday after Trinity. Similarly, cycles *de sanctis* comprise sermons for the saints feasts, again arranged according to the chronology of the church year, from the feast of Saint Andrew to that of All Saints or St. Catherine.[2] In distinction to cycles, random sermon collections lack such order; not only do

---

1. See S. Wenzel, *Preachers, Poets, and the Early English Lyric* (Princeton, NJ: Princeton University Press, 1986), 4–8; and *Macaronic Sermons: Bilingualism and Preaching in Late-Medieval England* (Ann Arbor, MI: University of Michigan Press, 1994), chap. 3.

2. Smaller cycles are made up of sermons for Lent, which also follow the church calendar. Other sequences of sermons, such as those for special occasions or sermons that deal with one or several psalms or the opening verses of the gospel of John, could also be included among cycles, though they lack the chronological order.

they gather sermons *de tempore* and *de sanctis* without separation, but they do so without any regard to their position in the church year. They are also selective, in that, in contrast to cycles, they do not present at least one sermon for each Sunday or feast day; and they are often heterogeneous, in that their pieces may differ noticeably among themselves in form and treatment.

One can assume that these two forms came about in fundamentally different ways. Sermon cycles evidently are the result of a single author composing or compiling individual pieces. Often such cycles are provided with prologues that name their authors and specify their intentions and occasion. For example, some time in the fourteenth century the English theologian Ralph Acton wrote:

> As I was residing quietly in my church and made it a habit to speak to the people on Sundays and feast days, some of our companions asked urgently that I should be willing to commit to memory in some form of writing the things I was preaching to the people. Pondering in silence within me whether I should satisfy them, I find four reasons. . . . Urged by these reasons, I have yielded to the request of our brothers. But since I composed these little homilies for the benefit of simple people, I tried to avoid allegorical obscurities, scriptural profundities, and rhetorical or-nateness as much as possible and sought everywhere for the moral truths that are necessary to human life. If anyone should, in this work, find authorities quoted incompletely or in other words [than the original], he should understand that this happened because, being summoned to the court of the prince, I wrote much of it on the way and much of it in the fields and did not have the original sources available.[3]

After giving his name, "Radulphus" then provides over two hundred short sermons on the epistles and the gospels, first of the *de tempore* and then of the

---

3. Prologus. Cum in ecclesia mea quietus residerem et loquendi ad populum per dies dominicos et festos mihi consuetudinem fecissem, quidam nostratum sociorum nostram efflagitauere pronitatem quatinus ea que ad populum sermocinabar qualicumque scriptura memo-rie commendarem. Quibus an satisfaciendum esset dum mecum ipse tacitus deliberarem, causam reperio quadrifariam. . . . Hiis itaque causis compulsus postulacioni fratrum nostrorum adquieui. Quoniam autem ob vtilitatem simplicium omeliunculas istas composui, obscuritatem alle-goriarum, profunditatem scripturarum, ornatumque sermonum euitare curaui pro posse meo, in vniuersis inquirens moralitatem vtpote vite hominum necessariorum. Ceterum si quis in hoc opusculo autoritates semiplenas sub aliisve verbis reppererit, nouerit hoc inde contiguisse quoniam ad curiam principis raptus plerumque in via, plerumque inter ipsa arua scriptitabam et copiam exemplarium non habebam. Oro igitur vt quicumque hoc mee deuocionis opusculum perspexerint, non temere iudicare set pocius pro peccatore Radulpho intercedere misericorditer meminerint. (Manchester, John Rylands Library, MS Lat. 367, f. 1.)

de sanctis cycles.[4] In contrast to such well organized labors, collectors—one assumes—went about picking up sermons that they happened to come across and that struck their fancy as worth collecting.[5] What do the resulting collections look like, and what problems do they pose for the taxonomy of medieval manuscripts?

In approaching these questions, I will discuss three major aspects of random collections: the authorship of individual sermons they gather, principles of arrangement, and the homogeneity of their contents. As my material I use the manuscripts I have identified and studied in connection with a larger investigation of bilingual sermons, together with some further collections that are entirely in Latin or have only marginal English elements.[6] This corpus, naturally, represents only a fraction of the large mass of Latin sermon manuscripts

---

4. Other late-medieval Latin sermon cycles made in England are the *Sermones dominicales* by John Felton (completed before 1431; see Alan J. Fletcher, " 'Magnus predicator et deuotus': A Profile of the Life, Work, and Influence of the Fifteenth-Century Oxford Preacher, John Felton," *Medieval Studies* 53 [1991]: 125–75), and a set of sermons on the Apostles' Creed by John Waldeby, which he wrote up at the request of Thomas de la Mare, abbot of St. Albans. Waldeby provided this set of sermons with a *prohemium* in which he says, among other things: "Venit in memoriam quedam materia moralis in exposicione simboli quam dudum populo predicaueram in Eborum. Ne vero dicta materia per obliuionem dilaberetur a posterum memoria . . . , quicquid fuerit de illa materia in cedulis et membranulis sparsim intitulatum recolligerem in seriosum tractatum 12 sermones . . . / Quicquid placuit Deo mihi peccatori diuinitus inspirare conatus sum in scripturam redigere" (Oxford, Bodleian Library, MS Laud Misc 296, f. 57ra–b).

5. I am not aware that collectors of this kind provided prologues to their work in any way similar to Acton's or Waldeby's. The note written in Oxford, Merton College, MS 248 quoted later in this essay was plainly written by a later owner of the manuscript.

6. Wenzel, *Macaronic Sermons,* provides a detailed discussion of thirteen manuscripts that contain macaronic sermons, including a number of codicological features (chap. 3), and inventories the sermons found in them (app. A). Both sections provide full documentation of many of the points made in this article. The following manuscripts analyzed there are quoted in this article by their respective sigla.

A: Cambridge, University Library, MS Ii.3.8
B: Cambridge, University Library, MS Kk.4.24
D: Dublin, Trinity College, MS 277
Q: Oxford, Bodleian Library, MS Lat.th.d.1 (SC 29746)
T: Oxford, Magdalen College, MS 93
W: Worcester, Cathedral Library, MS F.10
X: Worcester, Cathedral Library, MS F.126
Z: Arras, Bibliothèque Municipale, MS 184 (254).

In addition, I am here also using the following manuscripts.

U: Oxford, Merton College, MS 248
F: Fitzralph's sermons as contained in Oxford, Bodleian Library, MS Bodley 144.

produced in England from the thirteenth through the fifteenth centuries. But its members are sufficiently diversified in contents, style, and affiliation[7] to ensure that the corpus provides a reliable sample.

Not all random collections are anonymous. Those preserved with an individual's name include, for instance, the collected sermons of Archbishop Richard Fitzralph[8] or those of Bishop Brunton of Rochester.[9] But even in these cases, where the whole collection is ascribed to one churchman, we cannot be sure whether the pieces in the collection were gathered by himself or by a later collector. Nonetheless, the individual pieces are likely to have come from the pen of the named churchman.[10] Much more normally, the collections have come to us without any indication of who made them. There are at least two important and well-known exceptions. One is Oxford, Merton College, MS 248 (U), in which an owner's note tells us that this is "the third volume of sermons that were collected by Dom John of Sheppey, doctor of theology, a monk and later bishop of Rochester, during his stay at Oxford."[11] This volume gathers, with some other material, over two hundred sermons, of which a number are ascribed to more than half a dozen Franciscan and Dominican preachers active in the late 1320s and 1330s.[12] The other well-known manuscript that comes to us with a name is Oxford, Bodleian Library, MS Lat.th.d.1 (Q).[13] It contains approximately fifty-seven sermons, many of which bear dates between 1432 and 1436 and place names where they were preached. They also bear a personal name, that of Nicholas Philip, who at some point tells

---

7. Their collectors, where they are known, range from an archbishop (F) to simple preachers (Q); their affiliations include Benedictines (W and X), Franciscans (Q), and Dominicans (B).

8. Unedited. They have been studied in Aubrey Gwynn, S.J., "The Sermon-Diary of Richard Fitzralph, Archbishop of Armagh," *Proceedings of the Royal Irish Academy* 44 C (1937): 1–57. See also Katherine Walsh, *A Fourteenth-Century Scholar and Primate: Richard Fitzralph in Oxford, Avignon and Armagh* (Oxford: Clarendon, 1981).

9. Edited in Sister Mary Aquinas Devlin, O.P., *The Sermons of Thomas Brunton, Bishop of Rochester (1373–1389),* Camden Series, 3d ser., vols. 85–86 (London: Royal Historical Society, 1954).

10. In his review of Devlin's edition, however, H. G. Richardson queries the authenticity of several sermons in the collection; see *Speculum* 30 (1955): 267–71.

11. "Tercium volumen sermonum per dominum Jo. de Schepeya, sacre theologie doctorem, monachum Roffensem, et postea ibidem episcopum, pro suo tempore in vniuersitate Oxon' collectorum (U, f. v [flyleaf]). A similar inscription appears on the endleaf of Oxford, New College, MS 92, which also contains sermons collected or made by Sheppey.

12. Sheppey's sermons have been studied in an unpublished Oxford B.Litt. thesis by George Mifsud: "John Sheppey, Bishop of Rochester, as Preacher and Collector of Sermons" (1953). See also A. G. Little and F. Pelster, *Oxford Theology and Theologians c. A.D. 1282–1302,* Oxford Historical Society 96 (Oxford: Clarendon, 1934), 176–77 n. 5.

13. See Alan J. Fletcher, "The Sermon Booklets of Friar Nicholas Philip," *Medium Aevum* 55 (1986): 188–202.

us that he owned this book, belonged to the Franciscan custody of Cambridge and the convent of Lynn, and wrote the book at Lichfield in 1436. Since his name frequently appears with a date at the head or foot of a sermon, he probably preached these himself. Whether he also composed the respective pieces is impossible to say.

With these and possibly some other exceptions, random collections more usually do not furnish the names of the collectors. But whether the collector is known to us or not, such collections normally gather sermons of diverse authorship. John Sheppey's collection of Oxford sermons by named preachers (U) has already been mentioned. Another example is a fifteenth-century manuscript now in France (Z), containing fifty-seven sermons, most by unknown authors, except for one by an otherwise unidentified Master Henry Chambron, who preached it at Oxford in 1382,[14] and another preached at Oxford by Robert Lychelade, B.A., probably in 1395.[15] A third piece in this manuscript, without identification, turns out to be a sermon by Robert Grosseteste delivered at Lyons in 1250.[16] Another case worth citing is Cambridge, University Library, MS Kk.4.24 (B). This early fifteenth-century codex contains two sets of sermons, one of which is a cycle, the second a random collection. The ninety-two pieces in the latter are all anonymous, but one of them is a sermon by Richard Fitzralph, which he preached at St. Paul's Cross, London, on February 26, 1367.[17] Its presence here is somewhat startling, because Fitzralph's antimendicant stance ill agrees with the otherwise Franciscan character of the collection in general. But affiliation of their material with specific orders and individuals seemingly meant very little to our collectors, as is also demonstrated in a third case: Worcester, Cathedral Library, MS F.126 (X), a large tome belonging to the Benedictine priory of Worcester, contains some sermons of named Benedictine authorship[18] and with them a sequence of fifty-five sermons on the Sunday gospels that were written by the Franciscan John Pecham.[19]

The diverse authorship in the given examples is determined either by the authors' names recorded in the collections or by the fact that the respective

---

14. Z-1, f. 4rb.

15. Z-12, f. 36vb. Lychelade was expelled in 1395; see J. I. Catto, "Wyclif and Wycliffism at Oxford 1356–1430," in J. I. Catto and Ralph Evans, eds., *Late Medieval Oxford,* vol. 2 of *The History of the University of Oxford* (Oxford: Clarendon, 1992), 226, 233.

16. Z-22, f. 69rb.

17. B-158, f. 286rb.

18. Sermons ascribed to John Sene, a monk of Gloucester; his name occurs several times in the manuscript, and it is likely that all of ff. 235–46 is his work.

19. The *Collationes dominicales de evangeliis,* appearing on ff. 165–83v.

pieces are identical with sermons whose authorship is known from elsewhere. In addition, difference in authorship can also be reasonably established by significant structural and stylistic differences. Another random collection made at Worcester priory, Worcester, Cathedral Library, MS F.10 (W), for instance, contains several pieces with an unusually florid style as well as the address "patres conscripti," both features I would consider signatures of a particular preacher[20] who shares this collection with a number of other sermon writers.

The overall order in which items in these random collections appear seems to lack any rationale. The conventional separation of *de tempore* and *de sanctis* sermons, and further sermons *de diversis,* is as a rule not observed, so that pieces appear in a helter-skelter mixture. For example, the sermons of Thomas Brunton begin with two for saints' feasts (on Thomas of Canterbury and Eleazar) and are followed by sermons for the third, second, and third Sundays of Advent; after this we get two more saints' sermons, on the Assumption and St. Thomas of Canterbury, which are in turn followed by a sermon to the clergy; and so forth. Even a random collection whose overall layout seems to distinguish between *de tempore, de sanctis,* and *de diversis* sermons (MS X) constantly mixes individual pieces from one division into the other.

Even where several sermons in sequence belong to one of these major divisions, they tend not to follow the chronological order of the church year. We already noticed that the cited temporal sermons in Brunton's collection follow the order 3 Advent, 2 Advent, 3 Advent. This is absolutely typical of random collections. To cite one more case, a section of MS Q contains sermons for the following occasions as noted in a table at the end of the manuscript.

Q-15	4 Lent	T22[21]
Q-16	1 Lent	T19
Q-17	4 Advent	T04
Q-18	Passion Sunday	T23
Q-19	Advent	T01+
Q-20	Nativity	T06
Q-21	Lent	T19+

---

20. Author of W-71 and W-167; the former is ascribed to Master John Fordham, a monk at Worcester from 1396 to 1438, who held a D.Th. from Oxford (ca. 1407) and was president of the general chapter from 1420 to 1426.

21. These sigla are taken from Johannes Baptist Schneyer, *Repertorium der lateinischen Sermones des Mittelalters für die Zeit von 1150–1350,* 11 vols., Beiträge zur Geschichte der Philosophie and Theologie des Mittelalters 43 (Münster: Aschendorff, 1965–90), 1:17–21. They mark the occasions for sermons *de tempore* (T) and *de communi sanctorum et de occasionibus* (C) in their liturgical order. I use them here to emphasize the helter-skelter order of sermons collected.

Q-22	Easter	T28
Q-25	Easter	T28
Q-26	Easter	T28
Q-27	Synod	C14

Similar haphazard sequences can be found in virtually any manuscript that contains a random sermon collection.

The just cited case of Q, however, poses the question whether this sequence may yet have its rationale, even if it is not that of liturgical order. Could the sermons have been copied thus because they had been preached in this order? MS Q is a good case with which to investigate this question further. Its sermons 16, 17, 18, 21, and 22 all bear the date 1432, and while it is not absolutely certain whether the dates on the sermons refer to their delivery or rather to their being copied by Nicholas Philip, the former possibility seems altogether more likely. That other pieces in this sequence of eleven sermons lack a date is unfortunate but no great impediment, since—among other reasons—they may originally have had such an indication, but it may have been lost in the process of binding the volume. What is more unsettling is the fact that Q-27 is dated 1435. But this may be explained by observing that the sermons dated 1432, with some other material, apparently are part of one booklet in MS Q,[22] and it is possible that Q-27 was added, on the remaining blank pages of the manuscript, four years after Philip had done his "1432 booklet."

But the dates that appear in the remainder of the codex, insofar as they are legible, do not run in chronological order either. Before the cited section, we find 1432 (f. 5) and 1433 (f. 38v); after it occur 1436 (f. 90), 1430 (f. 100v), 1436 (ff. 113, 114), 1434 (f. 118v), 1433 (f. 126v), 1434 (f. 132v), 1430 (ff. 139, 142, 143v), 1436 (f. 153), 1430 (f. 157, perhaps beginning a new booklet, and perhaps an error for 1431), and 1431 (ff. 159, 161v, 164v, 166, 170v, 175). At this point it would be mandatory to examine the composition of the codex intimately. This, unfortunately, is not possible, because of the extreme brittleness of its paper folios and the losses they have already sustained. Even so, it would seem that, while one could speak of a 1432 booklet and a 1431 booklet,[23] though bound in reverse chronological order, the other dates appearing in the volume appear to be wildly erratic.

Because of the presence of these dates, MS Q has been called a sermon diary. If the term *diary* suggests an orderly chronological progression through

---

22. This would comprise ff. 43–90; see Fletcher, "Sermon Booklets," 199 n. 2.
23. Ff. 157–77 and 43–90, respectively.

days, weeks, months, and years, it is clearly inapplicable to this manuscript as a whole. The same is true of another sermon collection to which the term has been applied, those of Richard Fitzralph. Its entries—ninety-two sermons[24]— are highly "personalized," in that they bear indications of the preacher's name or ecclesiastical rank and of the occasion, place, and date at which they were preached. These indications make it clear that the collection, as it has come to us in the major, uncontaminated manuscripts, actually comprises two different sequences of sermons. The first sixty-eight pieces, with exception of the initial three, occur in a precise chronological order from November 28, 1344, to March 12, 1357, and were preached, mostly in the vernacular, to congregations in and around Lichfield, London, and various towns in Ireland. They also contain many reflective remarks by their author, such as "then I said," "first a prayer was said; then, after repeating the thema, it was shown that . . . ," "the remainder of the sermon was spoken to the people in their language, and first the things that here immediately precede were repeated in the vernacular, and then the development was given as follows," and so on. This is clearly a personal record of the writer's preaching activity and, given the chronological sequence, can well be called a sermon diary. But in the major manuscripts, this section is followed by some twenty-four more sermons that lack such reflective annotations, bear various dates between 1335 and 1359 in no chronological order, and were given before various audiences in Latin at Avignon. Hence, the entire collection of Fitzralph's sermons, as it now stands, combines a sermon diary with sermons preached at Avignon, the latter out of chronological order.

If neither their liturgical occasions nor, in special cases, the chronology of their delivery played a dominant role in the arrangement of sermons in random collections, can one perhaps think of still other principles of arrangement? MS Q, despite or beyond its dates, suggests such a possibility. A number of its sermons seem to be grouped around a common subject. Thus, five sermons for Easter occur in sequence (22 through 26), as do six on the Passion (38–43) and four written for the visitation of friars (34–37). In addition, several sermons occur in sequences that deal with a particular *thema* ("Ecce nunc tempus," 29–31; "Nunc clamemus in celum," 45–48)[25] or topic ("sanguis," 38–40). Finally, four sermons (61–64, associated with Melton, probably the well-known Franciscan, who may even be their author) and the fully macaronic sermons in the manuscript (19–25) form distinct groups. Similar groupings, whether by

24. I follow the count and numbering given by Gwynn, "Sermon-Diary."

25. Q-46 is explicitly intended as part of Q-45.

topic, *thema,* author, or language, can be found here and there in other random sermon collections.[26]

The presence of such grouping would mean that the collectors, or more precisely the scribes who produced the manuscripts we now have, did not copy items completely haphazardly. Somewhere in the transmission of these pieces—and it is nearly impossible to tell at which point in the process of collecting, copying, and making up a codex from individual gatherings or booklets this happened—some attempt was made, even if only a partial one, to arrange the items according to some principle. Hence the term *random* may not be entirely accurate for describing this kind of sermon collection and should be taken as only a provisional label. Why such grouping occurred is not difficult to see: the respective collections were made not simply as repositories of items found by chance and deemed interesting or useful but as books to be consulted by either the collector himself or his fellow preachers. In other words, they constitute preaching tools. Their utilitarian purpose is further revealed in the fact that the respective codices usually lack decorative features and are written in undistinguished hands and in the fact that many of them were provided with such devices as foliation and various kinds of tables that would make it easy for a busy preacher to locate and look up material for his work.[27]

I now turn to the third major feature of random sermon collections, their homogeneity. I have so far discussed them as if all they contained were complete sermons. But this is not the case. The majority of pertinent manuscripts I am familiar with hold, next to complete sermons, other material of various kinds. Very often, their sermons appear interspersed with short passages that must have been felt to be useful for preachers: theological commonplaces, distinctions, mnemonic verses, exempla with or without moralizations, and the like. Occasionally such material seems to be topically related to an immediately preceding or following sermon, but more often than not any such topical connection is hard to see. In a good many cases, such short items are introduced with the word *nota;* hence, to call them theological or sermon notes, as many older catalogs do, reflects accurately what their scribes had in mind. Alongside such notes also occur parts of sermons (such as an individual *pro-theme*), sermon outlines, or partial sermons. These can pose frustrating prob-

---

26. A fine example is MS W, where several entire quires show such grouping. Thus, quire V (W-13 through W-15) contains sermons that are entirely in English; quire VI (W-16, W-17, and perhaps more) comprises sermons attributed to "Folsam," apparently a monk at Norwich; and quires XXI–XXIII (W-122 through W-137) gather sermons preached to a clerical, academic audience.

27. See especially my discussion of MS B in chap. 3 of *Macaronic Sermons.*

lems to someone attempting to inventory the sermons in a collection. Cambridge, University Library, MS Ii.3.8 (A), for example, contains many extended distinctions—such as would have been used for the division or subdivisions or development in a scholastic sermon—as well as skeleton sermons; as a result, the reader is frequently not sure whether a given entry is a full sermon or not. In listing the sermons a collection contains, one can of course proceed from the assumption that a full sermon should begin with a *thema* (which in the case of scholastic sermons leads to the division) and should end with the standard concluding formula that expresses a pious wish or blessing ("To which glory may He bring you and me who . . . "), followed by a standard trinitarian formula ("He who reigns with the Father and the Holy Spirit, world without end. Amen."). But limiting one's inventory to pieces that have these characteristics would exclude many sermons that, for some reason, have been preserved incomplete, and it could therefore seriously distort the nature of a collection or the oeuvre of a known preacher and its popularity. Furthermore, the point at which an item breaks off may come at various places in the sermon's structure. If it does so in the development of the third principal, there is no reason not to consider the item a sermon. But what if the item breaks off in the first principal or soon after the division? Does it then still constitute a sermon, or should it be considered only a *protheme?*

Another and much weightier factor that works against homogeneity is the presence of entire treatises that are not themselves sermons. A number of collections I have examined contain such works as *artes praedicandi,* commentaries on the Lord's Prayer or the Ten Commandments, treatises on confession, and much else. Again, it is not difficult to explain their presence: they were obviously gathered with the sermons as material of use to preachers. The problem is in deciding at what point a manuscript stops being a sermon collection with some additional material and becomes a miscellaneous collection with some sermons. A good illustration is the already mentioned MS Z, which contains, together with its fifty-seven sermons, a large number of short theological notes, stories, and fables; two Wycliffite tracts in English; a short *ars praedicandi;* Origen's Latin homily on St. Mary Magdalene; miracles of the Blessed Virgin; Nicholas de Hanapis's *Liber de exemplis sacre scripture;* Odo of Cheriton's *Fabulae;* a treatise on confession by William of Auvergne; and several other pieces. This may be compared with Oxford, Magdalen College, MS 93 (T), one of the volumes made and given to the college by John Dygoun. MS T is composed of several booklets, many of which end with blank leaves. One booklet actually was to have an alphabetical index, which however did not advance very far. The whole volume contains excerpts from and complete copies of a wide variety of works that range from the Fathers to Rolle, Hilton, and Thomas a Kempis.[28] These works include, like MS Z, a Wycliffite treatise, Origen's homily on St. Mary Margaret, a commentary on the Lord's Prayer, and theological notes, commonplaces, and exempla. With this material appear ten complete "modern" sermons, one of which enjoyed a good deal of popularity in fifteenth-century England.[29] If one is willing to consider MS Z a sermon collection (its complete sermons occupy about 125 of its total 227 folios, i.e., more than half the volume), can one say the same of MS T, whose "modern" sermons occupy only 27 folios out of 309?[30]

At this point students of sermon collections are faced with their major taxonomic problem. Of the various factors I have surveyed that make for diversity in random sermon collections—authorship, arrangement, and contents—the latter is the crucial cause of much variation in the manuscripts and hence of uncertainty among manuscript students and bibliographers on how to label the respective volumes. Terms like *sermon collection, notebook, commonplace book, preacher's handbook, anthology,* and perhaps some others offer themselves and demand clear and firm distinctions. Making these distinctions requires students of medieval sermon manuscripts to engage in discussion based on careful attention to the contents of a given volume, to their putative purpose or motive for collecting them,[31] and to formal, codicological features, such as their composition, layout, appearance, variety of hands, and apparatus. The following remarks aim to stimulate such a discussion.

The distinction with which I began this chapter, between a sermon cycle and a sermon collection, yields two categories that are clearly distinguished from each other and pose no taxonomic problem. Either could be by a known author or collector or anonymous. The label *sermon collection* is not affected by whether the individual pieces included in it are anonymous or by named authors. The same holds for the arrangement of the pieces, since by definition a collection lacks a liturgical order. The presence of a partial arrangement by

---

28. A list of contents can be found in H. O. Coxe, *Laudian Manuscripts,* vol. 2 of *Bodleian Library, Quarto Catalogue* (reprint, with corrections and additions, etc., by R. W. Hunt, Oxford: Bodleian Library, 1973), 49–51. The volume has been recently refoliated, and an updated inventory appears in Wenzel, *Macaronic Sermons,* app. A.

29. This is the Good Friday sermon "Amore langueo," preserved in three other manuscripts. I am unaware of further occurrences of the other nine sermons.

30. By "modern" I refer to sermons written after ca. 1200. In addition, MS T gathers several sets of patristic homilies by or attributed to Origen, Augustine, Gregory, and Remy of Auxerre. These make up approximately another ninety-six folios.

31. "Putative" because random sermon collections characteristically do not bear any statements by their collector about why or for what purpose their contents were collected.

topic or occasion is an interesting feature but seems to pose no problem for the overall taxonomy. More important is the possibility that the collected sermons may be arranged by some kind of chronology, such as the order in which they were preached. In this case, *sermon diary* is a good term for a subtype of sermon collection.[32] In all these cases, the respective volume holds predominantly, if not exclusively, full sermons.

Where full sermons are accompanied by a significant amount of preaching material (such as exempla, theological notes, distinctions, and so forth—and of course it is debatable how much is significant) and beyond this of separate works that might have been useful to preachers (such as *artes praedicandi,* commentaries on the Lord's Prayer, and so forth), terms like *preaching tool* and *preacher's handbook* are often used. The former term is far too general, since beyond sermon collections and cycles it covers separate collections of exempla, distinctions, and commonplaces, as well as such works as *artes praedicandi,* Bromyard's *Summa praedicantium,* Mirk's *Festial,* and even Peraldus's *Summa de vitiis*—so many different books and works for the use of preachers that require finer taxonomic distinctions. The other term, *preacher's handbook* or *manual,* similarly is of little help here, since it defines a single work that furnishes explicit instruction for the performance of a certain task, in our case composing or delivering a sermon.

Some of the miscellaneous collections may be called *notebooks,* a term that is relatively easy to define and to apply. A notebook is a document into which someone enters a variety of things, which are normally not very extensive and are either composed by the writer or copied from elsewhere. These entries stand in the order in which they were entered. The order may reflect the writer's current and possibly changing interests, so that over many pages the entries may well be unified by a common topic; at the same time, the document might also contain bits and pieces that are unrelated to their context and that could betray the temporary musings or wanderings of the writer's mind.[33] If the writer is very orderly, he or she may identify his or her sources, even the date when the notes were taken. And finally, when the book was filled, its

---

32. It remains debatable, however, whether the term *diary* should require that the texts in such a volume contain "personal" remarks concerning their delivery, such as the ones I quoted earlier in this essay in discussing the collection of Fitzralph's sermons. By definition, a diary is a more personal document than a repertory, systematic collection, or anthology.

33. For example, "Mr John Arundel recorded in his logic lecture-notebook sums of money received and paid by him in 1424" (M. B. Parkes, "The Provision of Books," in Catto and Evans, *Late Medieval Oxford,* 408).

maker might go so far as to paginate it and provide it with an index. This description fits some medieval manuscripts very well. Of the sermon collections I have examined, MS T has many of the features mentioned, except perhaps that the pieces copied into it include several complete and lengthy treatises. Even so, the label *notebook* is appropriate.[34]

Although notebooks thus contain material that was commonplace among medieval preachers, including complete sermons, they should be differentiated from *commonplace books,* or *florilegia.* The individual units gathered in the latter would normally be shorter than those in notebooks, thus excluding full sermons. A well-known example is Friar John Grimestone's collection of *materia praedicabilis.*[35] If the term *commonplace book* is acceptable for this work, we must allow this category to include collections that are arranged by a predetermined plan, here the alphabetical order of the entries.[36]

If commonplace books, with respect to the size of individual entries, stand to one side of notebooks, we find on the other side a kind of collection that comprises items, or a larger number of items than notebooks do, that are longer and in fact separate works. For such collections the term *anthology* might be appropriate.[37] Their distinguishing feature is not just the length of the pieces collected (which in our case include full sermons) but some sort of thematic unity. Dublin, Trinity College, MS 277 (D) furnishes a good case for discussion. It is a thick fifteenth-century paper codex into which a large number of treatises and excerpts have been copied. In contrast to T, this manuscript does

---

34. Several notebooks containing lecture notes and occasionally also sermons are mentioned by Catto in "Wyclif," in Catto and Evans, *Late Medieval Oxford,* 198, 247, 255, 268, 273; by Parkes in "Provision," ibid., 408; and by R. B. Dobson in "The Religious Orders 1370–1540," ibid., 574–75. G. R. Owst, *Preaching in Medieval England: An Introduction to Sermon Manuscripts of the Period c. 1350–1450* (Cambridge: Cambridge University Press, 1926; reprint, New York: Russell and Russell, 1965), 59, called attention to a "sermon notebook" in Cambridge, Gonville and Caius College, MS 356, which, as I show in an article forthcoming in *History of Universities* 14 (1995), has chronological features that transcend the notion of a simple notebook. For the notebook of a priest in York, see Roy Martin Haines, *Ecclesia anglicana: Studies in the English Church of the Later Middle Ages* (Toronto: University of Toronto Press, 1989), 156–79.

35. See Edward Wilson, *A Descriptive Index of the English Lyrics in John of Grimestone's Preaching Book,* Medium Aevum Monographs, n.s., 2 (Oxford: Basil Blackwell, 1973), vi–xxiv. I have reproduced the section on "Adulacio" in *Preachers,* 102–6.

36. On changing principles of order in medieval exempla collections, see Jean-Claude Schmitt, "Recueils franciscains d'*exempla* et perfectionnement des techniques intellectuels du xiiie au xve siècle," *Bibliothèque de l'École des Chartes* 135 (1977): 5–21.

37. An alternate term is *library,* as it is used in discussions of literary anthologies of the fifteenth century; see Julia Boffey, *Manuscripts of English Courtly Love Lyrics in the Later Middle Ages* (Woodbridge, Suffolk: D. S. Brewer, 1985), chap. 1.

not contain booklets with partially blank pages for further material, nor does it contain dates and scribes' names. Being thus physically different from T, it is not a "notebook." However, at least some of its voluminous material is grouped by major devotional topics or interests, such as the Blessed Virgin, Christ's Passion, the religious life, penance and the vices and virtues, the Lord's Prayer, the trials and tribulations of life, and finally the duties and neglect of the pastoral office.[38] If one can make a convincing case for such grouping—and I emphasize that the matter needs further study—the manuscript may be considered an anthology. It also contains a few sermons, including the popular macaronic one on "Amore langueo" (mentioned in n. 29). In MS D this appears after excerpts from several meditative works on Christ's Passion, such as the *Stimulus amoris,* the *Horologium sapientiae,* and the tract *De fletu et lacrimis,* and it would therefore seem that the collector was interested in "Amore langueo" not as a sermon (MS D does not evince much interest in preaching materials) but for its meditative quality. In other words, though MS D contains some sermons, it is not a sermon collection but perhaps an anthology containing some sermons. One major objection manuscript students and catalogers could have to this designation is that sermon or meditative anthologies like MS D completely lack such deluxe features as decoration, illustrations, and dedications—features that characterize, for example, the anthologies discussed by Sylvia Huot later in this book. The objection may be countered by postulating that a common theme of the material collected and a clear intentionality are essential characteristics of anthologies, while high-quality decoration, illustrations, and dedicatory prefaces are accidental.

This argument, however, needs further investigation, just as it still needs to be shown that the material in MS D is gathered and grouped around common topics or subjects. Until such investigations of many codices like D are to hand, what are we to call such a volume? For lack of a better term, *miscellany* suggests itself as a provisional term for a manuscript of mixed contents. Professor Marvin Colker, who has given us a detailed catalog of the Dublin Trinity College manuscripts, refrains from giving D any label whatever, and perhaps such silence is wisdom. I can also imagine that some medievalists shrink from using classifying labels altogether on the grounds that such labels are deceptive and that every manuscript is an individual that, like a person, should be known by its name, not its race or party affiliation. Yet there seems to be something in human nature that wants to sort things into folders and boxes. I see two very good reasons why we should not give up on taxonomy altogether. One is that

---

38. For further details, see Wenzel, *Macaronic Sermons,* chap. 3.

the uncertainties connected with labeling a medieval manuscript force us to think more precisely about how it came into being and what it was intended for. In my work with sermon collections, the urge to label has again and again sent me back to the codices to look for physical as well as textual clues about what might have compelled their scribes to select these pieces, transcribe them, and put them in the order in which they now appear. Taxonomy thus can be a way toward literary history, toward understanding the rationale and genesis of book production and a good many other things.[39] The other reason for finding an adequate label is much more practical. As in the near future much bibliographical material will become available in electronic form, with its magnificent search capabilities, short descriptive terms are essential for efficient archiving. Maybe *miscellany* will do for that purpose, but I think we should aim at finding a better label.

---

39. An interesting recent case study that attempts to infer major thematic concerns and the intended audience for which several French "miscellaneous" manuscripts were made is Pamela Gehrke, *Saints and Scribes: Medieval Hagiography in Its Manuscript Context,* University of California Publications in Modern Philology 126 (Berkeley: University of California Press, 1993).

Iter per miscellanea: Homer's *Batrachomyomachia* and Johannes Reuchlin

Georg N. Knauer

Gathering the Latin and early vernacular translations of Homer's works for the Catalogus Translationum et Commentariorum has turned out to be a much more exciting job than even Professor Kristeller had foreseen in 1977, and in this search, codices that contain large amounts of miscellaneous material have provided surprising and most welcome help. One of them is Munich, Bayerische Staatsbibliothek, Codex Graecus Monacensis (Cgrm) 582a, which furnishes a missing link in the later history of the pseudo-Homeric *Batrachomyomachia.*

During the Renaissance, this short Hellenistic mock epic, now dated not before the first century B.C.,[1] was normally considered to have been a youthful work of Homer. It was then, perhaps because of its brevity, often translated into Latin and the vernaculars. The first translation, in Latin hexameters, was made by Carolus Marsuppinus Aretinus of Florence (ca. 1399–1453), probably finished in 1429.[2] Marsuppinus's translation of the roughly three hundred lines of the Byzantine vulgate into—it seems—331 Latin hexameters begins with a clever rendering of the Greek title *Batrachomyomachia* into a hexameter:

Professor Knauer informs the editors that since submission of this essay he has continued to work on the manuscript here discussed and has been able to identify further texts in it.

1. Reinhold Glei, *Die Batrachomyomachie: Synoptische Edition und Kommentar,* Studien zur klassischen Philologie 12 (Frankfurt am Main and New York: P. Lang, 1984), 34. Commonly used is the edition by Thomas W. Allen in *Opera Homeri,* 5 vols. (Oxford: Clarendon, 1912–1920; reprinted with corrections, 1946), 5:168–83; the codices are listed on 164–67.

2. Remigio Sabbadini, *Biografia documentata di Giovanni Aurispa* (Noto: F. Zammit, 1890), 179 f.

23

"Ranarum murumque simul crudelia bella." Marsuppinus dedicated it with an interesting *epistola* to his friend, the Sicilian poet Johannes Marrasius (Giovanni Marrasio, 1400/1404–September 1452), who replied with a poem entitled "Ad Carolum Aretinum de Batrachomiomachia Hecatombe,"[3] which actually surpasses the announced one hundred lines ("hecatombe") by two.

This translation was very successful, although it was not normally included in sixteenth-century editions of Homer's works, excepting that printed at Venice in 1516. The list in preparation for the Catalogus Translationum et Commentariorum comprises sixty-six manuscripts and nine editions of Marsuppinus's translation; no critical edition has yet been made, though the material for it is ready to be used.[4]

The translation and its dedicatory epistle were destined to cause a considerable amount of bibliographical confusion. The two were several times separated, and each began a life of its own. Thus, the epistle served as an example of letter writing and became incorporated in collections of letters or orations.[5] Similarly, the translation could be copied without the epistle.[6] It is interesting to note that Marsuppino's translation of the *Batrachomyomachia* attracted attention for its own merits: it was usually copied without the original Greek text[7] and is rarely found with Marsuppino's other translations of Homer, that is, his hexametrical renderings of a large part of *Iliad* 1 (which is accompanied by an *epistula dedicatoria* to Pope Nicolaus V) and of a section from *Iliad* 9 (308–

---

3. Johannes Marrasius, *Angelinetum et carmina varia,* ed. Gianvito Resta, Centro di Studi filologici e linguistici siciliani, Bollettino, Supplementi Serie Mediolatina e Umanistica 3 (Palermo, 1976), 155, with a short biography on 9–33 and a photo of his portrait in Noto, Sicily, facing 34.

4. An edition should comprise all three items: the *epistola dedicatoria* to Marrasius Siculus, the translation proper, and Marrasius's *Hecatombe,* at least the text from Antonio Altamura's edition, *I carmi Latini di Giovanni Marrasio* (Palermo: Edizioni Sansoni Antiquariata, 1954), 27–30. The *epistola dedicatoria* has been edited in Resta's edition of Marrasius cited in n. 3, 152–55. Lisbon, Biblioteca Nacional, Cod. ilum. 45 seems to be one of the earliest dated manuscripts (1436).

5. Bergamo, Biblioteca Civica, MS Lambda II 32 (MA 613), f. 77r–v; Como, Biblioteca Comunale, MS 4.4.6, ff. 380v–381v; München, Clm 5369, ff. 45v–46v. The *orationes* appear in Basel, Universitätsbibliothek, MS F V 27 (1466), f. 141r–v.

6. E.g., Arezzo, Biblioteca Consorziale (formerly della Fraternita dei Laici), MS 150 (fifteenth century, before 1466), ff. 43–49v; Erlangen, Universitätsbibliothek, cod. 621 (fifteenth century), ff. 275v–278; Vat. lat. 2795, ff. 77–82v; the 1516 edition of *Homeri opera e graeco traducta* (Venice: Venetus de Vitalibus), item 6, ff. BBii^vo–[BBiv^vo].

7. Exceptions are (1) Vat. Lat. 11536, which bears the Latin translation on the rectos of ff. 97–111, the Greek text on the versos, ff. 96v–110v; (2) Paris, BN gr. 2600, in which the Greek text precedes the translation, ff. 130–44v; 145–51v are blank; then follows the *epistola dedicatoria* on ff. 152–55v and *Batr.* in Latin on ff. 155v–67.

422a).[8] Because both the translation of the *Batrachomyomachia* and its dedicatory epistle were short (the translation covering normally about six folios), they could be copied quickly into a single gathering, which then became a free-floating, independent small manuscript that could be given away, copied again, and finally gathered with other material into a miscellaneous volume. Therefore, these texts, either together or separated, are found—with or without titles and names—in miscellaneous manuscripts that contain all sorts of classical Greek texts in Latin translations or Latin classical or humanist texts. Thus they occur, for instance, in the company of Aesop (a natural connection because the *Batrachomyomachia* belongs to the same genre of ancient animal fables), Appianus, Lucian, Diogenes' letters, Terence, Juvenal, Persius, Vergil, parts of the *Appendix Vergiliana,* Livy, Ovid, and the *Ilias latina.* Another occasional companion is Plato, because Plato's works had been translated by Leonardus Brunus Aretinus, with whom Carolus Marsuppinus Aretinus was confused several times.[9] The manuscripts that contain these texts are very often, and quite appropriately, called miscellanies and cannot be further distinguished into orderly categories.

In these diverse lines of transmission, Marsuppinus's name was sometimes lost, and his translation was then copied as an anonymous work.[10] The translation was published for the first time perhaps in 1474, by an anonymous editor and without the dedicatory epistle, and it does not bear Marsuppinus's name. The unique surviving copy of this editio princeps of twenty-four leaves, now in Manchester, gives no place, publisher, or year of publication.[11] Here, Marsup-

---

8. With *Iliad* 1: Torino, Biblioteca Reale, Varia 14, ff. 127v–36v, epist. dedic. ff. "125/126"– 27 (mistake in pagination); the epist. dedic. to Nicolaus V, ff. 110v–16; and the translation of *Iliad* 1 on ff. 116–25v. With *Iliad* 1 and 9.308–429: Firenze, Biblioteca Laurenziana, MS Strozzi 100, ff. 19–26v; and Biblioteca Nazionale Centrale, MS II.IX.148, ff. 274–80v. In both, the *Batr.* is preceded by the *epist. dedic.* to Nicolaus V and the translations from *Iliad* 1 and 9.

9. Firenze, Biblioteca Riccardiana, MS 913; Oxford, Bodleian Library, MS Canon. Misc. 308; Padova, Biblioteca Universitaria, MS 1527.

10. Cambridge, MA, Harvard University, MSS 145 and 271; Colmar, Bibliothèque de la Ville, MS 493; Leiden, Bibliotheek der Rijksuniversiteit, Cod. Voss. lat. O 20; London, British Library, MSS Additional 17812, Harley 2695, 5198; Naples, Biblioteca Nazionale, MS IV. F.18; Siena, Biblioteca Comunale, MS I IX 1; St. Petersburg, Publičnaja biblioteka im. M. E. Saltykova-Ščedrina, MS. lat. Q. XVII 18 (lost); Vatican City, MS Vat. lat. 2795, Urb. lat. 643; Venezia, Biblioteca Nazionale Marciana, MS Lat. Cl. XIV, nr. 109 (4623); Vicenza, Biblioteca Comunale Bertoliana, MS G.3.7.20.

11. Manchester, John Rylands Library, Inc. 3325, ff. [1]v–[24]v, without date (1474?) or place (Brescia?), the printer perhaps being Thomas Ferrandus. See *Catalogue of the Printed Books and Manuscripts in the John Rylands Library, Manchester* (Manchester: J. E. Cornish, 1899), 879b ("Muobatrachomyomachia, Florence, 1480"). For this incunabulum, see Hain 8783; British Library, "Incunabula Short Title Catalogue" (electronic database, henceforth referred to as ISTC),

pinus's hexametrical translation appears on the versos of the earliest Greek text ever printed, the *Batrachomyomachia.*

This Greek text, however, is also accompanied by an anonymous interlinear prose translation, which begins:

> Incipiens primum musarum chorum ex helicone
> venire in meum cor opto causa cantus
> quem nuper in libellis meis super genibus posui.

The source for this odd edition was probably a manuscript in which Marsuppinus's name, as that of the verse translator of the *Batrachomyomachia,* had already been suppressed.[12] The sources of the Greek text and the prose translation have so far remained unknown. The latter was published again at Basel in 1518 by Beatus Rhenanus, in a revised form;[13] it—and not Marsuppinus's hexametrical translation—found its way into dozens of sixteenth-century editions and reprints of Homer's works with Latin translations.

About thirty-five years later, Joachimus Vadianus, then a very young professor at Vienna University, published a translation of the *Batrachomyomachia* under the title *Homeri Batrachomyomachia Ioanne Capnione Phorcensi metaphraste,* with a dedication dated 1510. The "Johannes Capnio" here named as the translator is Johannes Reuchlin of Pforzheim. On the title page of his edition, Vadianus also printed an epigram. The latter is indeed by Reuchlin, but the translation is not. It is, rather, the hexametrical rendering by Marsuppinus.

---

under "Homerus"; Johann Albert Fabricius and Gottlieb Christoph Harles, *Bibliotheca Graeca,* vol. 1 (Hamburg: C. E. Bohn, 1790), 338; Jacopo Morelli, *Bibliotheca Maphaei Pinellii Veneti,* vol. 2 (Venice: C. Palesi, 1787), 281–83, no. 4262; Georg Wolfgang Panzer, *Annales typographici,* vol. 4 (Nürnberg, 1796), 143, no. 636; Thomas F. Dibdin, *Bibliotheca Spenceriana,* vol. 2 (London, 1814), 53–55, no. 254: "purchased by Count Reviczky at the Pinelli sale"; Robert G. C. Proctor, *The Printing of Greek in the 15th century* (Oxford: Oxford University Press, 1900), 83; Robert A. Peddie, *Printing at Brescia in the Fifteenth Century* (London: Williams and Norgate, 1905), 5 and 13; Hansjörg Wölke, *Untersuchungen zur Batrachomyomachie,* Beiträge zur Klassischen Philologie 100 (Meisenheim am Glan: Hain, 1978), 44 and n. 132; *Graecogermania, Griechischstudien deutscher Humanisten, Die Editionstätigkeit der Griechen in der italienischen Renaissance (1469–1523),* unter Leitung von Dieter Harlfinger bearbeitet von Reinhard Barm, Ausstellungskataloge der Herzog August Bibliothek, 59 (Weinheim and New York: VCH, Acta Humaniora, 1989), 43, no. 16.

12. The editor, realizing that Marsuppinus apparently had left out three lines (i.e., 214, 214a, and 215 in Allen's edition of *Homeri opera,* 5:178), exclaims in capital letters: "Hic tres reliquit versus Homeri interpraes" (i.e., Marsuppinus; f. 19v). Allen's *apparatus criticus* lists no such lacuna.

13. *Homeri Batrachomyomachia, Hoc est, Ranarum et murium pugna: Graece et Latine* (Basel: Ioannes Frobenius, 1518).

This "Pseudo-Reuchlin" was transmitted in six further printed editions and three manuscript copies.

Vadianus may have made this remarkable error in good faith, perhaps because he had used one of the anonymously transmitted manuscripts mentioned earlier in this paper (at n. 10). But how did Vadianus get access to the genuine epigram by Reuchlin? It is addressed to one "Erhart confessor" ("Capnionis ad Erhartum confessorem epigramma modestissimum") and begins:

Muribus et ranis fuerint quae praelia: *nostrum* [1510: saeva]
Hoc translaticium que*n*que docebit opus. [1510: -m-]
Calle quidem scabro non laevia verba *mea*bunt [1510: niteb-]
Et sine mensura singula iuncta vides.
Non sic graeca sonant, non est ridendus Homerus,
Spirat enim vivus si modo graecus erit.
Sed verbum verbo dum curo cuique referre
Non color ille prior, nec sonus ullus adest.[14]

Line 7 plainly states the point of the epigram: a word-by-word—that is, prose—translation will never reproduce its Greek original appropriately. But evidently Vadianus did not understand this point, or he would not have printed a rendering in verse. Had he understood Reuchlin's lines correctly, he should have searched for a prose translation by Johannes Reuchlin instead of printing Marsuppino's verse translation. His failure to do so has been shared by many later scholars.[15]

---

14. The text here reproduced is taken from Cgrm 582a, f. 206, col. a. For the italicized letters and words, I add in brackets variants from the Vienna 1510 edition.

15. It is possible that Maittaire saw this edition; describing Marsuppinus's *Batr.* edition of 1509, he wrote: "Eandem hanc versionem [i.e. Marsuppini], sine anni, loci, et typographi indicio editam vidi, a Johanne Capnione sibi adscriptam"(*Annales typographici ab artis inventae origine*, vol. 1 [The Hague: Isaac Vaillant, 1741], 497). Ludwig Geiger, *Johann Reuchlin, sein Leben und seine Werke* (Leipzig: Dunker und Humbolt, 1871; reprint, Nieuwkoop: B. de Graaf, 1964), 95 n. 5, prints the epigram with a few variants, having no doubts about Reuchlin's authorship as translator of the *Batr.* (see 95 f.). This is rather astonishing, as Geiger used and praised Christian Fr. Schnurrer, *Biographische und litterarische Nachrichten von ehemaligen Lehrern der hebräischen Litteratur in Tübingen* (Ulm: Wohlerische Buchhandlung, 1792), 62, convincingly listing the translation not as a genuine work of Reuchlin. Schnurrer refers to and quotes Michael Denis, *Wiens Buchdruckergeschicht* (Vienna: C. F. Wappler, 1782), 306 f., who reports that in 1741 Michael Maittaire had already recognized that Vadianus's text was not Reuchlin's but Marsuppinus's translation; but he evidently thought that Reuchlin himself had appropriated this translation ("a Joanne Capnione sibi adscriptam"). Strangely enough, Denis then considered it likely that Reuchlin got a copy of Marsuppinus's translation in Florence in 1487, and by adding the epigram to Erhard, he easily misled Vadianus. Denis tried in vain to identify Erhard Confessor. Alexander

This hitherto "lost" prose translation of the *Batrachomyomachia* by Johannes Reuchlin has survived in the manuscript with which this paper is concerned, Munich, Bayerische Staatsbibliothek, Cgrm 582a, ff. 206–7v. The codex belongs to the group of Greek manuscripts that reached the Bayerische Staatsbibliothek after 1812. These codices still lack a printed description and have not been dealt with in the *Iter italicum*.[16] The "Greek supplement" can only be found in the photocopy of the undated handwritten list in the reading room of the Handschriftenabteilung (p. 2), where Reuchlin is listed; or in the brief and insufficient description by Wolfgang Hörmann published in 1958, where Reuchlin is not listed (pp. 56 f.).[17] Cgrm 582a is a paper codex of 280 folios in twenty-one gatherings, written by several hands in the late fifteenth and early sixteenth centuries, with a probable terminus ad quem of 1512 or 1513.[18]

Reuchlin's prose translation in Cgrm 582a is headed: "Ioannes Reuchlin phorcensis LL [legum imperialium] Doctor S.P.D. Erharto Confessori Dilectissimo."[19] This is followed by the dedicatory epigram,[20] and the latter in turn

---

Brückner, *Średniowieczna Poezya Iacińska w Polsce,* Rozprawy Akademii Umiejętności, Wydział Filologiczny, ser. 2, vol. 1 (Kraków: Nakładem Akademii Umiejętności,1892; reprint, 1894), 304–72 (reprint, 1–69), esp. 332 f. (29 f.), 353 (50), and 372 (68), in a modest addendum to his description of the lost St. Petersburg (formerly Warszawa) manuscript, is the only other scholar who has realized that Vadianus had made a mistake. But neither he nor any other reader followed up this hint or Denis's and Schnurrer's obvious and justified doubts; cf. Josef Benzing, *Bibliographie der Schriften Johannes Reuchlins im 15. und 16. Jahrhundert* (Bad Bocklet: W. Krieg, 1955), 32 f., nos. 109–12a.

16. Paul Oskar Kristeller, *Iter italicum,* 6 vols. (London: Warburg Institute, 1963–93); henceforth referred to as *Iter italicum.*

17. For the inventory see München, Bayerische Staatsbibliothek, "Codices graeci Monacenses, Inventar 575–619," 2; cf. Wolfgang Hörmann, "Das Supplement der griechischen Handschriften der Bayerischen Staatsbibliothek," in Χάλικες, *Festgabe für die Teilnehmer am 11. Internationalen Byzantinistenkongress, München 15.–20.9.1958* (Freising: F. P. Datterer, 1958), 56 f.

18. The latest works excerpted seem to be Georg Simmler's *Isagogicum* (Tübingen, 1512), on ff. 127 and 194v, or Giraldus in Ptolemy, *Geographia* (Strasbourg: J. Schott, 1513), on f. 116. The latest date I have found in the volume is February 7, 1517, on a small slip glued onto f. 266, with a schedule, it seems, for the exequies of abbots of the monastery of Ebersberg. The volume may have been bound at about this time. The gatherings in the volume have been determined by Mr. Andreas Daum, of the Institute for Modern History at the University of Munich, in January 1993. It is not easy to establish how many hands are present in it. The "main hand" wrote most of the manuscript, but three or four additional hands responsible for shorter parts are discernible. Original blanks at the end of gatherings or in the margins were used for later additions, written in very small letters; it has not yet been established whether these are by the "main hand" or not.

19. The title page of Vadianus's edition of 1510 seems to indicate that he did not see the title in the form of the Munich manuscript.

20. The text of the dedicatory epigram to Erhard Confessor in Vadianus's edition of 1510 has been cited previously in this essay.

is followed by the subscription: "Vale feliciter. Ex Stutgardia. Translatio Ioannis Reuchlin phorcensis De verbo ad verbum propter addiscentes" (f. 206). After the title "Homeri Batrachomyomachia: In quibusdam autem Tigretis Caris,"[21] the translation begins:

> Incipiens primum musarum chorum ex helicone
> Venire in meum pro "cor animum" per cantilenam
> Quam nuper in libris, meis super genubus posui
> contentionem ingentem, bellimotivum opus martis
> [5]   orans hominibus in aures universis mitti
> Quomodo mures in ranis fortiter pugnantes invaserunt
> terrigenarum hominum imitati facta gigantum.
> Ut sermo in mortalibus erat tale autem habuit inicium
> . . . .

It ends on f. 207v:

> Inque fugam vertebantur. occidebat autem sol iam
> [299/303]   Et belli opus uno die completum est. Finis.

The translation is followed by two subscriptions (f. 207v). The first contains a Latin translation of the subscription Leonicus Cretensis had added to his edition of the Greek text of the *Batrachomyomachia* (Venice, April 22, 1486).[22] In the Munich codex, the same hand that copied Reuchlin's Latin translation also copied this printed Greek text, which here precedes the translation (ff. 197–204). This Greek text is followed by an epigram of Michael Apostolius not translated by Reuchlin: "Praesertim in tanta rerum aliarum occupatione" (f. 207v). The identification of the source of the translation

---

21. "Vale feliciter . . . Tigretis Caris" is missing in Vadianus's edition of 1510. For the form *Tigres* instead of *Pigres* see Arthur Ludwich, *Die homerische BATRACHOMYOMACHIA des Karers Pigres* (Leipzig: B. G. Teubner, 1896), 17 and n. 45 on the editio princeps of 1486.

22. Walter Arthur Copinger, *Supplement to Hain's Repertorium bibliographicum,* 3 vols. (Milan: Gorlich, 1950), no. 8782; cf. Emile L. J. Legrand, *Bibliographie Hellénique,* vol. 1 (Paris: E. Leroux, 1885), 6–7, no. 3. Reprinted in Michael Maittaire, ed., *Batrachomyomachia Graeca* (London: William Bowyer, 1721), f. i.i ff., cf. p. xiii. The subscriptions read: "Sequuntur [i.e., on f. 204] Carmina Doctoris Michaelis [Apostolii] quae ipse appellat Heroica sed quia mensura versuum non est ut arbitror servata. Idcirco transferre nolui praesertim in tanta rerum aliarum occupatione. Sequitur ad finem [i.e., bottom of f. 204, in Greek]: In nomine sanctae trinitatis patris et filii et sancti spiritus:—Compositio mei Laonici Cretensis et praepositi Chaniorum in anno Millesimo quadringentesimo octuagesimo sexto mense aprili vigesima secunda Apud Venetiam [i.e., April 22, 1486]."

provides also the terminus post quem for it: Reuchlin must have bought his copy of Leonicus's edition after its publication at the end of April 1486. The end of this subscription confirms the statement following Reuchlin's dedicatory epigram: "Haec ego Ioannes Reuchlin phorcensis LL [legum imperialium] doctor verbum a verbo de graeco sermonem in Latinum traduxi. Finis." Since Reuchlin identifies himself twice as its author—once in the dedicatory epigram in Stuttgart, and again in the subscription—there can be no doubt that this is the "lost" prose translation by Reuchlin.

But the hand of the Greek text and of the translation is not Reuchlin's. It probably is that of the individual named in the second subscription (f. 207v), written in poor Greek: "Brother Johannes of Grafing, Bavarian, from the monastery Ebersberg." Grafing is just four kilometers south of Ebersberg, thirty-five kilometers east of Munich. Brother Johannes also dated his copy with date and year—to the feast of Saint Afra of Augsburg, August 7, and the feast of Saints Cyriacus and Smaragdus, August 8, in 1495.[23] Hence, Reuchlin must have translated the *Batrachomyomachia* between May 1486 and July 1495, perhaps in 1491.[24]

His translation would fit well into these years. It comes after his second trip to Italy in 1490, when he met, perhaps, Marsilio Ficino and, certainly, Pico della Mirandola, and studied Latin in Rome with Hermolaus Barbarus[25] and

---

23. F. 207v, bottom: ἄδελφος [sic] ἰωννης γραφίνγιως ἐκ Cυσθρόφης ἐβερσπεργ / υωιοαριοC ἔτι [sic] ᾶ ῦ ῥ ἐ [i.e., "in the year (for ἔτει) 1495"] ἄφρασ. μαρτυρ [squeezed in the right margin] ἐν ἡμερα [sic] κυριακοῦ, καὶ σμαραγδοῦ [last line].

24. Johannes Trithemius (1462–1516), abbot of Sponheim, reports that Reuchlin had translated the duel between Paris and Menelaos (*Iliad* 3. ca. 264–382) into German verses (*Catalogus illustrium virorum* [Mainz: Peter von Friedberg, 1494], f. LXIv: "Monomachiam quoque Iliados Homeri de Paridis et Menelai duello in linguam Germanicam metrice vertit"); see Geiger, *Johann Reuchlin,* 67 and 68, n. 1. It is probable that Dalburg thanks Reuchlin for this translation in his letter of December 12, 1491, published in *Clarorum virorum epistolae . . . missae ad Ioannem Reuchlin* (Tübingen: Thomas Anshelm, 1514), ff. g6v–g7r. Both sources are printed in Franz Worstbrock, *Deutsche Antikerezeption: 1450–1550,* Veröffentlichungen zur Humanismusforschung 1 (Boppard am Rhein: Boldt, 1976), 164: "Nempe cum alias tuas translationes quas vel nostro vel fratris amore absolvisti, e graeco in Germanicam vel latinam linguam vertens libellos, vehementer probaremus, tum has tuas lucubrationes maxime sumus admirati, Alemannica videlicet in lingua tam apte, tam lucide, tam suaviter et in ligata et ita ad certum numerum perstricta oratione, ea nihilo in sententiis immutato potuisse explicare, tantoque id mirabilius visum est quod te illo genere carminis quod octonis septenisque pedibus vicissim procedit concinnat similiterque cadit desinitque quam aptissime nunquam te antea usum esse aiebas." The German translation is lost. See Thomas Bleicher, *Homer in der deutschen Literatur (1450–1740): Zur Rezeption der Antike und zur Poetologie der Neuzeit* (Stuttgart: J. B. Metzler, 1972), 40–46.

25. Who instead of Latinizing Reuchlin's name turned it into Greek, Καπνίων: Capnion, Capnio, from καπνός, German "Rauch"; cf. Geiger, *Johann Reuchlin,* 23 f.; Rudolf Pfeiffer, *History of Classical Scholarship 1300–1850* (Oxford: Clarendon, 1976), 87.

Greek in Florence with Demetrius Chalkondyles, the editor of the editio princeps of Homer (1488). Reuchlin was entrusted with important diplomatic tasks, studied Hebrew, built up his library, but held no university post.[26]

Reuchlin's translation of the *Batrachomyomachia* seems to be unfinished. In some cases, ditto marks apparently indicate different options for the translation (lines 2 and 30); in others, Reuchlin simply transcribes the Greek words into Latin (line 30; cf. lines 255 and 298 f.), more or less following his itacistic pronunciation: in line 298 he has "Octapodes Dicareni Achirrees" for ὀκτάπο-δες, δικάρηνοι, ἀχειρέες; in 299, "Carcini" for καρκίνοι.[27] As it is the only extant translation of a "Homeric" text by Reuchlin, it should be published soon.

Who was Reuchlin's friend Erhardus Confessor? In 1978, Professor Sicherl published the following note by Johannes Cuno (ca. 1462/63–1513).

> Hec [i.e., poems by Gregory of Nazianzus] transtulit venerandus pater Erhardus de Pappenheim hebraice admodum peritus neque ignarus litterarum grecarum vir prudentissimus, confessor in Altenhohenau Ibique sepultus 1497.[28]

Altenhohenau was a monastery of Dominican nuns in the neighborhood of Kloster Ebersberg. Erhardus's hand had already been identified by the late Professor Bischoff in a manuscript from Tegernsee, Clm 18526b. His identification has made it possible to realize that the translations of Gregory's poems that Cuno had identified as being by Erhard are indeed preserved in his hand in yet another Munich manuscript, Cgrm 323. Moreover, Erhard—"hebraice admodum peritus"—rendered into German "selected judicial documents generated by the ritual murder trial" against the Jews of Trento in 1475.[29] This

---

26. Born in Pforzheim near Stuttgart in Suevia on January 29, 1455, Reuchlin died on June 30, 1522, in Stuttgart. Besides Geiger, *Johann Reuchlin,* see also Stefan Rhein, "Reuchliniana I: Neue Bausteine zur Biographie Johannes Reuchlins" and "Reuchliniana II: Forschungen zum Werk Johannes Reuchlins," *Wolfenbütteler Renaissance Mitteilungen* 12 (1988): 84–94; 13 (1989): 23–44.

27. In line 2, he has "in meum pro cor animum" for εἰς ἐμὸν ἦτορ ἐπεύχομαι εἴνεκ' ἀοιδῆς; in 30 "[*genuit*] (the reading is uncertain) autem me in Calyba" for γείνατο δ' ἐν καλύβῃ με (ed. 1474?: genuit autem in tecto); in 255 "tetrachytrum" for τετράχυτρον.

28. Martin Sicherl, *Johannes Cuno, ein Wegbereiter des Griechischen in Deutschland: Eine biographisch-kodikologische Studie,* Studien zum Fortwirken der Antike 9 (Heidelberg: Winter, 1978), 78. The note appears in the Sélestat manuscript 331 (K 892d), f. 2: "1497." The last digit is damaged; but after inspecting the manuscript (on October 26, 1993), I can confirm Sicherl's reading. The remark in *Iter italicum,* vol. 3, no. 348b—"1494 (? last digit unclear)"—is not correct.

29. Ronnie Po-Chia Hsia, *Trent 1475: Stories of a Ritual Murder Trial* (New Haven: Yale University Press in cooperation with Yeshiva University Library, 1992), xix.

manuscript, written after 1478 and provided with the parted coat of arms of Count Eberhard (1445–February 24, 1496) and his wife, Barbara di Gonzaga (died May 21, 1503), has now, after many adventures, been deposited as MS 1246 in the Yeshiva University Museum Library in New York.[30]

The discovery of Reuchlin's complete prose translation of the *Batrachomyomachia* in Cgrm 582a is important enough in itself, but it provides some further insights. Professor Sicherl has recently discussed the contents of another miscellany, the just mentioned Cgrm 323, and the two codices together furnish precious insights into the workings of Renaissance scholars.[31] Both manuscripts come from Kloster Ebersberg, where they must have stood close to each other on the library shelves.[32] Both contain a remarkable collection of miscellaneous texts. For many of those in Cgrm 323, Professor Sicherl

---

30. The coat of arms appears at the bottom of p. 4 of the manuscript. The German version must have been written after June 20, 1478, the date of the bull of Sixtus IV declaring the case "rite et recte factum," also on p. 4. The decisive passage proving that Erhard Confessor is the author of the German translation is to be found in Munich, Clm 18526b, f. 190; see Bernhard Bischoff, "Frater Erhardus O.Pr., ein Hebraist des XV. Jahrhunderts," *Historisches Jahrbuch* 58 (1938), reprinted in *Mittelalterliche Studien,* vol. 2 (Stuttgart: Hiersmann, 1967), 189: the entry of the librarian (attested since 1481) of the Benedictine monastery St. Quirinus in Tegernsee, Ambrosius Schwerzenbeck: "Anno Domini etc. 1492 scriptum istud factum est ab Erhardo religioso de ordine predicatorum." On f. 192v (f. 6rb of the copy in Chm 200) Erhard wrote: "Illas enim ut Tridentinorum Iudaeorum prodit confessio, prout iudiciarius ibidem contra eos formatus processus continet, quem multo tempore sub magna servare cogebar custodia, ne furto auferretur aut in aliquo falsificaretur. Qui per me in nostrum vulgare [i.e., German] translatus plus quam 24 integrorum arcuum sexternos continet." Bischoff, "Frater Erhardus," *Mittelalterliche Studien* 2:189, gives his own German translation; cf. Bernhard Walde, *Christliche Hebraisten Deutschlands am Ausgang des Mittelalters,* Alttestamentliche Abhandlungen 6.2–3 (Münster: Aschendorff, 1916), 178–82; Willehad Paul Eckert, O.P., "Aus den Akten des Trienter Judenprozesses," in Paul Wilpert and W. P. Eckert, eds., *Fudentum im Mittelalter,* Miscellanea mediaevalia 4 (Berlin: De Gruyter, 1966), 293 n. 38. Hsia, *Trent 1475,* is the most recent study of the trial and the manuscript.

31. Professor Sicherl has generously provided me with a photocopy of his typescript of his most recent article, "Neue Reuchliniana," in *Graeca recentiora in Germania: deutsch-griechische Kulturbeziehungen vom 15. bis 19. Jahrhundert: Vorträge eines ersten und zweiten deutsch-griechischen Arbeitsgespräches vom 19. bis 22. August 1989 und 11. bis 13. Februar 1991 in der Herzog August Bibliothek Wolfenbüttel,* edited by Hans Eideneier, *Wolfenbütteler Forschungen* 59 (1994): 65–92, in which he discusses the contents of Cgrm 323. Without his help, and without his earlier studies on Johannes Reuchlin, Johannes Cuno, or Beatus Rhenanus, the following remarks and identifications would have been impossible.

32. The provenance of Cgrm 582a is noted at the bottom of f. 1: "Residentiae Societatis Jesu, Ebersbergae 1596." On the spine appears an old call number: B I 0. Cgrm 323 is bound in the same way and has on its spine the same type of call number: B I 10. The latter volume is half the size of Cgrm 582a.

has been able to establish their general source, which is Reuchlin's library in Stuttgart. The same can now be said for Cgrm 582a.[33]

Both manuscripts contain many excerpts from the same texts. The excerpts in the two miscellanies may be identical, may differ in length, or may come from different sections of the same source. Latin translations may be added in one miscellany but not in the other. In all instances, the source of the excerpts in both manuscripts is the same: either an identifiable manuscript, an incunabulum in Reuchlin's library, or excerpts Reuchlin had made previously from manuscripts he had seen in his years of studying in Basel and Paris or on his trips to Italy. Professor Sicherl has identified many of these manuscripts—which often contain notes in Reuchlin's hand—in Paris, Sélestat, Heidelberg, or Basel, where Reuchlin was the first to recognize and make use of the Greek manuscripts in the Dominican priory, that is, of the famous library of Cardinal John Stojković of Ragusa.[34]

The contents of Cgrm 582a fit into roughly three groups.

First, most of the longest items are copied from incunabula listed in the catalog of Hebrew and Greek manuscripts and of printed books in Reuchlin's library, preserved in Vat. Palat. lat. 1925 and published by Karl Christ in 1924. Some examples are

Ff. 1–93: Reuchlin owned two editions of Johannes Crastonus, *Lexicon Graeco-latinum.* One, published in 1478 or 1480, is copied in Cgrm 582a, ff. 1–93ra. From the other, the 1497 edition, only Aldus's preface is copied in part, also on f. 93ra (Christ no. 29). In addition, on ff. 219–21v of Cgrm 582a, the anonymous *Lexicon militare,* published in the same two incunabula, is copied in part. This clearly proves that Reuchlin's own books were used as exemplars.

---

33. For editions copied or used in Reuchlin's library in Stuttgart, see Karl Christ, *Die Bibliothek Reuchlins in Pforzheim,* Zentralblatt für Bibliothekswesen, Beiheft 52 (Leipzig: Otto Harrassowitz, 1924); Karl Preisendanz, "Die Bibliothek Johannes Reuchlins," in Manfred Krebs, ed. *Johannes Reuchlin, 1455–1522, Festgabe Pforzheim* (Pforzheim: Selbstverlag der Stadt, 1955), 35–82; Wilhelm Brambach, *Die Handschriften der Badischen Landesbibliothek in Karlsruhe,* vol. 1, *Geschichte und Bestand der Sammlung, Neudruck mit bibliographischen Nachträgen* (Karlsruhe: C. T. Groos, 1891; reprint, Wiesbaden: Otto Harrassowitz, 1970); 2–13: "Die Bibliothek des Johannes Reuchlin"; vols. 3–5, *Orientalische Handschriften, Neudruck* (Karlsruhe: C. T. Groos, 1829; reprint, Wiesbaden: Otto Harrassowitz, 1969), 1–28.

34. André Vernet, "Les manuscrits grecs de Jean de Raguse (+ 1443)," *Basler Zeitschrift für Geschichte und Altertumskunde* 60 (1960): 75–108.

Ff. 117–ca. 187v: Constantinus Lascaris's *Erotemata,* in Greek with a
Latin translation, printed by Aldus Manutius in Venice, 1494 (HC 9924).
Pseudo-Pythagoras and Pseudo-Phocylides, in Greek with a Latin translation, were also copied from this edition and appear in Cgrm 582a on ff.
251–55.

Ff. 225–42v: excerpts from Isocrates, *Vitae* and *Orationes,* from Reuchlin's copy of the Milan edition of 1493.

Second, if these and many other texts were copied in Reuchlin's library,
further excerpts in Cgrm 582a may be from books that also belonged to
Reuchlin but have not yet been attested, especially Latin or vernacular prints.
Examples are

Ff. 94–111v: the incomplete copy of the *Introito e porta,* the curious
Italian-German glossary published in Venice in 1477.

The *Batrachomyomachia,* the editio princeps of 1486 with Reuchlin's translation (ff. 204–7v).

Long excerpts from Lactantius, *Divinae Institutiones,* including passages on
the sibyls (ff. 243–47, 255v–57), from one of the editions published after
the editio princeps (Subiaco, 1469). These are followed (ff. 247v–50), for
example, by excerpts on the sibyls from Robertus Caracciolus's *Sermones quadragesimales de poenitentia,* from one of the editions between
1472 and 1479 (f. 248), surrounding the famous acrostic from the Sib-
ylline Oracles (8.217–26), with St. Augustine's Latin translation (*De
civitate Dei* 18.23). Added were also passages on the sibyls from
Hartmann Schedel's *Libri cronicarum* (Nuremberg, 1493).

Third, numerous excerpts from other texts, some of them very short, were
evidently copied from Reuchlinian excerpts from Plato's *Phaedrus;*
Thucydides; Aristotle; the Platonist philosopher Albinus; four letters of
Diogenes; Marcus Aurelius; the paradoxographer Apollonius; Aphthonius;
Maximus of Tyre; Gregory of Nazianzus; and others. There are also excerpts
from poems of contemporaries, such as Conradus Celtis (ff. 93–93v), a number
of so far unidentified pieces, and a few pages with words written in Hebrew.

Very surprisingly, both manuscripts contain a Turkish text that translates the
Lord's Prayer, the Hail Mary, and the Creed.[35] In Cgrm 582a, the Turkish text

---

35. Cgrm 582a, f. 115; Cgrm 323, ff. 217v–19, followed by some exercises. Heading:

is preceded by the Lord's Prayer, the Hail Mary, and the creed in Hungarian (f. 114v).[36]

Cgrm 582a thus does not offer many "new" texts. Basically, it collects copies of printed material that were made between ca. 1495 and 1512, and hence it is likely to be looked at with scorn.[37] However, it does preserve one text so far not identified but clearly of importance in the appropriation of Homer's minor works during the Renaissance: the *Batrachomyomachia* translation by Reuchlin. In addition, the excerpts it contains, written by students who were often not very fluent in Greek, offer a welcome view into Reuchlin's interests: dictionaries, grammar, languages, the orators, historical texts, the Cabala, Pythagoreism, the sibyls. In a number of cases, one gets, for a few pages, the feeling that the scribe was taking notes during conversations with Reuchlin, who seems to have shared his knowledge generously with his visitors in his beloved and famous library in Stuttgart. Cgrm 582a does not represent a teaching curriculum, such as one finds in other humanistic manuscripts.[38] Yet its curious assortment of texts, modest relics from an exciting cultural period, surely reflects the interaction of encouraging teachers and receptive students.

Van Pelt Library of the University of Pennsylvania owns a moving example. In its copy of Johannes Aurispa's Latin translation of Hierocles' *In aureos versus Pythagorae* of 1474, Johannes Cuno copied Pseudo-Pythagoras's *Aurea verba* with a Latin translation from the same incunabulum of 1494 with Constantinus Lascaris's *Erotemata,* which the copyist of Cgrm 582a (ff. 251–52) had used in Reuchlin's library. Cuno visited Reuchlin in Stuttgart on August 10, 1496, and after copying both the Greek text and the Latin translation of the

---

Τουρκικῶς πατερ ἡμῶν [Pater noster, Inc.]: Ata mis quim [superscript: kym] coc da sen Algbisladir senin atin. Chelsin chanlichin senin . . . / . . . (6) yschalla fiat optatū ḍẹi [Ave Maria] χαιρε μαρια / (7) Süüntschla sen [superscript: laeta es] . . . / . . . (9) ischalla. [Credo] πιστευω συμβολον . . . .

36. A source for these exotic translations of the Lord's Prayer has not yet been found. But compare the "Apex Ascensianus" in the great Virgil edition with commentaries published by Iodocus Badius Ascensius in Paris in 1500. Ascensius feels it necessary to inform the reader about the Greek alphabet. He prints the Lord's Prayer in Greek, then in Latin transliteration according to the Byzantine (i.e., Reuchlin's) pronunciation, then in the Latin of the Vulgate. There are a few other examples extant that suggest a common source for using the Lord's Prayer as an introduction into other languages.

37. Cf. M. D. Reeve, "Manuscripts copied from printed books," in J. B. Trapp, ed., *Manuscripts in the Fifty Years after the Invention of Printing: Some Papers Read at a Colloquium at the Warburg Institute on 12–13 March 1982* (London: Warburg Institute, 1983), 12–20.

38. For example, Florence, Biblioteca Medicea-Laurenziana, MS 66.31.

Aurea verba, he recorded his debt to Reuchlin's hospitality: "Finis aureorum carminum pythagore scripta velocissime in Stutg[ardia] accomodante domino doctore Reuchlin Grece [*changed from* hebraice] lingue sui temporis apud germanos peritissimo" (f. 4).[39]

---

39. RBC Goff-H 151 S (formerly Inc. 6763). Sicherl, *Johannes Cuno* 208 and 214 (cf. *Iter italicum,* 5: no. 378, reference to p. 214 lacking), describes the four leaves written by Cuno at the end of the Latin translation of Johannes Aurispa of Hierocles' *In aureos versus Pythagorae* (Padova: Bartholomaeus de Valdezoccho, 1474; Hain 8545). Cuno had bought the book in Landshut (on the last page, f. [m5]v: "Emptum per F. Jo. Cuno conventus Nurembergensis in Lantshut cum ibi esset cursor pro 6 cruc[iferis]"). He then began to copy the Greek text with a Latin translation of Pseudo-Pythagoras's *Aurea verba* on the last, blank page of Hierocles' commentary (f. [m6]) and added one leaf for the rest of the text. Sicherl thought it not impossible that the book belonged to Pirckheimer. The University of Pennsylvania owns another book that preserves a student's notes of similarly unexpected value. Johannes Hartung (1505–79), professor of Greek and, for some years, of Hebrew at Freiburg University, had left an unpublished commentary on the *Odyssey* in manuscript form. Van Pelt's copy of the Homer edition published by Hervagius in Basel in 1551 and 1552 (RBC f.grC. H 7525.1552) belonged, in 1562, to a certain Johannes Schönlin from Miltenberg in Franconia, also Hartung's birthplace (on the title page of the *Iliad:* "Sum Ioannis Schönlini Miltenburgensis, Anno 1562"). The text of the *Iliad* contains no notes, but on the verso of the title page of the *Odyssey* appears a note that "Ioannes Hartungus publicus Graecorum litterarum professor Friburgensis Gymnasij" began his lectures on the *Odyssey* on January 27, 1562, and finished them on June 30, 1564. The text is covered with notes in Schönlin's hand, which agree with Hartung's commentary on the first three books of the *Odyssey* (1539; Van Pelt Library, RBC GC. P9994. 539p). These lecture notes, obviously, preserve to a certain degree Hartung's lost commentary.

Miscellaneity and Vernacularity: Conditions of Literary Production in Late Medieval England

Ralph Hanna III

The discussion of "miscellaneity" at the colloquium at the University of Pennsylvania in March 1993 testifies to a modern critical befuddlement about our subject matter. Those witnesses through which we receive medieval texts of all sorts often lack, for us, many of those organizational principles we associate with either the term *book* or with subject-oriented terms, for example, our customary generic markers. As manuscript scholars, we thus contend with difficulties inherent in a double act of mediation. First, a substantial portion of our befuddlement is of our own making: in explaining the past to ourselves, we necessarily adopt our own language, which is to say our own estrangement from the objects of our interest. But the books we examine can scarcely be perceived as lacking their own mediations. In the pre-1450 English situation with which I customarily deal, all books are probably "bespoke," the product of special orders. Rather than being publicly available renditions of texts, as are the printed books on which we still unconsciously model our researches, they represent defiantly individual impulses—appropriations of works for the use of particular persons in particular situations. In such contexts, the books may have required no explanation, the private quirks behind their manufacture being abundantly clear; certainly, the medieval disinterest not simply in expressing but even in developing any critical terminology like our own estranges us and renders the objects of our studies opaque.

In my past studies of miscellaneous volumes, mainly of books for religious instruction, I have been fascinated by the oscillation between the planned and

[handwritten marginalia: oscillat[ed] b/w planned & random]

[handwritten marginalia: • flexibility • readjustment • suppose[d] "finalized" plans" are disrupted]

the random.[1] I am especially struck by the degree to which producing these volumes required constant flexibility and readjustment of what may, at some points in production, have been a reasonably fixed program.[2] And as an opening argumentative move, I will indulge in a measure of repetitiveness—analyzing a miscellaneous volume in a way I have done several other Middle English books. But after an appropriate degree of codicological analysis, on this occasion I will back off a bit and examine my own fascination with productions of this type—to suggest how I want to interface the study of such complex manuscripts and the concerns of general literary history.

Winchester College MS 33 cannot be called totally unknown, but its arrival on the edge of scholarly ken has been significantly belated. The manuscript has attracted attention largely because of its two dramatic dialogues, "Lucidus and Dubius" and "Occupation and Idleness"—the last pieces of the Middle English dramatic corpus to be published.[3] But these unique materials are conjoined here with a variety of other vernacular spiritual productions, ranging from the learned—a Trevisan translation of narrow dispersal—to the popular—bits of *The South English Legendary* and the prose *Abbey of the Holy Ghost* and its *Charter*. The manuscript thus transmits not just the dramatic pieces but also prose and verse.[4]

Virtually all descriptions of Winchester 33 depend on the meticulous examinations of Walter Oakeshott, long Winchester College's librarian.[5] To these, later students—Norman Davis, Neil Ker, Kathleen Power, Manfred Görlach, and I—really add only grace notes.[6] Those of Davis on the paper stocks bear

---

1. See especially Ralph Hanna III, "The Origins and Production of Westminster School MS 3," *Studies in Bibliography* 41 (1988): 197–218; and "The Growth of Robert Thornton's Books," *Studies in Bibliography* 40 (1987): 51–61.

2. See especially Hanna, "Origins."

3. Norman Davis, *Non-Cycle Plays and the Winchester Dialogues* (Leeds: University of Leeds School of English, 1979). A new edition is forthcoming in a University of Wisconsin Ph.D. dissertation by Gerard NeCastro.

4. See the analysis of the manuscript and its contents in the appendix to this chapter.

5. See his typed in-house Winchester College catalog of manuscripts, frequently reproduced in whole or part, as for instance by D. Peter Consacro, "A Critical Edition of *The Abbey of the Holy Ghost* from all known extant English manuscripts," (Ph.D. diss., Fordham University, 1971), lxxxix–xcii.

6. Davis, *Non-Cycle Plays,* 135–39, with facsimile of ff. 54v–73v, 140–78; N. R. Ker (and, for volume 4, A. J. Piper), *Medieval Manuscripts in British Libraries,* 4 vols. (Oxford: Clarendon, 1969–92), 4:623–25; Kathleen H. Power, "A Newly Identified Prose Version of the Trevisa Version of the Gospel of Nicodemus," *Notes and Queries* 223 (1978): 5–7, at 6–7; Manfred Görlach, *The Textual Tradition of the South English Legendary* (Leeds: University of Leeds School of English, 1974), 104–5.

[handwritten margin notes: "series of separated 'booklets' combined as a miscellany"]

particular importance.[7] All except Görlach agree that Winchester 33 was produced by a single scribe at the middle of the fifteenth century: the paper on
which he wrote would suggest that this work took place sporadically over
about a decade, around 1450.

The scribe produced his book not as a single, ongoing activity, but as a
series of four separate "booklets" (see the appendix to this chapter). These may
be easily distinguished by a variety of customary identification procedures that
confirm one's initial suppositions of separate production, based on the coincidence of quire and text ends. Each booklet appears on a different paper stock
and has a slightly different page format; each has a separate signature system.
And putative booklet endings display features conventionally associated with
separate production—blank leaves at folios 47v and 109rv, a canceled blank
after folio 47, and adjustments of quire size to handle materials neatly in the
booklet-concluding quires 6 and 8.

[handwritten margin note: "material evidence of separate production"]

But despite separateness of production, and despite certain obscurities about
the manuscript's history at Winchester College (no conclusive evidence for all
four booklets conjoined predates the contents leaf of ca. 1660), these four
pieces of work seem to have remained in a single site and to share a common
history. Whatever their passing differences, the booklets show relatively homogeneous formats. And the manuscript contains evidence for at least three
separate binding programs, two of them in the fifteenth century (the earliest
one, as I will suggest, probably contemporary with part of the actual copying).
The oldest of these bindings (A), the Latin numeration of the quires, joins at
least the third and fourth booklets; Davis's categorical statement that the "secundus" at the foot of folio 13 "cannot be part of the same series"[8] seems to me
overly conclusive, and part of the first booklet, at least putatively, also belongs
to this codicological state. The second binding (B), identified by arabic numerals written in blue chalk, clearly joins these three booklets in their current
full extents. Only the second booklet, resembling the first in the inclusion of
South English Legendary texts (in addition to the dramatic dialogues), remains
outside the count. And, in some form, the booklets were at Winchester in the
early sixteenth century, since a hand that can be associated with one in college
records ca. 1540 wrote a medical recipe on one of the flies (f. 116). I see no
reason to believe that the whole manuscript may not have been produced in
Winchester or by a Winchester alumnus, whether in the neighborhood or at
Winchester College, Oxford.

[handwritten margin note: "history of binding"]

7. Davis, *Non-Cycle Plays,* 136.
8. Ibid., 135.

The result of collating Winchester 33 and dividing it into coherent production units does not fully explain how the book was produced. Despite recent
antipathy toward editorial procedures—expressed primarily by paleographers
like Mary and Richard Rouse,[9] but echoed by some textual critics—the only
basis one can use to discuss the compilatory procedures by which diverse texts
were joined is that of textual detail. To identify the scribe's source materials
and their prior configurations—to measure exactly how "miscellaneous" the
codex is—one must be able to specify, as narrowly as possible, the scribe's
sources. And this can only be accomplished by the book's coincidence in
shared error with other surviving copies.

On this basis, producing the book required that the scribe had access to at
least five, and probably six, separate exemplars. Booklet 1 involved at least two
different archetypes. As Görlach demonstrates,[10] the *South English Legendary*
texts that occupy folio 17v–47 display features distinctive to a limited recension of that huge composite work (Görlach's recension L). They were thus
acquired separately from the three texts that open booklet 1 (the Genesis
sections of the Old Testament history associated with the *Legendary,* the lives
of Pilate and Judas), all in non-L forms. These occupy folios 1–17v, that is, all
of quire 1 and the first five leaves of quire 2. In other words, the conclusion of
this copying and the gathering of these two quires with portions of the remainder would correspond with the binding directions "Secundus" on folio 13
succeeded by "Tercius" at folio 74. Thus, at least planning the initial binding of
Winchester 33 well preceded the conclusion of copying (after all, neither early
binding program envisioned inclusion of booklet 2). Consequently, booklet 1,
in the form we have it, reflects at least two different codicological programs
(although, if binding actually occurred, disbinding and extension of this portion cannot have been long delayed, given the scribe's use of a single paper
stock for the whole) and two different states of a work adjudged "finished"
enough to receive covers.

My hesitation about the number of *South English Legendary* codices to
which the scribe had recourse concerns the relationship of booklet 2 selections
to those of booklet 1. The six legends in the second unit of Winchester 33 resist
genetic classification save as derivatives of the widely dispersed A recension of
the work. They thus potentially might be of the same source as the opening
portions of booklet 1. But the compilatory procedures in this section of

---

9. Mary A. Rouse and Richard H. Rouse, *Authentic Witnesses: Approaches to Medieval Texts
and Manuscripts* (Notre Dame, IN: University of Notre Dame Press, 1991).

10. Görlach, *Textual Tradition,* 104–5 (summary statement) and 133–218 (detailed
discussion).

Winchester 33 differ from those in earlier portions of the book; in contrast to
the apparently random provision of lives in booklet 1, the scribe here attempted
a fairly straightforward, from-the-incipit copying of his *Legendary* exemplar,
although he did allow for excisions.[11] On the whole, this set of texts probably
reflects a third exemplar.

The remainder of the manuscript is much more straightforward. Booklets 3
and 4, the Trevisan *Nicodemus* and *Abbey* materials, each came from discrete
separate sources. The dramatic texts, unparalleled elsewhere, also required a
separate exemplar (and thus this booklet, like the first, has been compiled from
diverse sources). In all likelihood, the two plays came to the scribe as a unit—
although it is not entirely clear that they are of common genesis, either linguistically or in terms of authorship.[12] The partial blank leaf between the two
texts, unique in consecutive sections of Winchester 33, does not, I think,
necessarily imply separate acquisition. "Lucidus and Dubius," the first of the
dialogues, at least gives the impression of incompleteness;[13] the scribe may
have shared this impression, may have hoped to find a conclusion, and may
have hedged his bets by leaving space to continue copying (counting on inter-
calated bifolia to handle any remainder of the text that might have turned up).[14]

---

11. He chose not to copy two of the legends, Hilary (no. 4) and Wulfstan (no. 5), the latter a
puzzling exclusion, given booklet 1's emphasis on English figures (Oswald, Edward martyr, and
Cuthbert at ff. 17v–25; Gregory at ff. 30–31v). On the basis of evidence Görlach assembles about
manuscript contents (*Textual Tradition,* 306–9), these exclusions are likely to have been editorial,
not inherited from the scribe's exemplar. The only full copy without one of these texts is Bodleian
Library, MS Laud Misc. 108, which omits Hilary; but this codex cannot have been the scribe's
source here, since it lacks the standard prologue to the legendary, which opens booklet 2.

12. Norman Davis, "Two Unprinted Dialogues in Late Middle English, and Their Language,"
Revue des Langues Vivants 35 (1969): 461–72, at 467, 470–71; but see further discussion later in
this chapter.

13. Davis, "Two Unprinted Dialogues," 464; and B. S. Lee, "Lucidus and Dubius: A
Fifteenth-Century Theological Debate and Its Sources," *Medium Aevum* 45 (1976): 79–96, at 93–
94. "Lucidus and Dubius" lacks what "Occupation and Idleness" has, the conventional broken-
back morality structure in which the errant protagonist surrenders his sinful ways. And what one
might take to be a concluding rubric, the two Latin lines following 610, only indicates the source of
Lucidus's last speech.

14. Cf. the behavior of early scribes of the *Canterbury Tales* when faced with apparent textual
lacunae—e.g., the deliberate booklet conclusions to "The Cook's Fragment" in Hg El Ha4. For
some idea of the range of uses involving composite quires, with bifolia intruded to supplement
already completed materials, cf. such situations as (a) Salisbury Cathedral, MS 113, quire 5 (ff.
49–60), where ff. 57–58 (e 9+10) are an inserted bifolium to correct a large eyeskip noted by the
scribe; (b) British Library, MS Additional 31042, where the scribe seems to have worked by
inserting sheets into the centers of already in-progress quires to extend his textual units (see Hanna,
"The London Thornton Manuscript: A Corrected Collation", *Studies in Bibliography* 37 (1984):
122–30); (c) British Library, MS Cotton Caligula A.ii, quire 3 (ff. 34–55), where six leaves (ff.
44–49) appear to have been inserted after the original tenth leaf of a quire of 16, to accommodate a

Moreover, on the basis of the provenance and textual affiliations of Winchester 33 texts, one can speculate about the scribe's procedures for acquiring texts. These point toward two discrete sources for his materials, the most prominent of these broadly southwestern, perhaps with an intermediary stop in Oxford or Salisbury. Although copies eventually show a fair scattering, *The South English Legendary* is fundamentally a western text, most prominently of Worcester/Gloucester provenance.[15] The specific L recension from which the scribe derived folios 17v–47 is known only in four other copies, the most proximate being Bodleian Library, MS Laud Misc. 108, from west Oxfordshire, and "The Vernon Manuscript" (Bodleian, MS Eng. poet. a.1), from north Worcestershire.[16]

Similarly western is an apparently coterie text of very narrow distribution, the translation of *Nicodemus* produced by John Trevisa, vicar of Berkeley, south Gloucestershire.[17] One of the two other surviving copies occurs in a book in the British Library, MS Additional 16165, which can be directly associated with Trevisa's patron, Sir Thomas Berkeley: its scribe, John Shirley, was personal secretary to Richard Beauchamp, earl of Warwick and husband of Berkeley's heir.[18] But the second survivor, textually closer to the Winchester copy, Salisbury Cathedral MS 39, belonged to Thomas Cyrcetur, an Oxford scholar (eventually B.Th.); later, when he was canon of both Wells and Salis-

---

lengthy romance text—after the scribe had already copied materials in an inappropriate page format into the head of what he planned as the following quire; (d) Cambridge, University Library, MS Ff.1.6, quires 2 and 5 (ff. 11–34, 61–76), where the final organization of the book involved the reduction of originally independent quires by inserting some (here ff. 17–20 and 21–28 after 2:6 and ff. 64–67 after 5:4) into others containing texts deemed relevant. See further John Thompson, "Collecting Middle English Romances and Some Related Book-Production Activities in the later Middle Ages," in Maldwyn Mills, Jennifer Fellows, and Carol M. Meale, eds., *Romance in Medieval England* (Cambridge: D. S. Brewer, 1991), 17–38, at 31 and n. 48.

15. See the map of the localizable copies in Görlach, *Textual Tradition,* 305.

16. The two other related copies are twins from the south Derby-Notts. border, Lambeth Palace MS 223 (G) and Cambridge, Fitzwilliam Museum, MS McClean 128 (F); see Görlach, *Textual Tradition,* 82–83.

17. Contrast the organized distribution of Trevisa's major translations, discussed in Hanna, "Sir Thomas Berkeley and his Patronage," *Speculum* 64 (1989): 909–13—a quite typical example of what I call the canonical "law of extent." Like the *Nicodemus* in British Library, MS Additional 16165, Trevisa's *De regimine principum* never escaped its coterie; the unique copy, Bodleian Library, MS Digby 233, f. 199v, has a swan badge one would associate with Richard Beauchamp. On *Nicodemus* see also David C. Fowler, "The Middle English Gospel of Nicodemus in Winchester MS 33," *Leeds Studies in English* 19 (1988): 67–83.

18. Although the manuscript postdates her death and Berkeley's remarriage. Cf. British Library, MS Additional 24194, a copy of Trevisa's *Polychronicon,* with accompaniments, produced for Beauchamp in London, s. xv in.

bury, he donated the book to the cathedral (before his death in 1453).[19] Given Trevisa's own Oxonian connections (at Exeter and Queen's College from 1361 to 1379 and at Queen's College at odd intervals thereafter), Cyrcetur may have acquired the text there during his university career (which covered at least 1395–1418). And the Winchester compiler might have got the text either from Oxford (as he may have got the *Legendary* texts in the Laud recension) or from interchanges between the cathedrals at Salisbury and Winchester—note the A30/303 complex, a major thoroughfare already in the fourteenth-century Gough Map.[20]

But equally, the scribe of Winchester 33 had a second source of textual supply, broadly East Midland. *The Abbey of the Holy Ghost* and its engulfing companion piece, *The Charter of the Abbey,* typically circulate together, and the Winchester renditions of these works show, so far as is known, identical textual histories.[21] The Winchester texts are closely associated with two other copies. British Library, MS Harley 2406 (siglum B) was produced by several scribes sharing the language of west Norfolk or the Soke;[22] Lambeth Palace MS 432 (siglum H) is probably to be associated with Syon Abbey.[23] And a manuscript derived from an exemplar like, but not identical to, that available to the Winchester scribe also has eastern affiliations: Harley 1704 (siglum F) shows the language of east central Leicestershire.[24]

One would initially presuppose that the dramatic texts share a similar history. For the great home of English moral plays (and of the alliterative stanza,

---

19. See Power, "Newly Identified Prose Version," 6. On Cyrcetur, see A. B. Emden, *A Biographical Register of the University of Oxford to A.D. 1500,* 3 vols. (Oxford: Clarendon, 1957–59), 1:531–32; and R. M. Ball, "Thomas Cyrcetur, a Fifteenth-Century Theologian and Preacher," *Journal of Ecclesiastical History* 37 (1986): 205–39.

20. See F. M. Stenton, "The Road System of Medieval England," *Economic History Review* 7 (1936): 1–21, at 9.

21. See D. Peter Consacro, "A Critical Edition of *The Abbey of the Holy Ghost* from All Known Extant English Manuscripts," (Ph.D. diss., Fordham University, 1971), cxiii–iv, cxvi; Clara Elizabeth Fanning, "*The Charter of the Abbey of the Holy Ghost:* A Critical Edition from All Known Extant Manuscripts" (Ph.D. diss., Fordham University, 1975), xciii–v, ci. Consacro's and Fanning's findings should probably be regarded as tentative: they predicate genetic relations only on isolated "major errors," especially omissions.

22. See Angus McIntosh, M. L. Samuels, and Michael Benskin, eds., *A Linguistic Atlas of Late Mediaeval English,* 4 vols. (Aberdeen: Aberdeen University Press, 1986), 1:112, no assigned linguistic profile (LP) (henceforth referred to as *LALME*).

23. George P. Keiser, "Patronage and Piety in Fifteenth-Century England: Margaret, Duchess of Clarence, Symon Wynter and Beinecke MS 317," *Yale University Library Gazette* 60, nos. i–ii (1985): 32–46, at 43.

24. *LALME* 1:110, LP 302. Its genetic twin, Stonyhurst College MS B.xxiii (siglum E), has never been dialectically surveyed, although the decoration may point to the borders of East Anglia.

which occurs five times in the Winchester dialogues, in "Lucidus" at the head only) is East Anglia. Thus, Davis, albeit tentatively, identifies the language of the dialogues with that of south Suffolk or north Essex.[25] But I am afraid that in this process he errs: the far broader conspectus of Middle English usage now available,[26] which may unsettle some widely accepted generalizations about Middle English dramatic development, would suggest that these, too, are western texts. Nothing about the language of the plays would seem to preclude such a provenance, and some items only make sense in a Gloucester/Somerset context, most notably an authorial form that cannot be artificial and that is common to both plays, *again* as *a3e* ("Lucidus," line 508; "Occupation," line 534) rhyming on "close e."[27] In addition, in the play Dubius characterizes himself as "a child of Bathe" (line 324), a detail strangely overlooked by Davis.

Thus, the acquisition of these texts points toward miscellaneous collection procedures from centers other than Winchester. And Winchester 33 certainly looks like a grab bag: simply consider the very different principles by which the *South English Legendary* texts were put together in booklets 1 and 2, from the incipit copying in the latter case to the selective hopping about an exemplar in the former. Yet I persist in thinking that the texts display a rough unity, one dependent on informatively consistent thematic concerns. To understand what miscellaneity means in a book like this, one cannot be satisfied with a reading demarcated by the tools of codicology or textual criticism: as did its compilers, one must *read* the texts, for they embody a rhetorical strategy.

The compilers of Winchester 33 are persistently, although not ubiquitously, interested in a well-focused historical point of view. In this regard, one may easily distinguish the codex from various other Middle English spiritual miscellanies that, in giving religious instruction, use the so-called Pecham program.[28] In contrast, numerous Winchester texts emphasize the "two-trees" or "Eva-and-Ave" patterns of historiography. The compilers present narratives of

25. Davis, "Two Unprinted Dialogues," 469–72.

26. Davis was forced to rely on extremely fragmentary maps for a limited number of features—printed in M. L. Samuels, "Some Applications of Middle English Dialectology," *English Studies* 44 (1963): 81–94—rather than the tool currently at our disposal, *LALME*.

27. Line references are to the edition in Davis, *Non-Cycle Plays*. The form *a3e* is apparently quite restricted; cf. *LALME* 1:362, dot map 231, which depicts all *-n*-less forms of *again* and shows them limited to the southwest (Gloucestershire, Somerset, Wiltshire, Dorset, and Devon). Similarly, sporadic reproduction of Old English *y* as *e* typifies this area as well; see, e.g., the differing distributions marked at *LALME* 1:400, 406, and 408, dot maps 384, 408, and 414 (*church, fire,* and *first,* respectively).

28. See Vincent Gillespie, "Vernacular Books of Religion," in Jeremy Griffiths and Derek Pearsall, eds., *Book Production and Publishing in Britain 1375–1475* (Cambridge: Cambridge University Press, 1989), 317–44, at 317–19.

the fallen human condition, our inheritance from Eden, and the mirroring, necessary redemption expressed both in prophetic promise and in the actual redemptive acts of the gospels. These emphases are quite overtly reflected in some of the texts the scribe copied. *Nicodemus,* for example, might well be considered "the fifth gospel": it reproduces the hopes and promises of the prophets in hell as they await Jesus' destruction of its gates. And *The Charter of the Abbey of the Holy Ghost* eschews the contemplative emphases of its enabling predecessor text, *The Abbey,* to narrate and explain the Fall, the prophetic promises of Jesus' coming, the Council in Heaven (with the debate of the Four Daughters of God), and the Incarnation.[29]

Other texts involve more subtle and careful selective procedures. For example, "Lucidus and Dubius" may have appealed to the compiler of Winchester 33 less for its dramatic form than because the playwright had adopted, for the most part,[30] only dialogue from book 1 of his source, Honorius of Autun's *Elucidarium,* which treats the relations of God and man, sin and beneficence, Fall and redemptive Crucifixion.[31] And although later portions of Winchester booklet 1 appear a grab bag, they significantly look as if they were collected by leafing about in the Eastertide portions of *The South English Legendary,* the textual locus where the compiler might reasonably have expected to discover tales of the fulfillment and undoing of Jewish failures. In some *Legendary* manuscripts, the compiler could even have found the legends of Pilate and Judas here;[32] certainly his later selections are anchored by two large chunks of explicit Easter materials, the treatment of the movable feasts (ff. 33–37) and the histories associated with the Cross (ff. 39v–47).

Indeed, this last text, which concludes the booklet, provides a fitting, though perhaps belatedly and accidentally conceived, balance with its head, the

---

29. See Stella Brook, "'The Charter of the Abbey of the Holy Ghost,'" *Modern Language Review* 54 (1959): 481–88.

30. The exceptional questions, on which the play as we have it ends (lines 515 ff.), concern issues of priestly authority and may be perceived as vaguely anti-Lollard (the author on several occasions associates Dubius with heresy). Like the companion "Occupation and Idleness" (see n. 34), the more or less original portions of the play, near the opening, suggest distant derivation from *Piers Plowman;* cf. the discussion of dinner-table heresy (lines 11–12, 40–59) with *Piers* B 10.39–119, and especially the question at lines 155–62 with "telleþ þei of þe Trinite how two slowe þe þridde" (*Piers* B 10.54; in George Kane and E. Talbot Donaldson, eds., *Piers Plowman: The B Version* [London: Athlone, 1975], 409).

31. See Lee, "Lucidus and Dubius," 79–82.

32. These are manuscripts DKNOPT in Görlach's classification; see Görlach, *Textual Tradition,* 217. But Winchester's reversed order of presentation is paralleled in but a single copy of the *Legend,* Ba. The materials on the Cross that I subsequently discuss appear in Winchester 33 in the order peculiar to Laud Misc. 108 (see Görlach's p. 165).

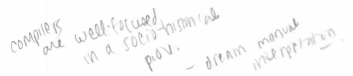

Genesis portions of the Old Testament history occasionally attached to *The South English Legendary* (ff. 1–12). For the "History of the Cross" proper[33] traces the Rood back to the tree of Adam's disobedience; this Seth sees in its redeemed form in Paradise (lines 195 ff.), where he is told it will eventually be the source of the salvific Oil of Mercy. But the Cross is also materially derived from the seeds Seth receives in Eden, which sprout into three shoots from the fallen Adam's grave.

Further, the *Inventio crucis* narrative appended to this history shows similar concerns. It ascribes the actual discovery of the redemptive implement to a second Jewish Judas. But unlike his predecessor, whose evil career is narrated at the head of the booklet (ff. 15v–17v), this Judas is converted by his discovery, becomes the good Christian bishop Quiriac, and is eventually martyred while attempting to convert the apostate Julian. Moreover, the text has been tailored to emphasize Quiriac and his status as the New Knight of Christendom heralded in the prologue to the *Legendary:*[34] the compiler simply expunges the last third of his source text, given over to "modern-day" miracles of the Cross.

The manuscript thus embodies a thematic reading of its archetypes. Its compilers' most persistent desire is to stimulate hope, to create in the book's audience a sense of omnipresent divine mercifulness, even in the face of human unregeneracy. Just as the compilers of the Vernon manuscript could envision that book's diverse contents as falling under a single thematic heading, "Sowle hele," so those of Winchester 33 may have seen the theme of their book as fall and redemption.

Yet, simultaneously, such thematic texts—which reflect a medieval sense of propriety quite removed from familiar categories of modern literary history—form only a core to the book.[35] And this core never thoroughly programmed

---

33. Lines 1–390 in the edition by Carl Horstmann, *The Early South-English Legendary, or Lives of Saints,* Early English Text Society, o.s., 87 (London: N. Trübner, 1887), 1–12. In the edition of *The South English Legendary* edited by Charlotte d'Evelyn and Anna J. Mill (3 vols., Early English Text Society, o.s., 235, 236, 244 [London: Oxford University Press, 1956–59]), the legend of the Rood appears at 1:167–80.

34. This text, in the current binding, immediately follows the Cross narratives, across the booklet boundary at the head of quire 5—a provocative collocation perhaps enabled by production accident. The moralities may have appealed for their similar conversion narratives; note especially the emphasis on "mercy" at that point when Idleness repents and, like Quiriac, is renamed, in his case Cleanness (lines 766–811—he has earlier masqueraded under the name Busyness). This play resembles "Lucidus and Dubius" in its reliance on *Piers* at its opening; cf. Occupation's association of holy manual labor, Reason, and Truth in lines 1–47.

35. Cf. Gillespie's comments on Bodleian Library, MS Laud Misc. 210 (for which see Hanna, "Origins," 210), in Gillespie, "Vernacular Books," 326. Histories of single texts often display such accommodations to differing thematic programs. For example, manuscripts of the alliterative

contents and production; the compilers remained open to the possible, as yet unforeseen usefulness that some audience might find in ancillary texts. Thus, "Lucidus and Dubius" would have piqued the thematic interests of the compilers, but they did not refuse to copy the less relevant, but probably exemplar-attached, "Occupation and Idleness." The same may be true of the thematic *Charter* and less relevant *Abbey;* and the *South English Legendary* texts provide even more overt evidence of such secondary selection procedures.

I think such a combination of happenstance acquisition and variously motivated selection is quite typical of a large range of Middle English manuscript books. And although such procedures are not a priori limited to Middle English, I think that they testify to certain aspects of late medieval vernacular literary (and not just book) production. For, down until almost the beginning of print culture in English, vernacular production proceeds in a situation of prenational literary culture. There exists no single literary canon and, consequently, no single set of institutions to stimulate literary activity and to mandate various forms of more or less standardized book production. Rather, there are plural literary canons, dependent on a good many variables—geography, gender, profession, and political affiliation leap immediately to mind—and miscellaneous books testify to highly individualistic canon-creating efforts by individuals variously inserted into discrete and fragmented social positions.

But precisely because "literature in English" exists as such a fragmented terrain, its reproduction will always approach miscellaneity as a limit. Although I used to think it an unduly mechanical explanatory procedure, in a precanonical period, exemplar poverty motivates much of the literary record. Quite simply, in any given locale, even a metropolis, one cannot be certain that exemplars of any given text were available. As a result, manuscript compilers, when they acquired an exemplar for any desired text, could not be certain that they could gain access to it a second time. Thus, they were constrained to make the fullest imaginable use of any book that came to hand, and their planned core selections would come to coexist with other items. Difficulties of textual supply, as numerous studies indicate,[36] contribute to the miscellaneous, not to say random, appearance of many Middle English books.

Siege of Jerusalem read the text as, variously, biblical history (Bodleian, MS Laud misc. 656), a romance (Caligula A.ii), specifically a crusader romance (British Library, MS Additional 31042), or learned secular history (Cambridge University Library, MS Mm.5.14).

36. E.g., Thompson, "Collecting Middle English Romances," 22–23; Julia Boffey and John J. Thompson, "Anthologies and Miscellanies: Production and Choice of Texts," in Griffiths and Pearsall, *Book Production,* 279–315, at 283–87, 297, 300; and Gillespie, "Vernacular Books," 325–27.

Miscellaneous NOT random

One can contrast such procedures with any variety of Latinate modes of book production, all of them supported by clearly demarcatable transmission networks generally supported by one or another sort of professional affiliation (schools, orders, legal institutions, etc.). These, almost automatically, prescribe more fixed notions of appropriate literary production, of canonical texts and presentations. Merely to take one well-known example, twelfth-century English monastic book production centers around a relatively limited schedule of patristic writers, generally in their most extensive works (literary canonization always privileges large works over small, *Aeneids* over *Eclogues,* for example).[37] Where the output of those designated central literary authorities, canonical figures, does not accord with such large-text formats, efforts occur to arrange their writings into comparable form. Outstanding examples of such procedures within monastic book culture are well known—for example, the stages by which diverse writings of Cyprian are arranged into volume-length anthologies with fixed text order;[38] or the similar stages in the production of St. Jerome's "epistolary," which often involved the importation of separate tracts, not epistles at all, simultaneously to reduce the appearance of oddments and to fill out large volumes.[39] In such contexts, canons become relatively fixed, and miscellaneity per se becomes a literary effect that compilers go to some pains to minimize.

With this situation, one can contrast the fate of what I think would pass for a vernacular canonical text, Winchester 33's *Abbey of the Holy Ghost* and *Charter.* This combined work—a bit of canonizing linking that may not correspond with the intentions of the translator of *The Abbey*—is, at both extremes of its transmission history, marked as a central spiritual text. In the late fourteenth century, the work appears in the massive Vernon manuscript within a carefully selected and organized religious anthology (booklet 4, ff. 319–93; the booklet extends through f. 406): this groups the absolute classics of English vernacular spirituality, with an emphasis on contemplative texts—Hilton, Rolle, *Ancrene Riwle,* as well as *Abbey* and *Charter,* a translation of Edmund Rich's *Speculum,*

37. Hence the vexed subject of the Chaucerian *minora*/apocrypha and courtly lyric corpus investigated so ably in Julia Boffey, *Manuscripts of English Courtly Love Lyrics in the Later Middle Ages* (Woodbridge: Brewer, 1985), 6–33; and in Boffey and Thompson, "Anthologies," 280–83. In the Middle Ages, such shorter pieces are apt to have been coterie work, limited in initial circulation (perhaps also an explanation for the visible form of transmission of *Piers Plowman* A), and they are apt to have been perceived as ephemeral/occasional. But see further n. 46.

38. Cf. the classic demonstration in Maurice Bevenot, *The Tradition of Manuscripts: A Study in the Transmission of St. Cyprian's Treatises* (Oxford: Clarendon, 1961).

39. Cf. Pierre Lardet, "Epistolaires médiévaux de S. Jérôme: jalons pour un classement," *Freiburger Zeitschrift für Philosophie und Theologie* 28 (1981): 271–89.

and other shorter works. Similarly, at the end of its tradition, the textual cluster *Abbey* and *Charter* achieved three incunabulum printings (STC 13608.7-610), further testimony to the work's classic status. In manuscript, the texts display a similar centrality: *Abbey* exists in twenty-five copies, *Charter* in twenty-four, in nineteen of the cases together. Yet if one examines the various copies, they display a minimal coincidence of other contents: no centralizing procedure insured universal availability of *Abbey* and *Charter,* even in narrowly spiritual circles; neither did other comparable spiritual texts achieve what we would consider canonicity in this way.[40]

In contrast to Latinate culture, fourteenth- and fifteenth-century vernacular book production tends to imitate prominent forms of literary production. For in the contemporary literary scene, which lacked any protracted tradition (prose spiritual literature had perhaps the most lengthy history, but only stretching back to the 1190s), the most typical production is the miscellaneous poem. Most obviously, the greatest work of the period—and the only one still securely canonical—Chaucer's *Canterbury Tales,* takes this form, being a group of stories joined by repeated thematic concerns, (revenge and sexual relations, for example). And typically of the period, *The Tales* presents its miscellanea within a frame we would identify with the Coleridgean "mechanical" (not the "organic unity" we have been trained to appreciate), a frame that provides a series of occasions for narrative eruptions, a pilgrimage with—at least originally—plans for four stories from each participant ("General Prologue," 790–95).[41]

Most Middle English single-work manuscripts (and most canonical Middle English poems) replicate this pattern. And this feature is not limited to such high literary productions comparable to Chaucer's own as *Confessio Amantis* or *Piers Plowman* C, for example. The great range of popular spiritual classics, texts desperately in need of extensive studies they have not, in most cases, received,[42] meld shortish discrete materials, ultimately of diverse sources, and hold them together through mechanical thematic devices. *The South English*

---

40. This demonstration could be extended to virtually any later Middle English spiritual text, with much the same results; a useful example would be a work of considerably greater dissemination than the *Abbey,* Rolle's *Form of Living,* which survives in more than forty copies, not counting quotations. Indeed, the only works of this sort that seem to achieve coherent patterns of transmission are a very few texts deliberately constructed as integral clusters, e.g., the translation of Isidore of Seville's *Synonyma* and its various companion pieces.

41. Chaucer texts are quoted from *The Riverside Chaucer,* ed. Larry D. Benson (Boston: Houghton Mifflin, 1987).

42. Cf. my comments in my review of Derek Pearsall, ed., *Studies in the Vernon Manuscript* (Cambridge: D. S. Brewer, 1990), in *Speculum* 67 (1992): 1026–29, at 1028.

Legendary, in its full forms, groups about ninety separate vitae of saints: it organizes them according to the calendar of the Sarum Lectionary.[43] *The Northern Homily Cycle* manages a relatively complete Incarnation narrative but presents it, along with interspersed exemplary materials, in the order of Sunday gospel lections, beginning with Advent. *The Prick of Conscience,* in its survivals the most widely dispersed of all Middle English poems, covers a wide variety of religious subjects within a framework provided by the topic "The Four Last Things." And William of Nassyngton's *Speculum Vitae* presents a huge amount of information on virtues (and secondarily vices) within a septenary format.

Thus, within Middle English literary production generally, miscellaneity forms a model procedure for creative work—as well as for its presentation in books. "The matere," the thematic subject, governs collections to an extent many students, still bound by modern categories, have not thoroughly appreciated. In this regard, one might recall Chaucer's pantheon of literary greats in *The House of Fame:* to take a single instance, six figures, including Homer, are described simply under the rubric "Troye" in lines 1464–72. Chaucer, of course, had no access to Homer—and, in any event, may not have minded, since Homer was reputed an untrue witness to "Troye" (see lines 1475–80). But similar problems of hearsay, of thematic unity, and of inauthenticity were to bedevil the dissemination of Chaucer's own contribution to "Troye," the *Troilus,* about whose text there is evidence of authorial care.[44] Something like one-third of the surviving copies of this large continuous poem were produced miscellaneously, from odd quires derived from more than one exemplar.[45] The continuous text was not universally available; book producers accepted the text of any available exemplar once they had exhausted their current stock of copy; and the texts of very mixed quality that resulted sufficed—they comprised the English "Troye."[46] The vicissitudes of so major a piece of vernacular scripture

---

43. Görlach, *Textual Tradition,* 29.

44. See the lyric to Adam Scriveyn, or *Troilus* 5.1793–99.

45. See Hanna, "The Manuscripts and Transmission of Chaucer's *Troilus,*" in Christian K. Zacher and James M. Dean, eds., *The Idea of Medieval Literature: New Essays on Chaucer and Medieval Culture in Honor of Donald R. Howard* (Newark: University of Delaware Press, 1992), 173–88.

46. For a recent demonstration of similar problems in the production of *Canterbury Tales* manuscripts, see Charles A. Owen, *The Manuscripts of the Canterbury Tales* (Cambridge: D. S. Brewer, 1991). Tellingly, in Owen's account, the miscellaneous work always dissolved into its constituent *membra disjecta.* Contrast contemporary French efforts with the failure of author-based collections in England (Cambridge University Library, MS Gg.4.27 and British Library, MS Cotton Nero A.x should be construed as exceptional); see Sylvia Huot, *From Song to Book: The Poetics of Writing in Old French Lyric and Lyrical Narrative Poetry* (Ithaca: Cornell University Press, 1987), 211–327.

should provide a salutary check to our expectations: modern generic (and print-driven) expectations may be of very limited application to the prenational Middle English literary scene.

create an appendix that organized texts by [fascile] ✱

APPENDIX: WINCHESTER COLLEGE MS 33

Booklet 1

ff. 1–47 = quires 1–3¹² 4¹² (–12, a cancel), signed a–d
paper of 1437?, 1445?, or 1449?
nineteen texts from *The South English Legendary,* presented as fourteen
f. 47v blank

Booklet 2

ff. 48–73 = quires 5¹² 6¹⁴, signed —, +
paper Briquet 14965 (Namur) of 1445
ff. 48–54v six further texts from *The South English Legendary*
ff. 54v–64v "Lucidus and Dubius" (most of f. 64v blank)
ff. 65–73v "Occupation and Idleness"

Booklet 3

ff. 74–93 = quires 7⁸ 6¹², signed a, b
paper of ca. 1454–66
John Trevisa's translation of "The Gospel of Nicodemus"

Booklet 4

ff. 94–109 = quires 9–10⁸, signed a, b
paper of 1430s? or 1447–50?
"The Abbey of the Holy Ghost" and (f. 99) "Charter of the Abbey"
f. 109rv blank
Binding A = quires 1–2, 7–10, signed —, *secundus–sextus*
copying break at f. 17v?

Binding B = quires 1–4, 7–10, signed —, 2–8

[Folios 110–15, from Erasmus, "De ratione conscribendi epistolas," s. xvi¹, appear to have been placed inside the front cover (s. xviii or xix) and to have been bound in their current place only in this century.]

Bodleian Library MS Arch. Selden B.24:
A "Transitional" Collection

A. S. G. Edwards

Sometime probably around the beginning of the last decade of the fifteenth century, in Dunfermline in Scotland, the poet Robert Henryson composed his great continuation of Chaucer's *Troilus & Criseyde,* the poem titled *The Testament of Cressid.* The action of Henryson's poem is precipitated by the narrator taking "ane quair . . . / Writtin be worthie Chaucer glorious / Of fair Cresseid and worthie Troylus." The naming of Chaucer's poem underlines the intertextual relationship between his work and Henryson's. But from the point of view of the student of fifteenth-century manuscripts, it simultaneously problematizes that relationship. For the "quair" Henryson's narrator reads seems to be the first explicit acknowledgment—albeit a fictional one—of the circulation of Chaucer's manuscripts in Scotland during the fifteenth century.

This is not to say that there were not indirect acknowledgments in Scotland of the influence of the dominant Chaucerian poetic tradition on the emergent Scottish one. It is clear that by the end of the fifteenth or beginning of the sixteenth century Chaucer had been absorbed into Scottish literary style and language. We have abundant evidence in the verbal borrowings from him in the poems of Henryson and Dunbar or in other works, some of which may be earlier, such as *The Book of the Howlett* or *Lancelot of the Laik*—evidence that testifies to a detailed awareness of Chaucerian idiom as well as other intima-

---

My thanks are due to Dr. Julia Boffey and Professor David Parkinson for their helpful criticisms of an earlier draft of this chapter.

tions of familiarity with his works.[1] But in contrast to the situation with Chaucer's main disciple, John Lydgate, a number of whose manuscripts can be shown to have had a Scottish provenance or to have circulated in Scotland during the fifteenth and sixteenth centuries,[2] there is, with one notable exception, virtually no direct evidence of the ways in which Chaucer was transmitted from England into Scotland in the fifteenth century.

At about the same time that Henryson was probably composing his *Testament,* there was being copied in Scotland[3] the manuscript that is now Bodleian

1. For discussion of the circulation of Chaucer's works in Scotland see Ethel Seaton, " 'That Scotch Copy of Chaucer,' " *Journal of English and Germanic Philology* 47 (1948): 352–56; John Durkan and Anthony Ross, *Early Scottish Libraries* (Glasgow: John Burns, 1961), 7; and J. A. W. Bennett, "Those Scotch Copies of Chaucer," *Review of English Studies,* n.s., 32 (1981): 294–96. The last draws attention to an allusion in John of Ireland, *The Meroure of Wisdom* (1490), which mentions Chaucer's *Parson's Tale,* Gower's *Confessio Amantis,* and Lydgate's *Fall of Princes.* For a recent discussion of the question of Chaucer's influence in Scotland see Walter Scheps, "Chaucer and the Middle Scots Poets," *Studies in Scottish Literature* 22 (1987): 44–59.

2. A manuscript of Lydgate's *Siege of Thebes* was in Scotland by the mid-sixteenth century, if not earlier (Boston Public Library MS F.med 94). For some discussion of Lydgate's influence on Dunbar and related manuscript evidence see P. H. Nichols, "William Dunbar as a Scottish Lydgatian," *PMLA* 46 (1931): 220–21. There are Scottish copies of his *Troy Book* in Cambridge University Library MS Kk.5.30 and Bodleian Library MS Douce 148, and of his *Dietary* in Cambridge, St. John's College MS 191, and University of Edinburgh MS La.III.149. In addition, there are other indications of interest in his works in the sixteenth-century Bannatyne and Asloan manuscripts discussed later in this chapter. Priscilla Bawcutt notes "increasing evidence for Lydgate's long-lasting popularity, from the fifteenth to the seventeenth century [in Scotland]," in "A First Line Index of Early Scottish Verse," *Studies in Scottish Literature* 26 (1991): 257; see also A. S. G. Edwards, "Lydgate Manuscripts: Some Directions for Future Research," in D. Pearsall, ed., *Manuscripts and Readers in Fifteenth-Century England* (Cambridge: Boydell and Brewer, 1983), 256. A manuscript of Gower's *Confessio Amantis,* British Library MS Add. 22139, was possibly in Scotland during the fifteenth century, when it was annotated in what seems to be a Scottish dialect; see R. J. Lyall, "Books and Book Owners in Fifteenth-Century Scotland," in Jeremy Griffiths and Derek Pearsall, eds., *Book Production and Publishing in Britain, 1375–1475* (Cambridge: Cambridge University Press, 1989), 240. This manuscript also includes copies of several Chaucer lyrics. Durkan and Ross (*Early Scottish Libraries,* 7) do note some copies of Gower in Scotland in the mid–sixteenth century, but these could be printed books. Priscilla Bawcutt records a work owned by James IV, *Gestorum de Gower* (*Dunbar the Makar* [Oxford: Clarendon, 1992], 79). In addition, Bawcutt has noted (in a private communication) the occurrence of an extract from Gower's *Confessio* on the flyleaf (f. 74v) of the Boston Public Library manuscript of Lydgate's *Siege of Thebes* cited earlier in this note.

3. Where in Scotland Selden might have been produced is a matter on which scholarship has not been disposed to speculate. The production of such an elaborately decorated manuscript might suggest the proximity of a book-producing center of some size. The only clue as to where this might be is the reference in a note by the first scribe to the birth of James IV "in monasterio sancte crucis prope Edinburgh" (f. 120). This reference is the only source for James's birthplace and could indicate some special local knowledge on the scribe's part that he was keen to impart, particularly

Library MS Arch. Selden B.24, a paper manuscript of 231 leaves, apparently copied by two scribes,[4] and carefully decorated. The contents of the manuscript are exclusively literary and exclusively in verse, including most prominently a number of the works of Chaucer. This manuscript has, I think, a certain amount to suggest to us about a variety of aspects of late medieval manuscript compilation and the ways we categorize manuscripts. It can be located in relation to several kinds of pressures—temporal, cultural, and geographic—that indicate the changing nature of such manuscript compilation in late fifteenth-century Britain.

The first and most obvious affiliations of the manuscript are with earlier fifteenth-century traditions of Chaucerian *compilatio*. Selden includes a number of works by Chaucer or otherwise connected to him in other fifteenth-century manuscripts. It contains copies of several of Chaucer's major works: his *Troilus & Criseyde, Parliament of Fowls,* and *The Legend of Good Women,* as well as his *The Complaint of Mars and Venus* and the lyric "Truth." It also contains a poem

---

since there is no evident necessity for recording the information in terms of what is being copied.

4. The first scribe wrote ff. 1–209v; the second takes over in the middle of this page (at line 1240 of *The Kingis Quair*) and continues to f. 228v. Facsimiles of the first hand appear in Walter W. Skeat, ed., *The Kingis Quair,* 2d rev. ed., Scottish Text Society, n.s., 1 (Edinburgh: William Blackwood, 1911), facing title page; R. K. Root, *The Manuscripts of Chaucer's Troilus* (London: Oxford University Press, 1914), pl. XXII; M. B. Parkes, *English Cursive Book Hands 1200–1500* (Oxford: Clarendon, 1969; reprint, London, 1979), pl. 13 (ii); and Jean Robert Simon, ed., *Le Livre du Roi,* Bibliothèque de Philologie Germanique 21 (Paris: Aubier Montaigne, 1967), facing 256. Plates of the second hand are reproduced in Skeat, *The Kingis Quair,* facing 1; Simon, *Le Livre du Roi,* facing 326 (illustrating the change of hands); and J. Norton-Smith and I. Pravda, eds., *The Quare of Jelusy,* Middle English Texts 3 (Heidelberg: Carl Winter, 1976), facing title page. The poems on ff. 230–31 are in different, less formal hands and appear to be later, early sixteenth-century additions to the manuscript. Attempts have been made to identify both the main hands, but they seem incorrect. The hand of the first scribe was once identified as that of James Gray, who is known to have been active as a scribe and illuminator in the late fifteenth and early sixteenth century. This identification was first made by George Neilson in "The Scribe of the 'Kingis Quair,'" *Athenaeum,* 16 December 1899, 835–36; and it was accepted by most subsequent scholars. On Gray see John MacQueen, "The Literature of Fifteenth-Century Scotland," in Jennifer M. Brown, ed., *Scottish Society in the Fifteenth Century* (London: Edward Arnold, 1977), 201. But this attribution has been authoritatively rebutted by N. R. Ker in *Medieval Manuscripts in British Libraries,* vol. 2, *Abbotsford-Keele* (Oxford: Clarendon, 1977), 1–2. The hand of the second scribe has been connected with that of the "V. de F." who copied Cambridge University Library MS Kk.1.5: see Margaret Muriel Gray, ed., *Lancelot of the Laik,* Scottish Text Society, n.s., 2 (Edinburgh: William Blackwood, 1912), xi and plate facing title page; and J. Norton-Smith, ed., *The Kingis Quair* (Oxford: Clarendon, 1971), xxxii n. 1. But this is not my own view or that of Dr. Julia Boffey, who kindly examined this manuscript with me.

by Chaucer's contemporary John Clanvowe and fifteenth-century verses by Lydgate, Hoccleve, and Walton, as well as a number of lyrics.[5]

The collection in Selden can be related to two different strands of earlier fifteenth-century manuscript compilation. One goes back to the first attempt to create an anthology of Chaucer's works in Cambridge University Library MS Gg.IV.27. This manuscript includes *Troilus, The Legend of Good Women,* the *Parliament of Fowls,* and "Truth" (all also in Selden), as well as *The Canterbury Tales* and a number of Chaucer's other lyrics. The model of Gg is partially reflected in subsequent traditions of Chaucerian compilation that most distinctively include his most substantial completed work, *Troilus & Criseyde,* occasionally in conjunction with other shorter works by or associated with Chaucer. Thus, Bodleian Digby 181 contains *Troilus, The Parliament of Fowls,* Lydgate's *Complaint of the Black Knight,* and Hoccleve's *Letter of Cupid,* all of which appear in Selden. In addition, *Troilus* and the *Letter of Cupid* occur together in Durham Cosin V.II.13.

On the other hand, Selden has considerably closer parallels to the manuscripts of the so-called Oxford group: Bodleian Library MSS Fairfax 16, Bodley 638, and Tanner 346,[6] a group of vernacular poetic manuscripts that reflect a primary interest in Chaucer's dream visions and lyrics and that derive from commercial London bookshops. These three manuscripts all include the *Legend* and the *Parliament,* as well as Lydgate's *Complaint of the Black Knight,* Clanvowe's *Boke of Cupide,* and Hoccleve's *Letter of Cupid*—all poems also in Selden, as are *The Complaint of Mars* and *The Complaint of Venus,* which appear in the Fairfax and Tanner manuscripts.

Gg dates from the first quarter of the fifteenth century. Fairfax is the earliest surviving manuscript of the Oxford group and dates from probably the 1440s; Tanner appears to be slightly later; Durham and Digby date from the second half of the fifteenth century; and Bodley dates from a point in the last quarter of the century. Selden seems to be the last of these Chaucerian collections: it contains the arms of Henry, third Lord Sinclair—arms that he only assumed in

[handwritten margin note: texts included in this manuscript & others (V. N)]

---

5. For a description of the contents see the appendix to this chapter. A more extensive account of them and a full physical description of Arch. Selden B.24 will appear in the introduction to a facsimile by Dr. Julia Boffey and myself (Woodbridge: Boydell and Brewer, 1996).

6. For facsimiles of all these manuscripts see J. Norton-Smith, introduction to *Bodleian MS Fairfax 16* (London: Scolar, 1979); Pamela Robinson, introduction to *MS Tanner 346* (Norman, OK: Pilgrim Books, 1980); Pamela Robinson, introduction to *MS Bodley 638* (Norman, OK: Pilgrim Books, 1981).

January of 1489. The manuscript has been variously dated between 1489 and ca. 1505.[7]

Selden is the last and also one of the largest of these collections. The merging of the two strands of compilation in Selden—those that include *Troilus* with those that contain most significantly Chaucer's dream visions—creates what is among the most substantial surviving collections of Chaucerian verse. The last major manuscript collection of Chaucer, Selden comes next after Gg in the actual quantity of his verse surviving in a separate manuscript collection.

It also serves to remind us of the distinctive problematic of the transmission of Chaucer's works enacted for us in Henryson's poem: that Selden provides our only surviving physical evidence for such Scottish manuscript transmission of Chaucer's works. The only other manuscript of any of them that was probably produced in Scotland during the fifteenth century is Cambridge University Library MS Kk.1.5, which, like Selden, includes Chaucer's "Truth" but contains only this single lyric. But the occurrence of the Selden collection seems to suggest the transmission of such commercially successful compilations to Scotland by the latter years of the fifteenth century, even if no other manuscript evidence does survive.

The parallels in content that link Selden with earlier fifteenth-century manuscript collections seem to have originally been the consequence of what has come to be termed "booklet"—or, more accurately, "fascicular"—circulation.[8] From fairly early in the fifteenth century, single texts or groups of smaller texts would often circulate as separate manuscript units, such units being collocated together by scribes or stationers into larger compilations to meet the needs of individual purchasers. Evidence of such separate exemplars can be discerned in the structures of both the Fairfax and Tanner manuscripts.[9] But it seems that during the fifteenth century the collocations of texts initially reflected in booklet compilations hardened into larger structural entities, in

---

7. "Almost certainly c. 1488," Norton-Smith, *The Kingis Quair,* xxxi; "shortly after 1488," Parkes, *English Cursive Book Hands,* pl. 13 (ii); "about 1490," Skeat, *The Kingis Quair,* xxxvii and lviii—but also "older than 1500" (lvii). A date ca. 1505 is argued by Matthew P. McDiarmid, ed., *The Kingis Quair of James Stewart* (London: Heinemann, 1973), 4.

8. For discussion of booklets in medieval English manuscripts see Pamela Robinson, "The 'Booklet': A Self-Contained Unit in Composite Manuscripts," *Codicologica* 3 (1980): 46–69; Ralph Hanna III, "Booklets in Medieval Manuscripts: Further Considerations," *Studies in Bibliography* 39 (1986): 100–111; and Julia Boffey and John Thompson, "Anthologies and miscellanies: Production and Choice of Texts," in Griffiths and Pearsall, *Book Production,* 279–315.

9. For discussion see Boffey and Thompson, "Anthologies and Miscellanies," 280–81.

[handwritten annotation: booklets inserted into larger structural entities of texts whose local sequences achieved a fixity of form as a single unit (the book / manuscript)]

which local sequences of texts achieved a fixity of form as a single unit, the book. Such appears to be the case with Selden, as with other of these later collections[10] in which there seems to have been through copying unconstrained by quire boundaries.[11]

Selden confirms the chronological durability of such collocations and their links with these earlier commercial, metropolitan forms of book production. Such links extend to even some of the briefer verse texts in the manuscript. For example, the extract from Walton in Selden appears elsewhere in three manuscripts associated with the famous fifteenth-century London scribe John Shirley.[12] Such smaller texts help to confirm the sense that this is not a collection that necessarily implies, in any sense, the imposition of personal taste on the selection of texts. The choice of even such minor items is explicable by preexisting factors of accessibility and collocation.

One can say that to this extent the compiling impulse was a retrospective one defined by the durability of earlier fifteenth-century English Chaucerian models. But while in certain respects Selden confirms such established principles of Chaucerian *compilatio,* in others it demonstrates the loosening of the parameters of Chaucerian attribution in ways that look forward to slightly later tendencies. As I have said, six of the texts in the manuscript are authentically Chaucer's: *Troilus, The Legend of Good Women, The Parliament of Fowls, The Complaint of Mars* and *The Complaint of Venus,* and the lyric "Truth." Most of these are so attributed in Selden—only *Troilus* and *The Complaint of Mars* are not identified as his. Five other texts are incorrectly ascribed to him: the extract from Walton's translation of Boethius, Lydgate's *Complaint of the Black Knight,* Hoccleve's "Mother of God," and two other lyrics (*IMEV*[13] 679 and

---

10. For example, Bodley 638; see Boffey and Thompson, "Anthologies and Miscellanies," 281.

11. A full account of the physical structure of the manuscript will appear in the forthcoming facsimile mentioned in n. 5. R. J. Lyall distinguishes at least seven different paper stocks that do not seem to fall into any clear codicological pattern apart from a break after *Troilus & Criseyde,* which ends on f. 118v (and which is written mainly on five of these stocks). It should be noted, however, that f. 1 is apparently a cancel and is from the paper stock used in the final part of the manuscript, ff. 213–30; see Lyall, "Books and Book Owners," 250–51.

12. British Library MSS Harley 2251, Add. 29729, Royal 20.B.XV; for the most recent listing of manuscripts associated with Shirley, see Jeremy Griffiths, "A Newly Identified Manuscript Inscribed by John Shirley," *Library,* 6th ser., 14 (1992): 92–93.

13. *IMEV* is used throughout to signify Carleton Brown and Rossell Hope Robbins, *The Index of Middle English Verse* (New York: Columbia University Press, 1943), and Rossell Hope Robbins and John L. Cutler, *Supplement to the Index* . . . (Lexington: University of Kentucky Press, 1965).

tendecy to adjust & expand the manuscript

IMEV 2461).[14] In addition, *The Parliament of Fowls* survives in Selden with a unique spurious conclusion that seems to be the product of local adaptation.[15]

In this tendency to adjust and expand the Chaucerian canon, Selden is set apart from the earlier Chaucerian compilations with their more conservative disposition to underascribe works to Chaucer. For example, none of the manuscripts of Chaucer's *House of Fame* actually identifies him as author, nor does any manuscript of the *Book of the Duchess*. In contrast, Selden is without parallel among fifteenth-century Chaucer manuscripts: no other contains so many misattributions to Chaucer. It does, however, adumbrate the sixteenth-century tendency toward a wilder measure of canonical optimism about Chaucer's achievement.[16] This tendency was to receive its fullest expression in the first early printed collected editions of Chaucer, those by Thynne in 1532 and Stow in 1568, each of which added about twenty noncanonical works to Chaucer's oeuvre. In degree and also in kind Selden's attributions can be differentiated from these later tendencies. As a collection, it achieves a significant degree of coherence through the subject matter of the majority of the poems it contains. All the substantial ones are concerned in various ways with love. In addition to all the major Chaucer poems—*Troilus,* the *Legend,* the *Parliament, Mars,* and *Venus*—many of the others share this common subject, including *The Kingis Quair,* Clanvowe's *Boke of Cupide,* Hoccleve's *Letter of Cupid,* and Lydgate's *Complaint of the Black Knight,* as well as "The Lay of Sorrow," "The Lufaris Complaynt," and "The Quare of Jelousy." What is curious is that almost all the works misascribed to Chaucer—the antifeminist lyric *IMEV* 679, the religious lyric *IMEV* 2461, the extract from Walton, and Hoccleve's "Mother of God"—do not take love as their subject. Only the Lydgate poem has any clear relationship, in terms of subject matter, to the main collection, and its misattribution may be explicable by the general association of the poem with other, earlier manuscript collections primarily of Chaucer's

as a collection, the manuscript contains a degree of coherence through subject matter

---

14. For an inaccurate account of these misattributions see J. T. T. Brown, *The Authorship of the Kingis Quair* (Glasgow: James MacLehose, 1896), 7–9.

15. This ending is printed in *Supplementary Parallel-Texts of Chaucer's Minor Poems,* Chaucer Society, 1st ser., 22 (London: Kegan Paul, Trench, Trübner, 1871), 23–26; it comprises lines 603–78 there.

16. On this enlarging of the Chaucer canon in the fifteenth and sixteenth centuries see F. W. Bonner, "The Genesis of the Chaucer Apocrypha," *Studies in Philology* 48 (1951): 461–81; and the chapters on William Thynne (by E. D. Blodgett) and John Stow (by Anne Hudson) in Paul Ruggiers, ed., *Editing Chaucer: The Great Tradition* (Norman, OK: Pilgrim Books, 1984).

poems.[17] In part, then, these misattributions may be the result of some attempt to link poems that were manifestly not congruent with the main subject matter of the manuscript to a Chaucerian focus that at least associated them with his primacy in the collection.[18]

There are, however, other factors related to these misattributions that suggest they can be seen as part of a peculiarly Scottish misappropriation of Chaucerian identity in the 1490s and early 1500s. One of the most interesting illustrations of this tendency is Thomas Hoccleve's "Mother of God," a poem that was also copied, virtually contemporaneously, into another Scottish manuscript where it is also ascribed to Chaucer, John of Ireland's *Meroure of Wisdom* (1490),[19] a work that provides other testimony to Scottish interest in English literary texts. Thus, two of the three surviving manuscripts of Hoccleve's work are of Scottish provenance, both apparently independently derived. In addition, Lydgate's *Complaint of the Black Knight,* in Selden titled "The Maying and Disport of Chaucer," was issued under the same title by the Edinburgh printers Chepman and Myllar in 1508.[20] The relationship between the two texts, one manuscript, the other print, extends considerably beyond identity of title. It seems clear that if Selden was not the direct source for Chepman and Myllar, the print derived from a copy not very far removed from it.[21] The manuscript and the print share over a hundred significant common variants against all these other witnesses, in addition to their close dialectal connections. Another poem ascribed to Chaucer in Selden, the lyric "Devise, Prowes and Eke Humility" (*IMEV* 679), was also printed by Chepman and

17. It appears elsewhere, for example, in such collections as MSS Bodleian Fairfax 16, Bodley 638, Tanner 346, and Digby 181, as well as in Cambridge, Magdalene College MS Pepys 2006.

18. It is, of course, possible that such misattributions antedated Selden. Four of the texts misascribed to Chaucer: the Walton extract, *IMEV* 679, the Lydgate, and Hoccleve's "Mother of God," form a sequence of about the length of a quire. It is possible that the Selden scribe received this part of his exemplar as a discrete unit.

19. National Library of Scotland MS Advocates 18.2.8; for discussion see Bennett, "Those Scotch Copies of Chaucer."

20. On Chepman and Myllar see *The Chepman and Myllar Prints: A Facsimile, with a Bibliographical Note by William Beattie* (Edinburgh: Edinburgh Bibliographical Society, 1950), xii–xiii; and William Beattie, "Some Early Scottish Books," in G. W. S. Barrow, ed., *The Scottish Tradition: Essays in Honour of Ronald Gordon Cant,* St. Andrews University Publications 60 (Edinburgh: Scottish Academic Press, 1974), 107–20.

21. See David Parkinson, "Scottish Prints and Entertainments, 1508," *Neophilologus* 75 (1991): 304–10. Parkinson suggests that Selden, Chepman and Myllar, and the Asloan manuscript all "derive from a common exemplar." He further observes a propos of Selden that "from such a book may well have come Chepman and Myllar's copytext" (305); see further on the textual relationship between these witnesses E. Krausser, "The Complaint of the Black Knight," *Anglia* 19 (1897): 216–23.

Myllar in 1508 and was there also ascribed to him. These links remind us that in another respect Selden is also a transitional manuscript, in this case in its possible connections with the movement from manuscript to print in Scotland.

And there are other links between Selden and an emergent Scottish literary culture, links that are reflected in a further significant strand in the compilation of the manuscript. For if it is the last major manuscript Chaucer anthology, it is also the first major anthology of vernacular Scottish verse. In addition to the works of English vernacular poets I have mentioned, it also contains several significant Scottish poems. Most notable among these is the unique copy of *The Kingis Quair* by James I of Scotland. In addition, it includes the related *Quare of Jelousy*—also unique—and several other shorter verse texts seemingly of Scottish origin, most extensively "The Luvaris Complaynt" and "The Lay of Sorrow." But for all their difference from the earlier poems, these additions may respond to the imperatives of established Chaucerian compilation: the newer, native poems are at least thematically consistent with the dominant amatory preoccupations of the preceding material.

The longer of these works all appear in the latter part of the manuscript (that beginning with *The Kingis Quair*), which part is notable because of its lack of affiliation to any antecedent collection. Indeed, most of these later contents appear unique.[22] But the Scottish affiliations of the manuscript are not restricted to this later part of the manuscript; a number of the shorter pieces in the earlier part of Selden seem to exist elsewhere only in later manuscripts of Scottish provenance, some of which also have parallels to some of the other contents of Selden. One lyric from this part, *IMEV* 2461, appears elsewhere only in the Asloan manuscript, compiled in the first half of the sixteenth century.[23] And it is followed there by a copy of "The Maying and Disport of Chaucer"[24] (Lydgate's *Complaint of the Black Knight*) that seems textually related to both the Selden text and the Chepman and Myllar print, the only other copies of Lydgate's poem with which it shares this title. At some point that manuscript also included a copy of Chaucer's "Truth,"[25] also, of course, in

22. Sally Mapstone,"Was There a Court Literature in Fifteenth-Century Scotland?" *Studies in Scottish Literature* 26 (1991): 422, links Selden to "the plethora of literary recopying [of Scottish works] around the late 1480s." The point seems valid; but Selden clearly differs from the other examples she cites in that there are no antecedent witnesses and hence there is no evidence that the poems in this part of the manuscript ever circulated together before their collocation in Selden.

23. See W. A. Craigie, ed., *The Asloan Manuscript*, 2 vols., Scottish Text Society, n.s., 14 and 16 (Edinburgh: William Blackwood, 1923–24); the lyric is printed at 2:245–46.

24. It is printed in Craigie, *The Asloan Manuscript*, 2:247–70.

25. The original table of contents for the manuscript is printed in Craigie, *The Asloan Manuscript,* 1:xii–xv; item "xlix" is "Itm a ballat of treuth" (xiv).

Selden. There are also connections with the slightly later, very large, mid-sixteenth-century, primarily verse collection, the Bannatyne manuscript.[26] This manuscript includes, for example, the selection from Walton's *Boethius* as well as three lyrics that also appear in Selden.[27] Two of these occur only in these two manuscripts; the third (*IMEV* 3660) is also in Pepys 2553, another Scottish anthology, the later sixteenth-century Maitland Folio manuscript.[28] In fact, all the lyric texts in Selden that circulated elsewhere did so exclusively in Scottish contexts. It would seem, then, that Selden demonstrates a distinct moment in Scottish as well as Chaucerian *compilatio*. Clearly, the manuscript contains both important unique Scottish texts—such as *The Kingis Quair* and *The Quare of Jelousy*—as well as others that were to assume a recurrent identity in subsequent Scottish manuscript traditions.

In these respects Selden looks forward to later compilational tendencies of form and attribution, and another important element in its construction is also less directly constrained by the force of earlier manuscript traditions: the manuscript's decoration. In demonstrating a shift from booklet compilation to book, Selden also demonstrates the disposition of such exemplar sequences into what is perhaps its most consistent and elaborate decorative form within the Chaucerian manuscript tradition. Individual texts have been laid out so that virtually all the major ones begin at the top of a leaf, as often do significant internal divisions in longer works. Many texts have demi-vinet borders at their beginning and at significant divisions.[29] In addition, there are numerous decorated initials of varying sizes, and the beginning of the text of *Troilus* contains a historiated initial.[30] Any form of illustration is rare in Chaucer manuscripts,

---

26. References are to *The Bannatyne Manuscript: National Library of Scotland Advocates' MS. 1.1.6,* with an introduction by Denton Fox and William A. Ringler (London: Scolar, 1980).

27. The Walton extract is no. 106, f. 75v. The three lyric texts are *IMEV* 679 (no. 349, ff. 262v–63; previously mentioned in this chapter and ascribed here as in Selden to Chaucer), 3660 (no. 97, f. 74v), and 3727 (no. 96, f. 74v); there are other texts common to both manuscripts, but some of these (though not no. 349) seem to have been copied into Bannatyne from the 1542 edition of Thynne's Chaucer; see further *The Bannatyne Manuscript,* xli.

28. See W. A. Craigie, ed., *The Maitland Folio Manuscript,* 2 vols., Scottish Text Society, n.s., 7 and 20 (Edinburgh: William Blackwood, 1919–27), 1:341. It was copied from this manuscript into a later Scottish anthology, the Reidpeth manuscript.

29. These appear on ff. 1, 1v, 41v, 67, 91v, 111v, 120v, 132, 134, 137v, 138v, 152v, 161, 163, 166, 172v, 177, 180, 185, 187v, and 192. They are all accompanied by initials varying in size between four and fifteen lines. Such decoration serves to mark the beginning of all major texts up to *The Kingis Quair* and of major divisions within the longer ones (like *Troilus* and *The Legend of Good Women*). In addition, the illuminated Sinclair arms appear on f. 118v, and there are a number of simpler flourished initials. For reproductions of those on ff. 41v and 192 see n. 4.

30. This is a narrative miniature, depicting Troilus's initial encounter with Criseyde and his falling in love with her.

and only two other manuscripts of *Troilus* contain illustration.[31] The very care with which such a late, nonmetropolitan piece of manuscript production was undertaken would seem to imply an unusually sophisticated awareness of the implications of the relationship between text and decoration derived from some experience of Chaucerian codicology or at least from some acquaintance with its forms. Parallels for the decoration of the Chaucer texts in Selden cannot be found. The general level of decoration seems untypically elaborate for Chaucer texts and/or manuscript collections. Thus, few of the other *Troilus* manuscripts are comparable in this respect—only the early Gg and Morgan manuscripts employ both illuminated initials and demi-vinets. The next longest text, *The Legend of Good Women,* is similarly unusual in the systematic elaborateness of its decorative program. Of the other manuscripts, both Gg.IV.27 and Tanner 346 have demi-vinets and illuminated initials at the beginning of the text but not elsewhere. No other manuscript of this poem has any equivalent decoration. But Selden has nine demi-vinets for the *Legend,* with accompanying decorated initials, marking virtually all the major divisions of Chaucer's poem.

If Selden is unusually elaborate for a Chaucer manuscript—or at least for one not comprised of his *Canterbury Tales*—it also appears to have been unusual among Scottish manuscripts of the period.[32] But the decorative elaborateness of Selden is not simply the manifestation of a developing sense of manuscript *ordinatio.* The decoration provides a visual correlative to the hardening of the compilational impulse into a fixed and stable form, imposing order on the manuscript. This stable pattern of decoration disappears in the latter part of the manuscript, that is, at the point where it is primarily concerned with newer, Scottish texts. Up to this point it is quite uniform. By furnishing a stable, decorative program, of a kind not previously established, Selden furnishes another demonstration of the way in which an originally variegated collection of texts had evolved into a larger, fixed form.

31. These are Cambridge, Corpus Christi College MS 61 (with the famous "Troilus frontispiece") and New York, Pierpont Morgan Library MS 817 (the "Campsall" manuscript); the latter also has a historiated initial at the beginning of the text. The Corpus frontispiece has been frequently reproduced; see, for example, the color reproduction in *Troilus and Criseyde: A Facsimile of Corpus Christi College Cambridge MS 61,* with introductions by M. B. Parkes and Elizabeth Salter (Cambridge: D. S. Brewer, 1978). The historiated initial at the beginning of the text in the Morgan manuscript, also depicting Troilus and Criseyde, albeit in more obscure circumstances, is reproduced in *The Pierpont Morgan Library Manuscript M. 817: A facsimile,* with an introduction by Jeanne Krochalis (Norman, OK: Pilgrim Books, 1986); for discussion see xxi–xxiii.

32. Lyall, "Books and Book Owners," 252: "The presence of at least twenty-one illuminated initials and borders suggests a much more elaborate production than was usual in Scotland."

The circumstances of the creation of such an atypical manuscript—in terms
of the culture and the traditions from which it is derived—merit some speculation. The manuscript demonstrates a decorative sophistication and access to
commercially circulating exemplars of Chaucerian works and to other indigenous poetic materials. How the Chaucerian works in Selden might have been
transmitted to Scotland is a matter for speculation. Such speculation centers
inevitably on the figure of James I himself. The author of *The Kingis Quair* had
clearly read a number of such works during his captivity in England.[33] His
marriage to Joan Beaufort in February 1424 connected him to a family of
distinct literary interests,[34] a family, moreover, related to Chaucer's own.[35] It
would seem plausible that he should have brought back to Scotland, on his
return in 1424, copies of works by Chaucer and his contemporaries and suc-
cessors. Such a collection, or such collections, would doubtless have remained
within a small courtly circle, one that would have restricted the making of
subsequent copies.

No obvious occasion suggests itself, however, for the creation of such an
elaborate and amplified conjunction of imported and native verse. The suggestion that the manuscript was prepared for Lord Sinclair's marriage to Margaret
Hepburn, daughter of Lord Hailes, on 4 December 1489,[36] lacks any evidential
or circumstantial support. Somewhat more attractive is the earlier hypothesis[37]
that relates the copying of the manuscript to family piety: Henry Sinclair's
grandmother was sister to James I, author of *The Kingis Quair*. But this is, at
best, a partial explanation that does not explain more than a single component
in the structure of the manuscript. For, as I have tried to show, the presence of
The Kingis Quair and related Scottish poems in the latter part of Selden is not
the only intimation of the merging of Scottish material with English traditions.
Perhaps a more general and more satisfactory explanation can be found in the
conjunction of familial *pietas* with more general bibliophilic and literary inter-

---

33. For a general account of this period in James's life, see E. W. M. Balfour-Melville, *The
English Captivity of James 1, King of Scots,* Historical Association Leaflet no. 77 (London:
Published for the Historical Association by Bell and Sons, 1929).

34. Walter Schirmer, *John Lydgate,* trans. Ann Keep (London: Methuen, 1961), notes that
Lydgate had "frequent dealings" with the Beaufort family (28); see also Ethel Seaton, *Sir Richard
Roos* (London: R. Hart-Davis, 1961), 215.

35. Chaucer's wife's sister, Katharine Swynford, was John of Gaunt's third wife; the Beaufort
line comes from this union.

36. See R. J. Lyall, "The Court as a Cultural Centre," *History Today* 34 (1984): 29. I owe this
reference to the kindness of Professor David Parkinson.

37. A. H. Millar, "The Scribe of 'The Kingis Quair,' " *Athenaeum,* 30 December 1899, 898.

ests[38] of the kind affirmed by the poet Gavin Douglas, who celebrates Henry, Lord Sinclair, as "fader of bukis" in the prologue to his translation of the *Aeneid.*[39]

The difficulties in clearly establishing the impulses that led to the creation of the manuscript are, in their turn, related to the taxonomic problems the manuscript occasions. It cannot be accommodated into any of the categories generally used to categorize late medieval English manuscript collections. It clearly does not belong with various categories of family or coterie compilations like the so-called Findern (Cambridge University Library MS Ff.I.6)[40] or Devonshire (British Library MS Add. 17492)[41] manuscripts. Nor can it be associated with the single author compilations that were undertaken for Hoccleve,[42] Lydgate,[43] or Charles d'Orleans.[44] I noted earlier the obvious parallels with earlier "booklet" collections containing most significantly the works of Chaucer. But such parallels do not comprehensively define Selden, which joins the works of Chaucer and his early followers to other, largely unique Scottish materials to create a unique transcultural collection, one that resists definition by any of the conventional terms we use to identify a manuscript that possesses no obvious single unifying principle. It is neither commonplace book, household book, miscellany, nor anthology.[45] It seems to constitute what I propose to term a "transitional" collection, one that embodies a number of elements that significantly modify earlier fifteenth-century English methods of literary manuscript compilation to meet the purposes of a later Scottish audience. It can also be linked to other new, apparently regional tendencies: most obviously its

---

38. On such interests within the Sinclair family see MacQueen, "The Literature of Fifteenth-Century Scotland," 197–98.

39. See D. F. C. Coldwell, ed., *Virgil's Aeneid Translated into Scottish Verse by Gavin Douglas,* Scottish Text Society, 3d ser., 25 (Edinburgh: William Blackwood, 1957), 1.prol.85.

40. On Findern see the facsimile of the manuscript with introductions by A. E. B. Owen and Richard Beadle (London: Scolar, 1977); and Kate Harris, "The Origins and Make-Up of Cambridge University Library MS Ff.1.6," *Transactions of the Cambridge Bibliographical Society* 8 (1983): 299.

41. On this manuscript see, most recently, Julia Boffey, *Manuscripts of English Courtly Love Lyrics in the Later Middle Ages* (Cambridge: Boydell and Brewer, 1985), 7–9, 69–70, 81–82, and the references cited there.

42. For Hoccleve one thinks most obviously of his own autograph collections: Durham University Cosin MS. V.III.9, and Huntington Library MSS 111 and 744.

43. In, for example, British Library MS. Harley 2255 and Bodleian Library MS. Laud Misc. 683.

44. In British Library MS. Harley 682.

45. For discussion and examples of these categories see A. G. Rigg, *A Glastonbury Miscellany of the Fifteenth Century* (London: Oxford University Press, 1968), 24–26; and Boffey and Thompson, "Anthologies and Miscellanies," 279–315.

decorative elaborateness, its extension of the Chaucerian canon, and its links to an emergent print culture. The manuscript is a form of cultural and compilational hybrid. It replicates aspects of earlier Chaucer manuscript traditions and simultaneously enlarges them through the incorporation of indigenous poetic material and its extension of the Chaucer canon, creating an admixture of the old and the new.

Selden clearly enacts these divergent pressures on the late fifteenth-century British manuscript book. The implications of Selden's form and content suggest the limited usefulness of conventional taxonomic terminology to define it as a collection by such terms as *anthology* or *miscellany,* and they locate the manuscript within contexts that more appropriately stress its genuinely literary and cultural transitional aspects.

APPENDIX: BODLEIAN MS ARCH. SELDEN B.24

CONTENTS

ff. 152v–91v	"Chaucere the legendis of ladyes", *The Legend of Good Women; IMEV* 100.
ff. 192–211	*The Kingis Quair; IMEV* 1215.
ff. 211v–17	Hoccleve, *Letter of Cupid; IMEV* 666.
ff. 217–19	"The Lay of Sorrow"; *IMEV* 482.
ff. 219–21v	"The Lufaris Complaynt"; *IMEV* 564.
ff. 221v–28v	"quod Auchen [?] . . ." "The Quare of Ielousy"; *IMEV* 325.
f. 229	John Russell, "My frende gif thou will be a serviture"; *IMEV* 2242; four eight-line stanzas.
f. 229v	"Thy begyning is barane brutelnes"; *IMEV* 3727.
f. 229v	"Man be as mery as tho . . ."; *IMEV* 2043.
f. 230	"[Go fro my] window, go, go fro my window / . . . [win]dow sir . . . si[r qu]ho ys at Four vndow?" Fragmentary (?), twenty-three-line text; *IMEV* 4284.
f. 231–30v	"O lady I schall me dress with besy cure"; *IMEV* 2478.
f. 231v	"In my defense god me defend / and bring my saull to ane guid end O lord." Couplet.

Short Texts in Manuscript Anthologies:
The Minor Poems of John Lydgate in Two Fifteenth-Century Collections

Julia Boffey

Lydgate is today perhaps best known for a number of long, very popular, and often very handsomely produced Middle English poems. *The Fall of Princes, The Troy Book, The Siege of Thebes, The Life of Our Lady,* and the substantial vitae of such saints as Alban and Edmund each take up somewhere between three thousand and thirty-six thousand lines.[1] The survival of some of these works in numerous copies has permitted fruitful textual, codicological, and art-historical studies that have revealed something of Lydgate's habits of publication and the forms and patterns in which his longer works circulated.[2] Relatively overlooked has been his huge body of short poems, which in number (depending on the certainty of some attributions) fall between 150 and 180; which in nature vary from courtly to moral, religious, didactic, informative,

---

1. For bibliography, see Alain Renoir and C. David Benson, "John Lydgate," in Albert E. Hartung, ed., *A Manual of the Writings in Middle English, 1050–1500,* vol. 6 (New Haven: Connecticut Academy of Arts and Sciences, 1980), 1809–1920, 2071–2175; Derek Albert Pearsall, *John Lydgate* (London: Routledge and Kegan Paul, 1970); Walter F. Schirmer, *John Lydgate: A Study in the Culture of the Fifteenth Century,* trans. Ann E. Keep (London: Methuen, 1961).

2. A. S. G. Edwards, "Lydgate Manuscripts: Some Directions for Future Research," in Derek Pearsall, ed., *Manuscripts and Readers in Fifteenth-Century England: The Literary Implications of Manuscript Study* (Cambridge: D. S. Brewer, 1983), 15–26; Edwards, "Lydgate Scholarship: Progress and Prospects," in Robert F. Yeager, ed., *Fifteenth-Century Studies: Recent Essays* (Hamden, CT: Archon Books, 1984), 29–47; and Kathleen Scott, "Lydgate's Lives of Saints Edmund and Fremund: A Newly Located Manuscript in Arundel Castle," *Viator* 13 (1982): 335–66.

and occasional; and which in some cases were evidently as popular as Lydgate's longer works.[3] Although they range in length and subject matter from, for example, the relatively substantial *Testament*—a devotional compilation that extends in its fullest versions to 897 lines—to a single stanza on *The Nine Properties of Wine* (*IMEV* 4175),[4] they are all works that because of their relative brevity have in the main been preserved only in composite collections of some kind. This is not of course to deny that the early circulation of many of them may have occurred in other quite distinct forms: single leaves, for personal record or perhaps for presentation; display copies, such as the English translation of the psalm *De profundis* produced for William Curteys, Lydgate's abbot at Bury St. Edmunds, "at his chirche to hang it on the wal,"[5] or such as the fable of *Bycorne and Chychevache* represented on a "peynted or desteyned clothe for an halle a parlour or a chaumbre";[6] even high-class gift wrapping, which seems to have been the function of the *Ballade on a New Year's Gift of an Eagle*.[7] But precisely because they were often not conceived as components of books, these poems had a precarious literary future, and those that survived were the fortunate ones that made their way at an early stage into a written collection of some sort. My concern in this chapter is the nature of some of the configurations in which these short poems have been preserved, in particular certain groupings of poems in single gatherings or booklets within larger compilations.

---

3. These statistics are based on the listings in Renoir and Benson, "John Lydgate," which includes some apocryphal attributions, and in Henry Noble MacCracken, ed., *The Minor Poems of John Lydgate,* 2 vols., Early English Text Society, e.s., 107, and o.s., 192 (London: Oxford University Press, 1911 and 1934). For a report of a computer-aided survey of authorship, see Stephen R. Reimer, "The Lydgate Canon: A Project Description," *Literary and Linguistic Computing* 5 (1990): 248–49. The pioneering work by Eleanor Prescott Hammond on the manuscripts of Lydgate's minor poems has still not been superseded; see, for example, the Lydgate texts edited in *English Verse between Chaucer and Surrey* (Durham, NC: Duke University Press, 1927) and "Two British Museum Manuscripts: A Contribution to the Bibliography of John Lydgate," *Anglia* 28 (1905): 1–28. The popularity of short works, such as the *Dietary,* is attested by the numbers of surviving manuscripts; in this case over fifty are listed by Renoir and Benson, "John Lydgate," 2092–93.

4. MacCracken, *Minor Poems,* 1:329–62 and 2:724. *IMEV* numbers, supplied here with anonymous texts or lyrics difficult to locate by title, refer to Carleton Brown and Rossell Hope Robbins, *The Index of Middle English Verse* (New York: Columbia University Press, 1943), and Rossell Hope Robbins and John L. Cutler, *Supplement to the Index of Middle English Verse* (Lexington, KY: Kentucky University Press, 1965), where editions are listed.

5. MacCracken, *Minor Poems,* 1:77–84, lines 161–68.

6. Ibid., 2:433–38. The information comes from the scribe John Shirley's introduction to the copy in Cambridge, Trinity College, MS R.3.20.

7. MacCracken, *Minor Poems,* 2:649–51.

Unlike other copious producers of short poems, such as Froissart, Machaut, or even Hoccleve, whose methods for organizing their minor poems can be partially documented,[8] Lydgate seems to have left no evidence of maintaining a portfolio of this material or of arranging to have it circulated in authorized collections. We can glimpse the flimsy forms in which his sources reached him in his reference to the "lytell bylle" on which the Latin *Legend of St. Giles* was brought to him for translation[9] and in his reference to the French "paunflet" from which he translated *The Churl and the Bird*,[10] and it may be that most of his own short poems circulated at first in comparable ways. London, British Library, MS Harley 2255, a large anthology of short poems on religious and moral subjects that seems to have been copied for William Curteys, Lydgate's abbot at the Benedictine house of Bury St. Edmunds, may in some sense (because of its likely preparation on Lydgate's home ground) represent an "authorized" selection,[11] but it comprehends by no means all of Lydgate's shorter pieces, many of which (particularly occasional poems or those on secular topics) circulated influentially in copies associated with the litterateur John Shirley and with the later scribe, associated with the London stationer John Multon, who used Shirley's exemplars.[12] A complete manuscript anthology of Lydgate's shorter poems—the handwritten equivalent of the two large volumes that Henry Noble MacCracken produced for the Early English Text Society—would have constituted an enormous book; and compilers of Lydgate anthologies (such as Harley 2255 and the Shirley-related anthologies) and of Lydgate manuscripts (such as Cambridge, Jesus College MS 56 or Oxford, Bodleian Library, MS Laud misc. 683)[13] seem to have contented themselves,

---

8. See W. W. Kibler and J. I. Wimsatt, "Machaut's Text and the Question of his Personal Supervision," *Studies in the Literary Imagination* 20 (1987): 41–53; Sylvia Huot, *From Song to Book: The Poetics of Writing in Old French Lyric and Lyrical Narrative Poetry* (Ithaca and London: Cornell University Press, 1987); and John M. Bowers, "Hoccleve's Huntington Holographs: The First 'Collected Poems' in English," *Fifteenth-Century Studies* 14 (1989): 27–51.

9. MacCracken, *Minor Poems,* 1:161–73, line 27.

10. Ibid., 2:468–85, line 35.

11. The arms of the abbey of St. Edmunds are included in the first initial in this manuscript. See further Pearsall, *John Lydgate,* 78–79; Hammond, "Two British Museum Manuscripts," 24.

12. On this scribe, see Julia Boffey and John J. Thompson, "Anthologies and Miscellanies: Production and Choice of Texts," in Jeremy Griffiths and Derek Pearsall, eds., *Book Production and Publishing in Britain, 1375–1475* (Cambridge: Cambridge University Press, 1989), 278–315 (at 287–89). London, British Library, MS Harley 2251, in particular, contains a large selection of Lydgate's minor poems.

13. Montague Rhodes James, *A Descriptive Catalogue of the Manuscripts in the Library of Jesus College, Cambridge* (London: C. J. Clay and Sons, 1895), 87–90; and H. O. Coxe, *Bodleian Quarto Catalogues,* II: *Laudian Manuscripts* (1858–85; reprint, with corrections, Oxford: Bodleian Library, 1973), 491–94. A further important small group of religious poems, copied by

whether through planned selections or simply through making do with available exemplars, with certain parts of the whole.

Other surviving manuscripts of Lydgate's writings demonstrate the compositional principle according to which a selection of short poems accompanied one of the longer works, as in, for example, British Library, MS Lansdowne 699 and Lincoln, Cathedral Library MS 129, where *The Lives of Saints Alban and Amphabel* occupy prime position,[14] and in a book recorded in the will of Sir Thomas Chaworth of Wiverton, Nottinghamshire, dated 1458/9: "ye which begynnyth with ye lyffe of Seynt Albon and Amphiabell and other mony dyvers lyfez and thynges in ye same boke."[15] The tentative identification of this with the first part of San Marino, Huntington Library, MS HM 140, in which *The Clerk's Tale* and a poem on Job seem to constitute the "lyfez," consigns Lydgate's short poems to the category of the remaining "thynges."[16] Certain recurring groupings of short poems are observable in these anthologies just as they are in the collections of exclusively short poems, such as Harley 2255. The Lincoln manuscript's grouping of *The Churl and the Bird, The Legend of St. Austin at Compton,* and the *Dance Macabre* is reflected in British Library, MS Lansdowne 699, whose remaining contents (apart from the long saints' vitae) recur in almost entirely the same order in a manuscript now in Leiden; and portions of Harley 2255 are duplicated in Jesus College 56.[17] It seems clear that Lydgate's short poems must in certain cases have been available to manuscript compilers in established configurations.

Richard Fox of St. Albans, is to be found in Cambridge, University Library, MS Kk.1.6; see Alexandra Barratt, "Dame Eleanor Hull: A Fifteenth-Century Translator," in Roger Ellis et al., eds., *The Medieval Translator: The Theory and Practice of Translation in the Middle Ages* (Woodbridge, Suffolk: D. S. Brewer, 1989), 87–101 (at 92).

14. *A Catalogue of the Lansdowne Manuscripts in the British Museum,* 2 vols. (London: R. and A. Taylor, 1819), 2:161; and Rodney M. Thomson, *Catalogue of the Manuscripts of Lincoln Cathedral Chapter Library* (Woodbridge, Suffolk: D. S. Brewer, 1989), 99.

15. J. M. Manly and E. Rickert, *The Text of The Canterbury Tales,* 8 vols. (Chicago: University of Chicago Press, 1940), 1:609–10.

16. C. W. Dutschke, *Guide to Medieval and Renaissance Manuscripts in the Huntington Library,* 2 vols. (San Marino, CA: The Library, 1989), 2:185–90. For a skeptical note on the identification, see Thorlac Turville-Petre, "Some Medieval English Manuscripts in the North-East Midlands," in Derek Pearsall, ed., *Manuscripts and Readers in Fifteenth-Century England: The Literary Implications of Manuscript Study* (Cambridge: D. S. Brewer, 1983), 124–41 (at 133 n. 16).

17. J. A. Van Dorsten, "The Leyden Lydgate Manuscript," *Scriptorium* 14 (1960): 315–25; this manuscript also includes *The Churl and the Bird, The Legend of St. Austin,* and *Dance Macabre,* but in reverse order. These texts of the *Dance Macabre,* which survives in two recensions, are according to Hammond all of the B-group; see *English Verse,* 125. A grouping of *Consulo Quisquis Eris, Midsomer Rose, Horns Away,* and *Look in the merour* is duplicated in Harley 2255 and Jesus 56.

To pursue this suggestion, it is helpful to explore in fuller detail the composition of two fifteenth-century manuscripts that draw together texts by Lydgate and others, to see what can be learned of the processes of their compilation. What decisions—intellectual, aesthetic, or pragmatic—determined the scope of their contents? Do we classify them as anthologies (that is, as a number of items brought together according to some governing principle) or as miscellanies, the fruit of more random incorporation? Is there a further option by which they might be classified as partly anthologies or miscellanies; or, as Siegfried Wenzel suggests in his contribution to this book, are we in need of some essentially other term?

The first compilation to consider is British Library, MS Harley 116, a folio-sized volume that sets its Lydgate in the company of mixed Latin and Middle English verse and prose.[18] Its main text, with which it opens, is Hoccleve's *Regiment of Princes,* copied throughout in one hand, which goes on to supply Benedict Burgh's translations of *The Distichs of Cato* and some short items of verse and prose. Lydgate is featured in the next four gatherings, which fall into two units, apparently both worked on by a further pair of scribes. In the first are his version of Psalm 53, *Deus in nomine tuo salvum me fac* and his *Dance Macabre,* separated by an anonymous mortality lyric addressed specifically to "jofenes dames" (*IMEV* 2136), and followed by Latin verses on the foundation of Carthusian houses;[19] in the second, *The Churl and the Bird* is sandwiched between a Middle English prose propagandist *Chronicle from Rollo to Edward IV*[20] and a verse elegy for Ralph Lord Cromwell (*IMEV* 2411). The remainder of the manuscript is occupied by a condensation of the Middle English prose translation of Geoffrey of Franconia's *Book of Trees and Wine;* translated sections of the treatise on arboriculture attributed to Nicholas Bollard, copied by a fourth hand;[21] and Lydgate's *Dietary* (in the hand of the scribe of the

---

18. Most recently described by M. C. Seymour, "The Manuscripts of Hoccleve's *Regiment of Princes*," *Transactions of the Edinburgh Bibliographical Society* 4 (1974): 253–97 (at 265–66).

19. The verses begin, "[S]alve frater mi salue tibi Quis locus iste / Est dom*u*s jhe*s*u non est ad nisi nomen . . . ."

20. Unedited; see Edward Donald Kennedy, "Chronicles and Other Historical Writing," in Albert E. Hartung, ed., *A Manual of the Writings in Middle English,* vol. 8 (Hamden, CT: Archon Books, 1989), 2702.

21. See W. L. Braekman, ed., *Geoffrey of Franconia's Book of Trees and Wine,* Scripta 24 (Brussels: Research Center of Medieval and Renaissance Studies of UFSAL, 1989); and Braekman, "Bollard's Middle English Book of Planting and Grafting and Its Background," *Studia Neophilologica* 57 (1985): 19–39. According to Braekman, the condensation of Geoffrey of Franconia is closely related to the text on ff. 20–46 of London, British Library, MS Harley 1785. On the evidence of notes on f. 54v, this belonged to one Robert Robinson, born in Lincolnshire in 1454, apprenticed in London in 1470, and married "in the parissh churche of saynt christofre in the

Dance Macabre and the *Elegy*), which has here spawned later additions in the form of various medical recipes.

Though the manuscript seems to fall into several distinct sections of rather different subjects of focus, and though these sections were copied by different scribes and constituted from gatherings that were tailored to fit,[22] the manuscript would appear from the outset, or from very near the outset, to have been used as a single entity. Gatherings throughout are comprised of eight leaves, unless they have been specially truncated or extended to accommodate a particular text. Quire signatures supplied by one hand run continuously from *a* to *v,* and are lacking (or have been cropped) only in the last two gatherings. A list of contents headed "Contenta huius libri," copied in an early sixteenth-century hand on the verso of the opening parchment flyleaf, confirms that the parts of the manuscript were together, in the order in which they now occur, from an early date.[23] Notes from the beginning and end of the volume also suggest that it was handled as a complete unit in the very early sixteenth century: beneath the list of contents, for example, is written "receyvyd of John Kymbell the ixth daye of auguste in / the xxti yere of the reigne of kyng henri the vijth by the hande / of John harrison—xxxiijs iijd," while on folio 170v the same individual features in the inscription "constat Jhon kymbel / of ludwell."[24] Though M. C. Seymour's opinion that the manuscript could well have been copied in a religious house[25] does not seem to accord precisely with the manuscript's

---

warde of Bradstrete" in 1482; it is also mentioned by Linda E. Voigts as related to the metropolitan "Sloane Group" of manuscripts: "The 'Sloane Group': Related Scientific and Medical Manuscripts from the Fifteenth Century in the Sloane Collection," *British Library Journal* 16 (1990): 26–57.

22. *The Distichs of Cato* and *The Churl and the Bird* sections conclude unusually with gatherings of four leaves.

23. Although the entry for the verses on Carthusian houses ("Item *tractatus fundacionis domus* Cartusiensis") is copied between those for Geoffrey of Franconia's *Book of Trees and Wine* and Lydgate's *Dietary,* a scribal correction mark indicates that it should be inserted between the *Dance Macabre* and the *Chronicle from Rollo to Edward IV*—the position the text now occupies.

24. This perhaps refers to Ludwell on the borders of Wiltshire and Dorset. Other inscriptions are as follows: "surgon Tirell" (recto of opening flyleaf), not identifiable in C. H. Talbot and E. A. Hammond, *The Medical Practitioners in Medieval England: A Biographical Register* (London: Wellcome Historical Medical Library, 1965); "Md þt I haue payd thomasse gese yn hyse barne þe same / day þt he & his wyfe mad hit clene þt wasse evyn vponne / þe tewysdaye nex before relyke sondaye sor a closse / vnto seynt petiir þe apostyll day nex folowyng / al hys owte fasse only— viiid before honde" (verso of the opening flyleaf); "Iste liber constat Willelmo Gygar teste Roberto holte / scriptum fuit a die sancte michaelis archangeli primo futuro / anno regum regis henrici octaui quartodecimo" (recto of the following parchment flyleaf); "md þt thomas bygnyll must haue of me / ij schyrtes a dowbelette redy made & a jaket / a payr of hose or xiiijd ij peyr schoys & / a gowne clothe & vijs yn mony" (f. 170).

25. Seymour, "Manuscripts of Hoccleve's *Regiment of Princes*," 266.

concern with secular conduct (including, interestingly, that of women, to whom the mortality lyric is specifically addressed), the manuscript certainly has the air of a generally planned compendium of useful and improving material, possibly worked on simultaneously by a number of associated scribes.

Of particular interest to the current discussion is the manuscript's construction from a group of units of which most in themselves form small anthologies or miscellanies of different kinds. The final *Dietary* section is perhaps best described as a small accretive miscellany, since it began life as a single text in a single gathering and only gradually acquired additions as later owners copied in medical recipes. The prose texts on arboriculture, which fill a single whole gathering, circulated (albeit in various redactions) as something of a unit, and there is ample precedent for their collocation in several other manuscripts. Both the *Regiment* and the *Cato* sections are composed, though rather differently, of one long text accompanied by short extras. The *Regiment,* occupying folios 1–97v and neatly tailored to fit eleven gatherings of eight leaves and a final extended ten, concludes with a copy of *The Short Charter of Christ* (*IMEV* 4184), which has been squashed into available remaining space on the final folio. Burgh's *Cato* translation, on folios 98–124, takes up three gatherings of eight and part of a final four, and remaining space here is filled by some short poems on moral subjects (*IMEV* 576 and 4230) and a prose note on sanctuary.[26] In both cases the assortment of items, seemingly brought about by a combination of the practical desire to fill space and the availability of texts of suitable lengths, has a general air of miscellaneousness.

The central Lydgate quires in the manuscript, three gatherings of eight and one of four (ff. 127–53), preserve rather differently a sequence of texts of various lengths in which distinctions between major and minor items are less marked and in which some rough areas of subject interest can be perceived. Death figures in the mortality lyric, in the *Dance Macabre,* and possibly also in the version of Psalm 53, which opens the section on an appropriately penitential note. The *Chronicle from Rollo to Edward IV*—a justification of the English title to France found elsewhere in Yorkist collections, such as Cambridge, Trinity College, MS R.3.19[27]—and the *Elegy for Ralph Lord Cromwell,*

---

26. The prose note begins, "The makynge of the sanctuarye to chaste theves extorcurers / with all other misdoers sente by the popes autorite vnd*er* / bulles of lede is as it apperith i*n* þt that folouth . . . ." (ff. 125v–26v).

27. See Bradford Y. Fletcher, *Manuscript Trinity R.3.19: A Facsimile* (Norman, OK: Pilgrim Books, 1987), xx, where the text is called *The Petigrew of England*. To the manuscript appearances listed by Fletcher can be added British Library, MS Harley 2252, ff. 51v–53v.

onetime lord treasurer of England, testify to an awareness of current affairs.[28] The inclusion of three poems by Lydgate—the psalm translation, the *Dance Macabre,* and *The Churl and the Bird*—together with a possible fourth, if as has been suggested he can be credited with the composition of the *Elegy* or some ancestor of it—indicates no little interest in his poems.[29] That the compilers of the manuscript may have worked from exemplars that were themselves anthologies containing other of Lydgate's works is suggested by a faint scribal note at the end of the *Elegy,* the final item in this section, which announces "hic scriba*tur* conueyed by a [lure] as / rigth as an ramhorne"—a reference of some kind to a satirical poem by Lydgate whose stanzas share the refrain "Conueyed by lyne—right as a rammes horne." One possible interpretation of this is that the scribe found the poem in the run of texts in his exemplar and yet decided to exclude it from his own copy, perhaps because he lacked space or because it was not to his taste or within his brief.[30] Such processes would seem to typify the small and often not actively desired modifications to which sequences of short texts are subject in their transmission.

Cambridge, University Library, MS Hh.4.12, which includes some of the same texts as Harley 116, demonstrates a range of interestingly comparable editorial and scribal activities. Made up in quarto, this collection opens with both the long and the short *Cato* translations and continues with an extensive selection of Lydgate's shorter works: *Stans puer ad mensam, The Legend of St.*

---

28. For Cromwell's career and associations, see E. M. Myatt-Price, "Ralph, Lord Cromwell (1394–1456)," *The Lincolnshire Historian* 2 (1957): 4–13; and Richard Marks, "The Glazing of the Collegiate Church of the Holy Trinity, Tattershall (Lincs.): A Study of Late Fifteenth-Century Glass-Painting Workshops," *Archaeologia* 106 (1979): 133–56. On f. 170v is also a series of scribbled Latin epitaphs, for figures including Guy of Warwick and Lydgate himself.

29. The *Elegy* appears elsewhere only in British Library, MS Cotton Caligula A. ii, an anthology of romances, saints' vitae, and moral and devotional poems (several by Lydgate). In this version it lacks the stanzas of specific application to Lord Cromwell and his wife, but as in MS Harley 116, it is headed, "O mors qua*m* amara est memoria tua." Henry Noble MacCracken, "A Meditation upon Death, for the Tomb of Ralph, Lord Cromwell (c. 1450), Lord Treasurer of England," *Modern Language Notes* 26 (1911): 243–44, pointing out certain features that the poem shares with Lydgate's *Dance Macabre* and arguing that Lord Cromwell could have known Lydgate, suggests that "the poem in its earlier form was written to hang by the tomb until the inscription should be needed to record the demise of its builders"; but it is also possible that Cromwell or those wishing to commemorate him adapted an existing text. For extensive personalizing funerary additions made by the London citizen Avery Corneburgh to a widely disseminated poem, see D. Gray, "A Middle English Epitaph," *Notes and Queries* 206 (1961): 132–35.

30. MacCracken, *Minor Poems,* 2:461–64; the variant states of the texts are discussed by Henry Hargreaves, "Lydgate's *A Ram's Horn,*" *Chaucer Review* 10 (1976): 255–59. There are of course other possible interpretations of the memorandum: the scribe might have expected to be able to find the poem and could have made the note in anticipation of this, or he might have registered an apparent omission in the exemplar.

Austin at Compton, Horse, Goose, and Sheep, Fabula Duorum Mercatorum, The Churl and the Bird, and an assortment of lyrics.[31] It concludes with an incomplete text of Chaucer's *Parliament of Fowls.* The contents were copied by two reasonably practiced scribes—one of whom (naming himself "Stok.t.") offers a supporting role in completing stints begun by the main copyist[32]—and their work has been rubricated and enhanced by penwork decoration. As with Harley 116, the component gatherings are, allowing for some losses, of a uniform length—twelve leaves here, rather than eight—and are more noticeably standardized, in that all are composed of mixed parchment and paper, with parchment serving strengthening purposes as the outermost and innermost leaves of each gathering.[33] The quire signatures, however, unlike those of Harley 116, are not continuous and seem to indicate that the component parts of the manuscript were conceived, or at the least worked on, as more distinctly independent units. The breakdown of visible signatures here gives first a unit or booklet of three gatherings, the second of which is signed *b,* and the third of which now lacks three leaves toward the end; this booklet contains the *Cato* texts, Lydgate's *Stans puer,* and some concluding blank leaves. What is now the fourth gathering of the manuscript, containing *The Legend of St. Austin,* Chaucer's *Former Age,* and an anonymous complaint of Christ with the refrain *Quia amore langueo (IMEV* 1463), contains only one visible signature (on f. 39), which although hard to decipher apparently reads "biij." This then, although the work of the same two collaborating scribes as the first booklet, was perhaps originally the second in a new sequence of gatherings.

It is followed by three gatherings devoted solely to Lydgate's verse. All in the hand of the main scribe, they seem to have been disarranged from their original order: the first, containing only *Horse, Goose, and Sheep* is signed *d;* the second and third, across which are copied *Fabula Duorum Mercatorum* and *The Churl and the Bird,* are signed respectively *a* and *b.* The missing *c* is nowhere visible in the manuscript, although it may have been one of the remaining two gatherings—a collection of lyrics mainly by Lydgate and the opening of *The Parliament of Fowls* (both, again, the work of the main scribe)—on which signatures are not now apparent. We are left, therefore, with

---

31. *A Catalogue of Manuscripts Present in the Library of the University of Cambridge,* 6 vols. (Cambridge: Cambridge University Press, 1856–67), 3:292–95.

32. The main scribe, A, copied ff. 1–28 (*Cato Major*), and B supplied 28v–33v (*Parvus Cato* and *Stans puer ad mensam*); A copied ff. 37–44 (*The Legend of St. Austin at Compton* and *The Former Age*), and B supplied 44v–47 (*Quia amore langueo*). The remainder of the items were copied by A.

33. Collation: $1-2^{12}$, 3^{12} (wants 9, 11, 12), 4^{12} (wants 2), $5-8^{12}$, 9^{12} (wants 7–12).

an "improving" Lydgate-associated anthology in one booklet, *Cato* and *Stans puer* (Benedict Burgh, the *Cato* translator, was an admirer of Lydgate's); an anthology of Lydgate's shorter poems in a further booklet that lacks at least one gathering; a small Chaucer and Lydgate anthology in a stray gathering marked *b;* and some currently unattached gatherings whose contents—Chaucer and Lydgate, again—could in different ways be seen to correspond to the focus of any of the other sections. The various parts seem almost deliberately conceived to constitute a puzzle for the would-be anthologist.

Once again, the evidence of later annotation indicates that the different parts of this manuscript were, from a relatively early date on, at least kept together, even if not necessarily in their present order. One annotator in particular has registered his perusal of the manuscript in the form of verses copied sporadically in an early sixteenth-century hand into the generous spaces left in the top margins of the pages; his additions, while sometimes echoing the sentiments of the formal copy that he enhances, cannot but add a certain air of miscellaneousness. In the first booklet, we find on folio 12 verses beginning: "When it is tyme of cost and gret expens / be ware of west and spend as by mesure . . . ." And on the top of folio 18, we read: "When that I lent then I was a frende / but nowe y aske y am vn kynde." At the end of the second booklet, on folio 47v, the same hand has made several attempts at verses beginning; "Of honest myrthe let be thy dalyaunce / swere no othes nor rebode dallyaunce / the best morsall thi selfe let be thy dalleance . . . ." And at the end of the penultimate gathering, on folio 96v, it copies "alas alas a made y whas a changyt / ys my chance let alle thyng passe."[34] This reader identifies himself on folio 18 as "ihon clerke of blomsbery dwellyng n*er* by" and again on folio 47v as "Joh*anni*s clerke." Nothing more specific than paleographical evidence suggests a date for these additions, although there is a distinct possibility that certain of the notes refer to early sixteenth-century songs: a note on folio 34v, "and y where a medyn / as meny hon ther ys / for alle the . . . ," cites the beginning of a well-known early Tudor song, and the reference on folio 48 to "A newe balade of a mayde that wolde go" may be in some way related to "alas alas a mayde y whas" on folio 96v.[35] John Clerk was perhaps connected to the annotator who writes on folio 47v, "thes boke howthe John peter ye menstrell"—possibly to be identified as the king's musician of this name who

34. Some Latin verses also appear among the additions (e.g., on ff. 3, 4, 24, and 25); they are perhaps the work of a slightly later hand.

35. John Stevens, *Music and Poetry in the Early Tudor Court* (London: Methuen, 1961; reprint, with corrections, Cambridge: Cambridge University Press, 1979), 418–19.

makes a brief appearance in the records in 1518, charged to carry a letter from Henry VIII to Alfonso d'Este, duke of Ferrara, and to return with the present of a lute for the king.[36]

The significance of these details for current purposes is their status as evidence that the booklets making up the manuscript were probably kept together. Losses of leaves from the end of the *Cato* booklet and from *The Parliament of Fowls* may suggest further that they were kept unbound and not necessarily in the order that they now occupy. The collection was flexible—potentially an anthology, but equally amenable to division or even to extension, should further desirable material become available or should the temptation to write in the invitingly empty margins prove impossible to resist. The ease with which certain of Lydgate's poems might be fitted into a single gathering or a small booklet made them especially suitable for collection (sometimes even serial collection) in this kind of environment, and the preservation in fifteenth-century manuscripts of such texts as *The Churl and the Bird, Horse, Goose, and Sheep,* and *Fabula Duorum Mercatorum,* both in sequences and in independent fascicles, testifies to their versatility.

The shorter lyrics in this manuscript present a slightly different problem. Several were clearly needed to fill one gathering or booklet, and assessing the extent to which lyrics were transmitted in groups is not easy. The appearance of Chaucer's *Former Age* in the autonomous fourth gathering (signed *b*) is surprising, since it survives otherwise only in a very early copy of Chaucer's translation of Boethius, in a context that has been plausibly explained as deriving from Chaucer's filing of the lyric at an appropriate point in his *Boece* working papers;[37] MS Hh.4.12 is the only testimony to its wider circulation. *Quia amore langueo* (in the version that attributes the complaint of love to Christ rather than Mary) similarly survives in only one other copy, a collection composed largely of religious lyrics that is now London, Lambeth Palace MS 853.[38] The cluster of Lydgate lyrics in the penultimate unsigned gathering,

36. J. S. Brewer et al., *Calendar of the Letters and Papers of the Reign of Henry VIII,* 21 vols. (London: Longman, Green, 1862–1910), 2:ii, entry 3744. Among other early sixteenth-century additions to the manuscript are a pen trial on f. 19v "be your hond thomas reuenyng"; a note on f. 32v, which reads, "this boke was made in yᵉ yer of owr lord / A god 1504 (?) as for the kyng name of this lond / I cannot say for here where . . . ."; the names of "John yarrade" and "Wylliam bryan" (f. 48), "jhon moke" (f. 68), and "John lyster" (f. 70v).

37. George B. Pace, "The True Text of 'The Former Age,'" *Medieval Studies* 23 (1961): 363–67.

38. Montague Rhodes James, *A Descriptive Catalogue of the Manuscripts in the Library of Lambeth Palace: The Mediaeval Manuscripts* (Cambridge: Cambridge University Press, 1932), 809–11.

however, does recall certain groupings in other manuscripts. *Consulo quisquis eris* (*IMEV* 1294), *Midsomer Rose* (*IMEV* 1865), and versions of *The Mutability of Man's Nature* occur in close proximity in the important Lydgate collections Jesus 56 and Harley 2255, as parts of short duplicate sequences;[39] MS Jesus 56 continues with *Why artow froward* (*IMEV* 3845), also present in MS Hh.4.12; and this latter poem is to be found in conjunction with *Midsomer Rose* in MS Huntington HM 140. More approximately similar groupings of poems also occur in Cambridge, Trinity College, MS R.3.21, booklet xiv; in Bodleian Library, MS Rawlinson C. 86; and in Harley 2251.[40]

The scribal note about Lydgate's *Ramshorn* in MS Harley 116 prompts the very elementary observation that compilers did not always slavishly reproduce the selection of items in their anthology exemplars; they sometimes exercised discretion in accordance with taste, with external direction, or with pressures of available space. Originally influential groupings or clusters of poems seem to have undergone subtle metamorphoses as they were gradually disseminated and as a variety of other texts became attached to them. The contents of MS Hh.4.12, in replicating another feature observable in MS Harley 116, confirm the tendency of texts of very localized or specific interest to be copied in the final position of gatherings or booklets that otherwise reproduce recurring configurations of texts. Gathering "v" in MS Harley 116 concludes with the *Elegy for Ralph Lord Cromwell* in what might be termed a user-specific version. The last two items in the gathering of Lydgate lyrics in MS Hh.4.12 are *The Lament of the Duchess of Gloucester* (*IMEV* 3720), supposedly the words of Eleanor Cobham, wife of Duke Humphrey of Gloucester, on her downfall in 1441 after charges of necromancy in a treasonable plot to murder Henry VI; and a verse discussion of *The Difficulty of Choosing a Profession in Religion* (*IMEV* 655). Both are long variant forms of poems that survive elsewhere only in single, much later witnesses.[41]

---

39. See n. 17.

40. Contents are listed, respectively, in Montague Rhodes James, *The Western Manuscripts in the Library of Trinity College, Cambridge,* 3 vols. (Cambridge: Cambridge University Press, 1900), 2:83–95; Julia Boffey and Carol M. Meale, "Selecting the Text: Rawlinson C. 86 and Some Other Books for London Readers," in Felicity Riddy, ed., *Regionalism in Late Medieval Manuscripts and Texts* (Cambridge: D. S. Brewer, 1991), 143–69; and Hammond, "Two British Museum Manuscripts."

41. The first is copied into an early sixteenth-century collection that is now Oxford, Balliol College MS 354, and the second into one of John Stow's mid-sixteenth-century anthologies, BL Additional 29729; see, respectively, R. A. B. Mynors, *Catalogue of the Manuscripts of Balliol College Oxford* (Oxford: Clarendon, 1963), 352–54; and *Catalogue of Additions to the Manuscripts in the British Museum, 1854–75,* vol. 2 (London: British Library, 1877), 696–701.

The manuscripts discussed here illustrate conveniently some of the processes of physical construction that can generate books including more than one text, books that we incline to consider as anthologies, miscellanies, compilations, or composite collections. Texts can be drawn together within individual gatherings or booklets, sometimes on the model of existing exemplars, sometimes in novel collocations; gatherings and booklets can be brought together to form larger units, sometimes preserved and bound into a specific order, and elsewhere simply loosely assorted, like the items in a ring binder or a filing cabinet. Both these processes can be planned in advance, with the work carefully apportioned to available scribes, or can simply underpin the gradual and more piecemeal accumulation of items copied as they come to hand (the extreme form of this latter process is sometimes characterized as the personal or collective commonplace book). Later scribes can also add further items, as they have done in the medical section of MS Harley 116.[42]

Some of the processes at issue here can be reconstructed, more or less precisely, from physical evidence: collation, signatures, paper stocks, hands, evidence of wear. Much more effectively concealed, however, are the intellectual, aesthetic, practical, and possibly even financial considerations in the minds of the scribes, compilers, patrons, and commissioners of the books. Modern scholars can attribute certain interests or intentions to these individuals—seeing, in the manuscripts described here, perhaps, one all-purpose anthology of morally improving and informative material (Harley 116) and one collection that illustrates the range of writings associated with Chaucer and Lydgate (MS Hh.4.12). But the defining and imputing of such interests is hedged with difficulty, and this difficulty very clearly focuses the need to unite literary with codicological speculation. Before making pronouncements on the collocation of Chaucer's *Parliament of Fowls* with Lydgate's *The Churl and the Bird* in MS Hh.4.12, for example, we need to ask if the items now drawn together in the manuscript were always intended to form an anthology or if the peculiar system of quire signatures indicates rather that the component sections were originally distinct undertakings that only accidentally came and stayed together. Similarly, we need to know if the lack of quire signatures in the final gatherings of MS Harley 116 suggests that the parts of the manuscript that deal with arboriculture and medicine (copied in part in a

---

42. Linda E. Voigts, paper delivered at this conference includes the suggestion that the compilers of these related and partially duplicated anthologies of medical texts similarly "personalized" certain individual anthologies for their prospective readers.

hand that appears nowhere else in the collection) were not conceived as part of the larger whole. The question raised by these instances is, reduced to its essentials, a simple but fundamental one: how is one to tell where an anthology, a miscellany, or even simply a compilation begins and ends?[43]

---

43. The significance of some of these issues for the understanding of collections of lyrics has been most recently aired by Theo Stemmler in "Miscellany or Anthology? The Structure of Medieval Manuscripts: MS Harley 2253, for Example," *Zeitschrift für Anglistik und Amerikanistik* 39 (1991): 231–37.

"Art" and "Nature": Looking for (Medieval) Principles of Order in Occitan *Chansonnier* N (Morgan 819)

Stephen G. Nichols

Two working hypotheses underlie this chapter. The first is that the various kinds of *recueils*—collections or compilations—that characterize the *mise en manuscrit* of so much romance vernacular literature in the thirteenth century, including the *chansonniers* of troubadour and trouvère lyric, should be thought of as miscellanies, that is, as a collection of varied texts. Too frequently, *recueils* or *chansonniers,* because they contain items that have been grouped generically, may not be recognized as containing a more heterogeneous collection of works than might be supposed from reading descriptions of them.

My second hypothesis follows as a consequence of the first. I believe that *recueils* or *chansonniers,* at least many of them, should be regarded as having an aesthetic (or other motivation) for the manuscript as a whole and therefore principles of order that convey reading programs to correlate the *dissimilar* individual texts they contain. The deep history of making manuscript books, at least like the Old French and langue d'oc *recueils* and *chansonniers,* comes from an innovation of the early Middle Ages that may no longer have been recognized as such by the thirteenth century but that nevertheless left its mark on medieval bookmaking of the period. I am referring to Cassiodorus's sixth-century innovation whereby he first conceived the idea of collecting the various sacred writings of Christianity into a *pandect,* a term previously re-

I would like to express my thanks to Ms. Tracy Adams, my research assistant, for her good offices in procuring many of the bibliographical items used in the preparation and writing of this chapter.

served for compilations of laws. As Pierre Petitmangin recently noted, "It was a retired government official, Cassiodorus († ca. 580), who first had the idea of collecting the books of scripture into a *pandecht* (a term previously reserved for juridical collections)."[1]

James Halporn, in a perceptive article on this subject, observes that *pandectes* refers "to a one-volume Bible, i.e., a Bible containing the entire text of the Old Testament and the New Testament under one cover." He emphasizes the unequivocal nature of this fact, citing Cassiodorus himself as witness:

> It is important to be clear on this point, namely that a Pandecht contains the entire Bible . . . . Cassiodorus himself specifically states that the *Codex Grandior* contained both Testaments: 'Tertia vero divisio [secundum LXX] est inter alias in codice grandiore littera clariore conscripto . . . in quo septuaginta interpretum translatio veteris Testamenti in libris quadraginta quattuor continetur; *cui subjuncti sunt novi Testamenti libri viginti sex* . . . .'"[2]

Cassiodorus's Bibles—he had two copied in his monastery at Vivarium in Calabria—not only provided the example for collecting the diverse and heterogenous texts of the Bible in one book but also initiated a number of technical innovations for displaying and facilitating the reading of biblical texts, some of which became standard in later medieval bookmaking—such as two columns on one folio, disposition of lines in units of meaning to facilitate reading aloud, initial letters in a slightly overhanging left-hand margin, rubrics in contrasting inks, and accompanying pictures.

Pandect means "all receiving," but its root, *dechesthai,* "to receive," is akin to Greek *dokein,* "to seem," but also "to show." The technical innovations of Cassiodorus and his Carolingian avatars, inspired by Alcuin's desire to produce Bibles easier to read from during services,[3] did indeed show (*dokein*) to better advantage the texts of Scripture. As my Hopkins colleague Herbert Kessler has argued, the great period of Carolingian illuminated Bibles produced at Saint-Martin of Tours under abbots Adalhard (834–43) and Vivien (843–51)—one thinks of the Moutier-Grandval or the Charles-the-Bald (Vivien) Bibles—established not only the preeminence of the Turonian Bible but

---

1. Pierre Petitmangin, *Mise en page et mise en texte du livre manuscrit,* ed. Henri-Jean Martin and Jean Vezin (Paris: Librairie-Promodis, 1990), 73. Hereinafter this work is cited as *MPMTLM.*

2. James M. Halporn, "Pandectes, Pandecta, and the Cassiodorian Commentary on the Psalms," *Revue Bénédictine* 90 (1980): 290–300, at 292 n. 1; Cassiodorus quoted from *Institutiones* 1.14.2 (40.6 ff. Mynors).

3. *MPMTLM,* 79.

also that of Jerome's Vulgate over the Old Latin translations of Scripture that still circulated in the ninth century.[4]

Pierre Petitmengin has pointed out that the Turonian Bibles set another precedent in medieval bookmaking: the sense of a clear internal structure for the page. He is referring to the five different kinds of script used in the *mise en page* of the different visual and interpretive components: capitals, the body of the text, incipits, explicits, and initials at the beginning of lines or sections.[5] Petitmengin observes that the Bibles of Saint-Martin de Tours gave to the manuscript page "an internal structure never before attained neither in Antiquity nor in the high Middle Ages."[6] Now while the exactitude and care of the precise material presentation of the Turonian Bibles may never again have been equaled, the conception of an aesthetic for the manuscript page that participated in and contributed to a conception of a structure for the work as a whole—both an aesthetic structure and an intellectual one—did survive into the period that concerns me. For the principle of the pandect provides a model for the book as a collection of diverse writings linked by an overarching theme: religious, political, philosophical, or historical.

The pandect principle can be particularly fertile for the older collections of vernacular texts, at least Occitan and Old French, that have survived from the late thirteenth and early fourteenth centuries. Both *recueils* and *chansonniers* have been, until recently at any rate, viewed more as repositories for texts to be edited as part of poet corpora issued in individual editions. And yet such collections can be studied for their own individual aesthetic, revealed not only in the internal structure of individual folios or sections but in terms of the principles of ordering and the underlying design of the whole. To do so, however, we need to appreciate that these manuscripts are indeed disparate collections of texts whose association in a given compilation must be sought in principles that may be reconstructed from studying the manuscript as a book.

What has impeded making this effort in a concerted way heretofore may be the fact that *chansonniers* have been given a misleading identity as generically homogeneous manuscripts by the very title *chansonnier.* Generic categorization was an extremely diverse proposition in the Middle Ages, more so than in modern times, perhaps. On close inspection, *recueils* and *chansonniers* often turn out to be quite diverse in terms of the materials they contain, and the

---

4. Herbert L. Kessler, *The Illustrated Bibles from Tours* (Princeton: Princeton University Press, 1977).

5. *MPMTLM*, 79–80.

6. Ibid., 83.

ordering of that diversity can impart to a manuscript its authentically medieval specificity.

One need only look at the description by Alfred Jeanroy of the codex that I will discuss here, *Chansonnier* N (Morgan 819) to understand just how driven by establishing generic identity were the classifiers of *chansonniers*. For Jeanroy is neither an isolated case nor aberrant. In his *Bibliographie sommaire des chansonniers provençaux,*[7] published in 1916, Jeanroy describes N, then in England and known as the Cheltenham *chansonnier.* His description of N is all the more interesting for our purposes because, while in the Phillipps collection at Cheltenham, N was notoriously difficult to access.[8] That he never saw the manuscript himself, must have known the difficulties of access and unreliability of the existing information on it, and yet insisted on giving a description of it confirms that the materiality of the mansucript as an artistic production in its own right played little role in the concerns of Jeanroy or his contemporaries.

Jeanroy's case is particularly salient because he had at his disposition a rather complete description of N published in 1875 by Hermann Suchier in the *Rivista di filologia romanza,* which, exceptionally, drew attention to the marginal illustrations keyed to words in the text by sigla.[9] Suchier's description respects the order of the manuscript, rather than dividing the contents up by genre or author. Jeanroy, like Curt Bühler in 1947 (see n. 8), was interested not in how the contents were organized in the manuscript but rather in their generic disposition. The location and classification of the individual texts of songs that could then be edited in author editions interested scholars like Jeanroy and Bühler. That is perhaps one reason why we find little difference between the description of *chansonniers* in Paris that Jeanroy studied at first hand and those from Italy for which he thanks Giulio Bertoni for supplying him with the details. Manuscripts were containers, not performative documents.

---

7. Alfred Jeanroy, *Bibliographie sommaire des chansonniers provençaux: Manuscrits et éditions* (Paris: Honoré Champion, 1916).

8. Curt F. Bühler observed of N in 1947 that it was of unusual interest as the only troubadour manuscript "illustrated by marginal illuminations of unusual spirit and interest but also a manuscript which has not been readily accessible to those interested in the poetry of the troubadours. Everyone, of course, knows of the difficulties involved in obtaining access to the manuscripts at Cheltenham or in getting satisfactory transcripts of the texts" ("The *Phillipps Manuscript* of Provençal Poetry Now *MS 819* of the Pierpont Morgan Library," *Speculum* 22 [1947]: 68).

9. Hermann Suchier, "Il canzoniere provenzale di Cheltenham," *Rivista di filologia romanza* 2 (1875): 49–52, 144–72. Jeanroy cites Suchier's article as the main descriptive source (*Bibliographie sommaire,* 11). Suchier underlines the interest of the initials and miniatures: "Non solo nelle iniziali ma anche ne'margini il codice ha miniature molto bene ed abilmente seguite da mano d'artifice" (51).

For *Chansonnier* N, Jeanroy gives a short, summary description followed by a slightly longer discursive one. The summary errs by omission, particularly in ignoring any mention of the fascinating poet portrait initials or marginal and *bas-de-page* illustrations that have captured the attention of recent scholars. Jeanroy simply says: "In-4°, parchment, 296 folios, with lacunae and numerous blank folios; 14th century; additions in diverse Italian hands from the 14th and 16th centuries."[10]

The notation "with lacunae" may refer to missing folios at folios 25 and 256, but the comment "numerous blank folios," like the fourteenth-century dating, is simply inaccurate. There are two blank pages in the body of the manuscript, folios 53 and 203, and partially used folios at 206 and 206v, but in each case the logical organization of the manuscript at these points accounts for the blank page. The manuscript dating from the late thirteenth century was written by five scribes, with the first hand being responsible for the initial folios and the last nineteen (f. 1–21 and 275–93), as well as a few in the middle (ff. 186v–91). Jeanroy's summary description does not mention the twenty-eight historiated initials, the thirty-nine pages of marginal illustrations, and the five more elaborate illuminated initials. Like many of his contemporaries, he seems not to have construed the vigorous role of pictures in the manuscript that add so much to its diversity and interest.

For Jeanroy, the lyric content mattered most of all, to such an extent that his discursive description of the codex, by focusing on the lyric, ignores the actual ordering of the manuscript disposition in favor of one proceeding by generic categorization and location. Jeanroy assumes a generic principle of ordering for the manuscript as a whole, even though a coherent presentation of his concept requires him to "disassemble" the manuscript as it exists and to describe an ordering remote from what one actually encounters firsthand.

Jeanroy speaks not of the manuscript but of "les pièces" that are, he asserts, "approximately distributed by genres."[11] In fact, genre does play an important role, but not in the way he conceives. He would have been closer to making his point had he, like Suchier, stuck with the manuscript disposition. Instead, for reasons not specified but undoubtedly linked to a conception of generic hierarchy, he uses Suchier's information to offer a synthetic description in which he begins with folios 20–26, where "one finds *saluts, comjatz,* and 'pièces diverses,'" that is, "minor" genres. He then moves to folios 46–51 to note the *descorts,* another "minor" genre in his classification. The "main" part of the

---

10. "In-4°, parchemin, 296 feuillets, avec lacunes et nombreux feuillets blancs; XIVe siècle; additions de diverses mains italiennes des XIVe et XVe siècles" (*Bibliographie sommaire,* 10).

11. "Les pièces sont approximativment réparties par genres" (*Bibliographie sommaire,* 10).

manuscript for him may be found on folios 54–100 and 107–271, which contain the "major" genres, *cansos* and *coblas* identified by the names of the poets. Anonymous songs may be found on folios 100–107, while the last twenty-odd folios, 272–96 (*sic*), contain *partimens* (*jocs partitz*). Only after describing the lyric poems does he return to the first twenty folios, which he does not fully account for even then, omitting Garin lo Brun's *ensenhamen*, folios 4–10, which follows Arnaut de Marueil's opening *ensenhamen*, folios 1–3.[12]

Besides the two didactic *ensenhamens* with which it opens, Morgan 819 contains a fragment of the *Roman de Jaufré* (f. 10–12v), the novella of Raimon Vidal (f. 14v–21), and an anonymous narrative, *Senhors, vos que voletz oïr* or *Cort d'amor* (f. 30–46). The first section accords no attribution to any of the works found there, although there are portraits in the historiated initials at the beginning of some of the poems like the ones found heading the author corpora later on. This is the case, for example, with the incipit of Morgan 819 (fig. 1), where we find a poet portrait at the beginning of an *ensenhamen, Raçons es e mesura.*

Arnaut de Marueil (Arnaut de Maroill)—active in the 1190s—was, according to his vida (contemporary with our manuscript), known for having composed a song, *La franca captenensa,* whose key word is also the leitmotif of the *ensenhamen.*[13] Another of his songs begins with the term *ensenhamen: L'enseignament el prez e la ualors.* Morgan 819 contains both of them, the former on folios 68b–d, the latter on folios 66d–67b. These indicators seem to suggest that the *ensenhamen, Raçons es e mesura* was sufficiently well-known as the work of Arnaut de Marueil so as not to require authorial ascription. In any event, the poet portrait on folio 1 does not have an accompanying identification. On the other hand, the image of the poet holding a stick that we find in the lower register of the *R* on folio 1 (fig. 1) is repeated in an author portrait on

---

12. Jeanroy is not alone in his disaggregating approach to the manuscript. Curt Bühler's 1947 description of N takes author identification as its principle, announcing itself as an "Index to Troubadours in *Morgan MS. 819*" ("The *Phillipps Manuscript*," 69). Bühler specifically critiques Suchier on the grounds that "the contents are there listed in the order in which they are found in the manuscript, mostly with only the author citations as found therein and not with the attributions now generally accepted" (69). In short, the manuscript as historical artifact does not enter the picture.

13. "Mas si avenc c'amors lo forsa tant qu'el fetz una canson, la quals comensa: *La franca captenensa . . .*" [But then it came about that Love worked so violently on him that he made a song [about his passion], that begins: *The noble treatment (deportment) . . .*] (Jean Boutière and A.-H. Schutz, *Biographies des Troubadours: Textes provençaux des XIIIe et XIVe siècles* [Toulouse: Privat, 1950], 18).

R agons es em
es mesura. m en
trom es seg
le dicta. Que
apprenda chac
sus. de cellsq
sa bon plus.

J al senz desala mon.
N il sabers de pla ton.
N ilen geing de uer gili.
D omer ni oepor fili
Q i uels altres doc tors.
E auez auiat plui sors.
N on fora ren presaz.
S a gues estat celac.
P er queu soi enconsire.
E om po gues far coure.
T al ren que fos honors.
E grazir pels meillors.
Q as la uns non m en da.
Q ueu aquest fais mi pren da.
Q ue len erim defollor.
N im tregna per docitez.
D e sabers nom sengey.
Q as danco cai apres.
E scol tan cue cen.
D e man dan caucen.

Q ue uns non a docta na.
S enz al trin disci plina.
Q os sabers non es granz.
V es quem tiral ta lanz.
A zan pentre carizir.
E on com de gues grazir.
E uen cus lo meu apenre.
S e nuls es de mi menre.
D e sen e de scienga.
S egon la conoi senga.
Q ue sen miuei nisai.
D el segle moshatai.
E om se deu captener.
Q ui bon laus uol auer.
Q as coben ben guar dar.
D n o deu comen car.
E ar seng non es graz.
Q as per los ei sernic.
E si es non ues guaire.
E per go uoil re traire.
A l rei cui es lentoa.
E ui iors e iouenz guida.
P er meira men mesoie.
S i con los ai esariz.
N on per tal queil so fingna.
R es ca bon prez atangna.
Q as car es conoi seng.

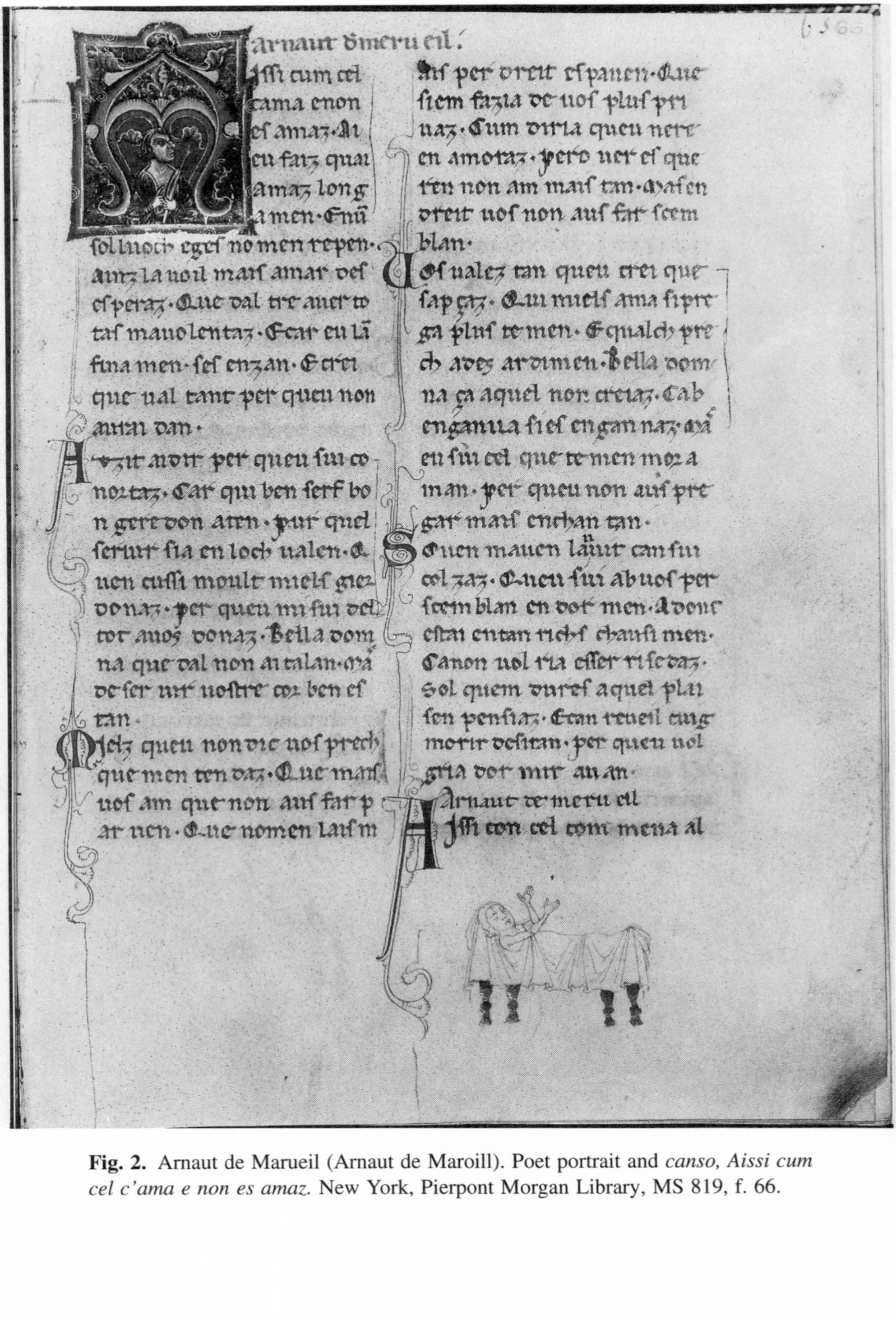

Fig. 2. Arnaut de Marueil (Arnaut de Maroill). Poet portrait and *canso, Aissi cum cel c'ama e non es amaz.* New York, Pierpont Morgan Library, MS 819, f. 66.

folio 66a (fig. 2), the first of twelve *cansos* by Arnaut de Marueil. Although the initial on the two folios differs—*R* on folio 1, *A* on folio 2—each has a lower register open at the bottom into which thrusts the portrait of the poet. The pose and features are identical in each case: the poet holds a stick in his right hand and wears a tunic open at the neck; his head, in three-quarter profile, has a prominent nose and deep-set right eye and is tilted slightly upward as though contemplating the beginning of the stanza immediately above. Adjacent to the top of the historiated initial on folio 66a, just above the first line of the song *Aissi cum cel c'ama e non es amaz,* occurs the rubric "arnaut de merueil."

These are the only two historiated initials in the whole manuscript whose close or nearly identical resemblance suggest intentional repetition.[14] That the portrait from folio 1 is repeated at the head of the section specifically identified as Arnaut de Marueil's (f. 66a) suggests both that the portrait was indeed intended to serve as identification for a specific poet (that is, Arnaut) and that he was known to those responsible for Morgan 819 as the author of the *ensenhamen* (f. 1a–4a). These facts strongly urge three observations: (1) that the manuscript possesses a coherence, indeed a "plan" linking its different parts; (2) that the role of the image in the historiated initials and other pictures plays a role in conveying those ordering principles and that, in consequence, the visual art cannot be dismissed as simply decorative or adventitious; and (3) that we can begin to sense the manuscript's role as a surrogate for the "live" performance of the poetic persona (poet or jongleur).

This makes it all the more strange that Jeanroy does not note one of the most puzzling aspects of the manuscript, although it is also one that weakens any assertion of a purely generic principle behind its organization. That is the long opening section with unascribed or anonymous works that occupy the first fifty-two folios of which *Raçons es e mesura* is a key example. Before following this lead, however, we need a sense of some historical details of the manuscript pertinent to the principles of internal structure that I shall elaborate presently.

Morgan 819 dates from the last quarter of the thirteenth century, between 1285 and 1300. Although the consensus of art historians who have studied the art varies, all parties seem to agree that the initials and the marginal pictures were executed in Padua by two different artists, the initials before the marginalia, but both prior to 1300.[15] Details of female costume and ecclesiastical

---

14. The Morgan's notice claims that the historiated *D* ("Domna") on folio 26d is identical to the same letter *D* ("Domna") on folio 21a. Though there are closer points of resemblance than one generally finds, they are not the same or as close in resemblance as the Arnaut portraits.

15. The fifteen-page typescript description and notice of Morgan 819 at the Morgan Library remains the principal authority regarding date and provenance. Angelica Rieger reviews the

insignia like the bishop's miter in the initial on folio 55 (fig. 2) have been cited as confirmation for the dating. The artists belong to the school of Giovanni Gaibana, curate of the cathedral at Padua, where he was buried on his death in 1293.[16]

Parenthetically, we might note that close consideration of the pictures, especially the marginal illustrations, reinforces the concept of variety in the subject matter. The *bas-de-page* and marginal pictures all occur in the portion of the manuscript devoted to author corpora and consequently in that portion that might be considered to correspond most closely to Jeanroy's idea of a homogenous *chansonnier.* The variety of the pictures reminds us that generic thinking can impose a false impression of homogeneity.

On folio 57v (fig. 3), for example, a male figure perches halfway up a gracefully elongated tree in the left margin, while a *bas-de-page* painting shows a musician singing and playing his *vielle* under the right-hand column. On folio 59 (fig. 4), a *bas-de-page* painting shows a fruit-bearing tree; a sun with a face and with pointed rays shining on a mountain; a tower; and a man holding in his right hand a mirror in which we see the tower reflected, while his left hand rests on the shoulder of the *domna* he addresses. These pictures all connect to different words and passages in the text of the song *Mout i fez gran peccat Amors* (Greatly does Love sin), through sigla easily discernible under

---

bibliography on this subject on pages 395–97 of her article " 'Ins e.l cor port, dona, vostra faisso:' Image et imaginaire de la femme à travers l'enluminure dans les chansonniers des troubadours," *Cahiers de civilisation médiévale* 28 (1985): 385–415.

16. The Morgan notice regarding these details deserves quotation in extenso since it is not readily available without going to the Morgan Library. Page 14 of the typescript states in part:

> *History:* Erroneously dated XIVth century (1355), because of the Charles IV document on f° 53v. The style of the miniatures however dates it [at the] end of the XIIIth century and includes M.819 within the group of North Italian MSS., chief of which is a Lectionary at Padua, dated 1259 and signed by Giovanni Gaibana curate of the cathedral at Padua where he was buried on his death in 1293.
>
> Prof. Jan Květ, in his discussion of Gaibana's MSS. and influence (*Italske vlivy*) considers them the work of several painters, schooled in the same place and style, to which he applied the term 'style gaibanesque'. Their locale was in the patriarchate of Aquileia, that is, Aquileia itself, Padua, Trieste, and Venice, in the second half of the XIIIth century. The date of M.819 can be fixed between 1285 and 1300 by certain details of costumes, iconography and calligraphic ornament.
>
> Among these are the types of costumes, the fillet worn by the women on their brows; the chain armor and shields, the shape of the bishop's mitre (f° 55); the type of filigrane ornament and the modelling and posture of Christ on the cross on f° 65. These are all before 1300.

See Jan Květ, *Italske vlivy na pozdne romanskou knizni malbu v Cechach* (*Les influences italiennes sur la miniature en Bohème à la fin de l'époque romane*) (Prague: Nakl. Filosoficke Fakulty University Karlovy, 1927). This book has a summary in French.

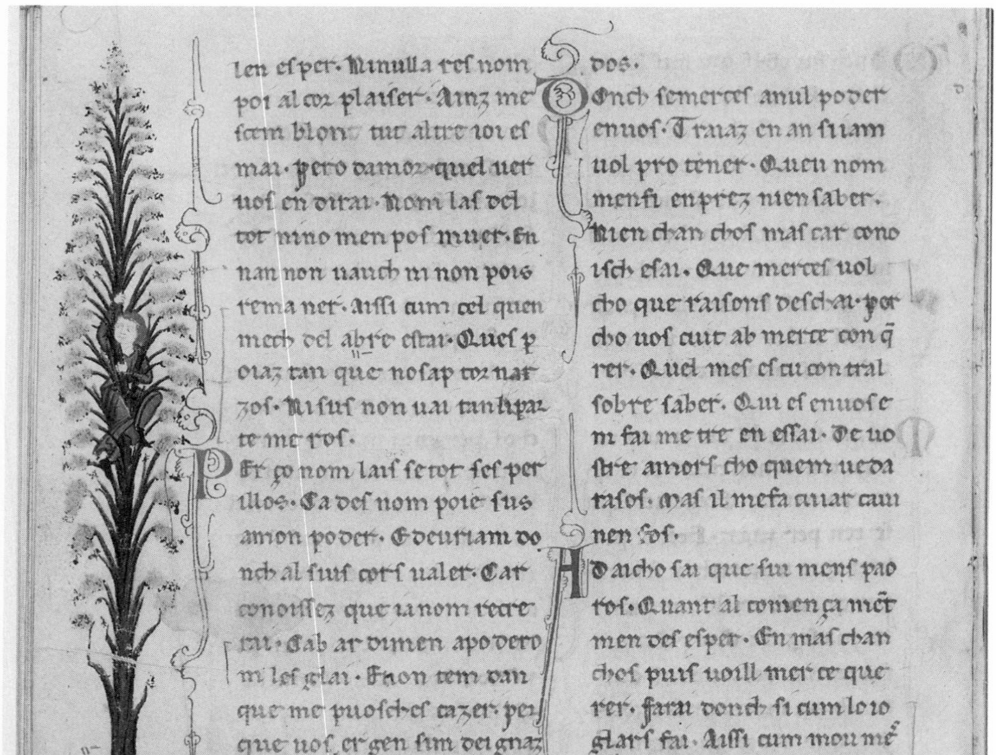

len esper. Ninulla res nom
poi al cor plaiser. Ainz me
faim blon tur altre roi es
mai. Pero damor quel uett
uos en oitar. Nom las del
tot mino men pos muet. En
nan non nauch ni non pois
rema net. Aissi cum cel quen
mech del abre estar. Ques p
oiaz tan que nosap tornar
zos. Ni sus non ual tan lipar
te me ros.
Er go nom lais se tot ses per
illos. Ca des nom pote sus
amon podes. E deuriam do
nch al suis cors ualer. Car
conoisses que ia nom recre
rai. Sab ar dimen apo dero
m les glai. Fa on tem uan
que me puosches cazer per
que nos er gen sim dei gnaz
retener. El guer dos est i
tals cum ses chan. Que nes
lo do lien es faz gier uos. Ace
l qui sap daui nen fait ses

uos.
Onch semerces amul poder
enuos. T raiaz en an suam
uol pro tener. Queu nom
mensi enprez nien saber.
Rien chan chos mas car cono
isch esai. Que merces uol
cho que raisons descha por
cho nos cuit ab merce con q
rer. Quel mes es cu con tral
sobre saber. Qui es enuose
m fai me tre en essai. De uo
stre amors cho quem ueda
rasos. Mas il mesa auat cau
nen sos.
D aucho sai que siu mens pao
tos. Quant al comença met
men des esper. En mas chan
chos puis uoill mer ce que
rer. faru donch si cum lo io
glars fai. Aissi cum mou me
lais lofeni rai. Des es petaz
puols donch noi posch saber.
Rasos per quel degnes de
mi ualer. Mas tant ator lo

Fig. 3. Illustrations showing poet in a tree and poet with *Vielle*. New York, Pierpont Morgan Library, MS 819, f. 57v.

Fig. 4. Illustrations showing fruit tree, mountain and sun, tower, and poet holding mirror reflecting the *domna* beside him; poet with *domna*'s image on his chest. New York, Pierpont Morgan Library, MS 819, f. 59.

the word in the text that corresponds to the picture in the *bas-de-page*. Sylvia Huot has recently written about the relationship between the visual image and memory in this song in an article published in *Gesta*.[17]

I have written about another marginal picture on this folio (fig. 4), the full-figure portrait of the poet with the face of his lady imprinted on his breast, a picture that both illustrates and problematizes stanzas from Folquet's *En chantan m'aven a membrar* (In singing I cannot help remembering). This song begins near the top of folio 59b, just where the marginal portrait occurs.

Another folio, 190 (fig. 5), has a *bas-de-page* with a small, double-ended, square-sailed boat under column one, while two stags walk in single file on the *bas-de-page* under the second column. Three quarters of the way up the right-hand margin, a lover sits bound hand and foot at the feet of his enthroned *domna*. Like the previous pictures, these belong to what Sylvia Huot calls the allegorical landscape that occurs when metaphor is visualized.[18] On folio 63 (fig. 6), something different occurs: a *bas-de-page* portrait sketch of the poet singing or the scribe both executing and performing the codex. On other folios, we find pictures of gambling, falconry (60), money changing, lovers in bed (214v), Christ enthroned (217v), a smith sharpening knives, poets pouring honey into vases observed by an enthroned Christ (188v), a deathbed scene (64v), a crucifixion of Christ (65), a grotesque feathered humanoid creature/demon (188), warriors (68), tents, a castle, a woman with a mirror (215), a school of fish (67), and a lion and whelps (72v).

What we need to bear in mind from this plethora of illustrations is not the dialectic between picture and text, which plays a vital role in the manuscript. Rather, the vividness and variety of the pictures remind us that heterogeneity, not homogeneity—variety, not sameness—mark the images of the world, both verbal and visual, in this miscellany. That the word *love* and its concept may stimulate these reflections only reminds us of the principle of the one and the many that plays so central a role in medieval aesthetics, as Plotinus showed. Art and poetry, Plotinus argued, are training grounds for the mind's progress in achieving inward contemplation. As he says at the beginning of *Ennead* 1.6.1,

Beauty is mostly in sight, but it is to be found too in things we hear, in combinations of words and also music . . . and for those who are advancing upwards from sense-perception ways of life and actions and

---

17. Sylvia Huot, "Visualization and Memory: The Illustration of Troubadour Lyric in a Thirteenth-Century Manuscript," *Gesta* 31, no. 1 (1992): 3–14.

18. Ibid., 11.

auos que no no sabetz. Tan
len ter sauenon en sems. Lo
senz. el prez elabeutatz. Etz
francx corg cane bona fos
natz.

E s im sueill eu tener clam. Co
uassalz delorg bons seingn
orz. E nomen soi deltor lauf
satz. Quel nesig corg abque
bataill feig contra leis euas
mi quetz. Ge dis quellam
son uele reinis. De manz
en con brietz cai passatz. En
quem fora deses peratz.

P Ero de cabrol ode dam. Si
prez en tendez mela morz.
E uiera fos auo mesiatz. mas
uos ma domna non assaill

O Lains nimertes
car non uezez. Los mals qui
en trac mils plantz nil gemg.
Q ue faz la nuez can soi col
gatz. E lorn non puesc estar
en patz.

E si per dieu eu forz estam. No
us platz quem trispas la do
lorz. Q ue mausira sinon

pen satz. E reu merse forgoill
nous tfail. E passatam si nõ
sentez. Con eg lorg freolitz
esems. Can de seruizi non
uengtatz. Sellm que neg mor
trebaillatz.

E s im tenez prez elciam. Enõ
ual forza niualorg. Nom deu
ualer humilitaz. Si fapos
enren. E ostres mang esim
destrignetz. Qui mais me
uol grafer rezems de mas
mutz ode reuelatz. Q uen
tal trebailla foluntatz.

P Er uos dompna quem de
strignetz. E uier ben en esse.
re gems de mas mutz ode
reue laz. Anz cassi fos uiste
zlatz. Dompna merces car
pen satz. Com eu non fos co
temps forsatz.

Giraut de burnel.

S Il corg nom lus tan oreg.
E mal son grat non la sta
ing. Enun chan tarer soul.
No meg uis quera lastraing
na. Si non eg forsatz. En n

Fig. 5. Illustrations showing boat and stags; poet bound and sitting at *domna*'s feet. New York, Pierpont Morgan Library, MS 819, f. 190.

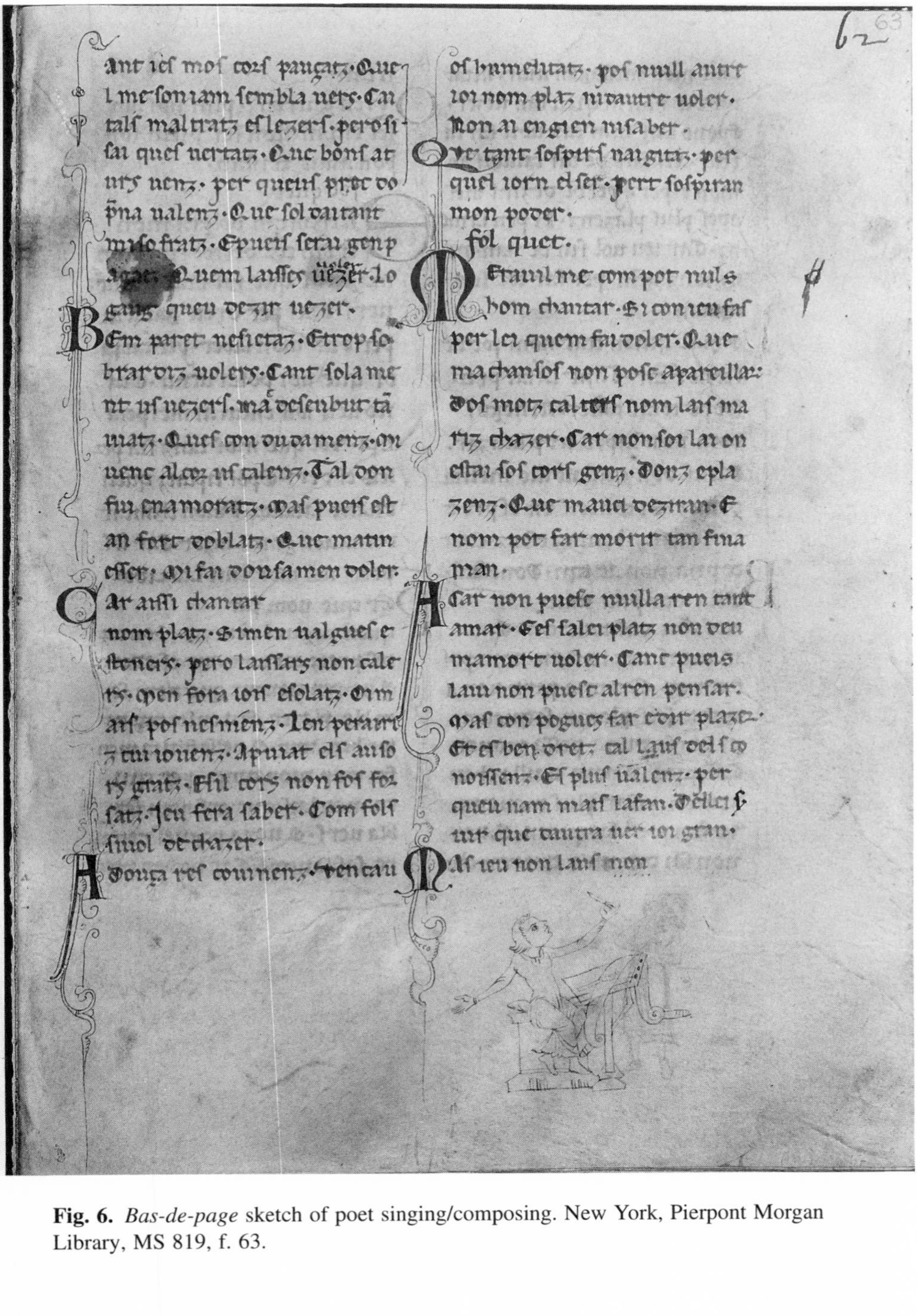

Fig. 6. *Bas-de-page* sketch of poet singing/composing. New York, Pierpont Morgan Library, MS 819, f. 63.

characters and intellectual activities are beautiful, and there is the beauty of virtue.[19]

Teaching the soul to look at the beautiful ways of life was, for Plotinus, the goal of contemplation, a contemplation that could begin, as this manuscript suggests with the close linking of sight and words in song. So the linkage between the words and pictures at key points in this manuscript plays a role in understanding the intention of the scribes who planned and executed it. In her 1985 article, the first ever to attempt to follow up on Suchier's observations about the interest of the art a century before, Angelica Rieger noted that Morgan 819's marginalia went back to the Carolingian tradition of literal or nominalist illustration whose most famous example is the Utrecht Psalter. While the practice of *Wortillustration* continued into the thirteenth century, its manifestation in what she terms "a resolutely secular context" is "tout à fait exceptionnelle."[20]

But just how "resolutely secular" is our manuscript? Perhaps Rieger, too, has been overly influenced by a kind of taxonomic nominalism, in this case the modern term *chansonnier provençal*. Evidence for this may be seen in her unsatisfactory explanation for why the manuscript contains marginal illustrations for only seven of over forty poets, with the chosen ones widely separate from one another in some cases at that. She argues that having illustrated the first two authors—Folquet de Marselha and Arnaut de Marueil—the illustrator would have realized that he could not do all of the troubadours and so chose Guiraut de Bornelh, who had a reputation as the greatest, and then skipped to the poets whose corpora were the last to have historiated initials.[21] But this

---

19. Plotinus, *Enneads,* vol. 1, *Enneads I.1–9,* trans. A. H. Armstrong, (Cambridge: Harvard University Press, 1989).

20. "Nous rejoignons ici la très ancienne tradition de l'illustration nominaliste ou littérale («Wortillustration») dont le plus célèbre exemple est le Psautier d'Utrecht. Cette tradition, qui remonte à l'époque carolingienne, a toujours été pratiquéeau XIIIe siècle; toutefois, son existence dans notre chansonnier, dans un contexte résolumment séculier, est tout à fait exceptionnelle. Elle ne repose pas sur une tradition antérieure bien établie, comme c'est le cas des mss sacrés. Or, l'iconographie du ms. *N* est d'une fraîcheur et d'une originalité étonnantes. Elle nous révèle un effort particulier de compréhension et d'interprétation de la part du peintre face au texte et à son créateur, le poète" (Rieger, "Image et imaginaire de la femme," 398).

21. "Or, l'illustrateur a dû opérer un choix sémi-occasionnel: après avoir commencé «par le commencement» il s'est rendu compte qu'il ne pouvait aller jusqu'au bout; aussi a-t-il sélectionné le troubadour qu'il considérait comme digne de ses illustrations, le plus grand, Guiraut de Bornelh; de plus, pour conférer une certaine symmétrie et une certaine unité aus enluminures, il a bouclé sa bande dessinée avec les derniers poètes ornés de lettrines historiées. C'est la seule explication logique, si on ne veut pas supposer des préférences tout à fait personnelles qui coïncideraient avec le début et la fin des lettres ornées: car, pour ce qui est et des sujets et des troubadours illustrés, il n'y a aucun point commun qui justifierait un tel choix. (Les troubadours illustrés n'ont ni la même importance poétique, ni les mêmes origines sociales ou géographiques et leur activité poétique ne se situe pas non plus dans la même période.)" (Rieger, "Image et imaginaire de la femme," 397–98).

does not explain why the illuminator began with Folquet, on folio 55, or why five of the seven poets chosen either were ecclesiastics (Folquet was bishop of Toulouse, Gausbert de Puicibot a monk, and Arnaut de Marueil a clerk), were like Guiraut de Bornelh, who was noted for rectitude and spirituality, or were like Pons de Capdueill, a crusade poet reputed to have died in the Holy Land. Nor does she attempt to suggest why the unnamed authors of *ensenhamens* and romances in the first section of the manuscript had historiated initials at the beginnings of their sections or why someone as well-known and prized as Bernart de Ventadorn (f. 83b, 137a–48a) did not.

I think we must cease trying to look at this codex piecemeal and try to understand, as Plotinus suggests, the principle of beauty to be discovered by viewing the manuscript as a coherent whole. It is a miscellany, but one that functions aesthetically and intellectually like a pandect, in the sense that the structuring principles derive not from the individual pieces but from the strength of the whole ordered very much as a series of rules or laws, meditations on conduct and self-governance. Let us see how that hypothesis might work.

In all the various descriptions of Morgan 819, no one has observed that there are three, not two, clear divisions in the manuscript. The first fifty-two folios, as we have seen, contain nonlyric works, unascribed or anonymous—beginning with two *ensenhamens* (literally teachings) by Arnaut de Marueil and Garin lo Brun. This first section contains ten miniatures in the form of historiated initials. The subject matter varies from author portraits to portraits of women who figure in the work.

Folio 55 introduces the longest section of the codex, the "body" of the manuscript as it were, containing lyric poetry by known poets, with a few anonymous sections (e.g., f. 86–87, 101v–2). This main section, beginning with eighteen songs by Folquet de Marselha, concludes with eleven songs by Marcabru, ending on folio 274, and contains the bulk of the portrait miniatures and all of the marginal illuminations.

The final section, folios 275–93, contains thirty-four *partimens* by various poets unascribed by the manuscript (and thus is symmetrical with the first section), although of course this is a genre that names the poet being addressed. *Partimen* literally means a shared poem, a debate between two poets about a topic proposed at the outset of the debate. The *partimen* may be viewed as a poetic version of the quodlibetal debates so much a part of the medieval intellectual scene, particularly in the university milieu. Quodlibetal debates were both a teaching or learning device—hence an *ensenhamen* as it were— and a means for showing off the level of an individual's wit (and rhetorical skill).

Whereas the *ensenhamen* offered a didactic exposition of the doctrine of a given social or amorous code of conduct, the *partimen* tended to be shorter and to pose the same kinds of topics as matters of debate or reproach in which each poet finds the other lacking in some crucial quality. "Per quel raçon avez sen tan venal" [Why do you have such a venal mind?], says Blancatz to Peire Vidal on folio 283b. In the final poem of the manuscript, a *partimen* between Guionet and Peirol/Pomeirol, the initiating poet seeks the advice (ironically or otherwise) of his interlocutor: "Peirols, dos barons sai / prez et ab bona genz. . . . a cal deu·m mais grazir / so[n] bon captemen" [Peirol, I know two barons, worthy and of good lineage. . . . which of the two should I reward the most for his good comportment?] (f. 292d).

The last section of Morgan 819, containing the *partimens,* was copied by the same hand responsible for the first twenty-one folios. The disposition of the verse does differ between the two sections, the first section having one verse per line, while the last section, perhaps imitating the disposition in the lyric section of the manuscript, runs the lines together, simply using periods to separate one verse from another. The same hand, then, is responsible for the *ensenhamens* at the beginning of the manuscript and the *partimens* at the end.

But why should this manuscript begin and end with genres that, from a modern standpoint, play so minor a role in the canon of troubadour poetry? Of the twenty-eight troubadour manuscripts, only one other, MS Q (Florence, Biblioteca Ricardiana), begins with an *ensenhamen,* also Arnaut's *Raçons es e mesura.* MS Q and MS G (Milan, Biblioteca Ambrosiana R71) are the two Italian manuscripts closest to N, but G buries Arnaut's *ensenhamen* far into the codex, at folios 116c–18c. Although relatively little appreciated in modern times, the *ensenhamen* was an important form of didactic poetry in Occitan. In Italy, Sordello composed a well-known example, the *Ensenhamen d'onor,* while the Catalan writer Ramon Llull dedicated the *Doctrinal pueril* to his son and composed another *ensenhamen,* the *Llibre del Ordre de Cavayleria,* to teach the principles of Christian chivalry.

The *ensenhamen* by Arnaut de Marueil that opens Morgan 819 teaches appropriate modes of conduct to different catagories of courtly society: chevaliers, clergy, and ladies. It begins with a vivid apothegm containing three principles for self-governance: reason, moderation, and learning.

Raçons es e mesura
Mentr'om es segla dura
Que aprenda chacsus
De cels que sabon plus.

                                                                    (f. 1a)

[It is right and meet so long as one lives in the world that each of us learn from those who know the most.]

Immediately following this apothegm, a twenty-one line *amplificatio* sets out a politics of knowledge that shows how vernacular literature can be a means to attaining wisdom for living. *Raçons* and *mesura* figure here as symbols of practical wisdom in contrast to learned philosophy. In a defense of displaying practical wisdom in vernacular texts, the poem asserts that all of the wit, the learning, and the ingenuity of Salomon, Plato, Homer, Virgil, or Porphyry would have accomplished nothing worthwhile had it remained hidden. Distancing himself from this company by excess of modesty, the poet says he will talk not about a learning he does not possess but about what he has learned from "listening and watching, from asking questions and hearing" the answers. He seeks only to show that no one can have a guide for living (*doctrina*) without some kind of discipline.

Que uns non a doctrina
sens altrui disciplina.

(f. 1b)

Both the *doctrina* and the *disciplina* can be summed up by a phrase key to the *ensenhamen: se captener,* "to govern oneself." Where good sense may be difficult to find in the world, the poet will press his understanding into the service of teaching self-governance to those who want to acquire a good reputation. It is the same terminology used by Guionet in the last line of the first stanza of his *partimen* (the last poem in the manuscript) "a cal deu·m mais grazir / so[n] bon captemen" [which of the two should I reward the most for his good comportment?] (f. 292d).

Arnaut's *ensenhamen* is unusual in including the clergy in its teaching. Clerks run the gamut in this catalog of exemplary human conduct, from those who give themselves to pastoral care, to those renowned for *cortesia,* to poets or preachers (*li un de gen parlar*), and to still others given to performing rich deeds (*de ricx fatz far*), great goodness, and largesse. The common thread here is the exemplarity of the clergy, their role as guides for *bos captenemens,* "good self-governance." Moreover, the guidance of the clergy and its exemplary value—whether for reasons that are humorous, ironic, or realistic—fall equally within the secular and the spiritual spheres. Morgan 819 clearly sets out to suggest a very broad definition of pastoral care. More exactly, it argues the role for self-governance, a mastery of one's own comportment, as a guide as crucial in secular as in religious life, in love as in church.

Arnaut de Marueil, whom his vida tells us was a "clergues de paubra generacion, E sabia ben trobar e s'entendia be" [a clerk of lowly birth, but a fine troubadour with a subtle mind], will himself become the exemplary figure of the poet-clerk who eschews dogma for a model of self-governing behavior (*se captener*) that combines the dignity of spirituality with sensuality. The opening poem offers a concept of *corteza vida,* a life of rule-governed sensuality, that Arnaut de Marueil articulates here and in the poems recorded in the lyric section of Morgan 819, where he is given the place of honor after Folquet de Marselha, bishop of Toulouse.

> Qui uol cortesa uida.
> demenar ni graçida.
> ab ferm cor e segur.
> per ço que sos pret[z] dur.
> sapcha deu retener.
> honorar e temer.
> car prez e cortesia.
> senz deu non cre que sia.
> pueis de totas contradas.
> estraignas e priuadas.
> apreignas de las genç.
> faiz e captenemenç.
> e demant eç enqueira.
> L'esser e la maneira.
> dels auols e dels pros.
> dels mal vaç e dels bos.

(f. 1c, ll. 4–19)[22]

[Whoever wishes to pursue and enjoy a refined, courteous life, with firm and sure heart, so that his worth may endure, must learn to accept, honor, and fear God, because I do not believe that worthiness and courtliness may exist without God. From every country, foreign and domestic, learn facts and behavior from people, asking and inquiring about the essence and the manner of baseness and worthiness, of good and evil ways.]

Cortesia and *captemen* bear the conceptual and ethical weight here by juggling tensions between the spiritual and the sensual. *Captemen*— linguistically conflating *cap,* "head," and the *demen, demenar,* "to lead, con-

---

22. This poem was edited by Mario Eusebi, "L'*Ensenhamen* di Arnaut de Marueil," *Romania* 90 (1969): 14–30. He used *Chansonnier* R as his base manuscript.

duct," of the second line of the quoted section—sets the ethical rules or limits for *cortesia,* whose end, however decorous, is always sensual. *Captemen/cortesia* here figure the mind/body problem so prevalent in medieval ethico-religious concerns. From that standpoint, we should not be surprised at the prominence of *captemen;* less obvious is the strongly sensual coloring given to *cortesia* and Arnaut's seeming refusal to subordinate it to *captenamen.*

In one of Arnaut's most famous poems, *Bel m'es quan lo vens m'alena / en abril* (How I love to feel April's breath), *cortesia* actually limns the corporeal charm of the lady, simultaneously analogized to Helen and, through her, rhymed with the wind's breathing (*alena/Elena*): "Bel m'es quan lo vens m'alena / . . . plus blanca es que Elena." Nature, myth, and history all—and each—suffuse the sensual image of *cortesia,* metaphor for the lady.

> Plus blanca es que Elena,
> belazors que flors que nais,
> e de *cortezia* plena,
> blancas dens ab motz verais,
> ab cor franc ses vilanatge,
> color fresc' ab soura cri;
> deus, quel det lo senhoratge,
> la sal, qu'anc gensor non vi.
>
> (St. 3, ll. 17–24)[23]

[Fairer than Helen, more beautiful than budding flowers, and courtly through and through, white teeth with true words, a noble heart without baseness, pellucid skin, red-gold locks; God, who gave her seigniory, save her, for I have never seen a nobler woman.]

Arnaut's subtlety does not run to crude binary oppositions. *Captenensa* can do the work of *cortesia,* just as *cortesia* can convey the rule-governed self-guidance of *captenemen.* In the opening of *La francha captenensa* (Morgan 819, f. 68a), *captenensa* has a similar denotation of corporeal sensuality to that of *cortesia* in *Bel m'es quan lo vens m'alena.* Arnaut personifies the qualities of conduct represented by the term, making it an allegory for the visual and emotional impact of the woman's physical presence on him. As used here, however, it is virtually untranslatable.

---

23. Text from Karl Bartsch, *Chrestomathie Provençale* (Elberfeld: R. L. Friderichs, 1880), col. 93.

La francha captenença.
qu'eu non pois oblidar.
e.l dols ris e l'esgar.
e.l scemblan que us ui far.
mi fan domna ualent.
meillor qu.eu non aus dir . . . .

[The noble presence that I cannot forget, and the sweet smile and the
gaze, and the appearance I saw you making, do more for me, worthy
lady, than I dare to say . . . .]

We appreciate better the unusual dynamics of the semantic field Arnaut
spins around these terms by looking at how the Comtessa de Dia uses them
later in Morgan 819, in her poem *A chantar m'er de so qu'eu no volria* (I have
to sing about that which I would not wish; f. 232c–d). On the fourth line of
stanza one, the Comtessa invokes *cortesia* in rhyming position linked with
merces, both referring to courtly attitudes manifested toward another—her
lover in this case.

car eu l'am mais que nuilla ren que sia.
ves lui no.m ual merces ni *cortesia*
ni ma beltatz ni mos prez
ni mos senz.

(f. 232c)

[for I love him more than any living thing, [but] my compassion nor my
courtliness avail me nothing in his case, / nor my beauty nor my worth
nor my intelligence.]

In the following stanza, at the rhyme for line 2, she invokes *captenensa* also as
a kind of behavior norm.

D'aicho.m conort car anc no[n] fis faillensa.
amics ues uos per tuilla[24] *captenensa.*

---

24. Morgan 819 reads, "tuilla captenensa"; other manuscripts, observing parallelism with
"nuilla ren" of the first stanza, read, "nuilla captenensa." Editors have adopted the latter reading for
obvious reasons.

[I take comfort from this: that never did I fail you, friend, through any kind of behavior.]

In neither case do the terms in *A chantar m'er* denote the tension between spirituality and sensuality that we find highlighted in Arnaut de Marueil's poems, for the Comtessa foregrounds other concerns. But we would miss the point by simply comparing the Comtessa with Arnaut. For it is less Arnaut's poems themselves than the way the manuscript positions them that reveals the tensions we have seen and that underlines how the tensions remain in delicate equilibrium, falling neither toward the sensual nor toward the spiritual. Morgan 819 performs Arnaut de Marueil in a very particular way. It is the manuscript's performance of its contents that we must now consider.

If we move on to the longest section of the codex, and the one receiving the most extensive and original illumination, we may now be in a position to understand how and why it presents as it does. Why should the lyric section begin with Folquet de Marselha and emphasize by the marginal illuminations three other churchmen and two laymen prominently associated with the church and spiritual governance? If we return to folio 55 (fig. 7) to look at the poet portrait that heads this main part of the codex, we see represented in the initial a full-figured bishop standing in the letter *T*. The portrait may represent Folquet as bishop of Toulouse; Raymond de la Torre, patriarch of Aquileia, the patriarchate that included Padua; or, most probably, both referents at once. In any case, the body of the manuscript begins on a visibly ecclesiastical note.

Folquet had completed his poetic corpus before becoming bishop of Toulouse, so it is not obvious that his troubadour corpus should represent him in episcopal regalia. And yet it was in that role that he acquired the formidable reputation for clerical self-governance that led him to fulfill all the clerical virtues Arnaut de Marueil enumerates in his *ensenhamen*. Legendary as a poet and as a warrior bishop, he plays a major role in the epic of the Albigensian crusade, where he is a principal architect of the defeat of the Toulousain heretics, ten thousand of whom he is said to have burned in an auto-da-fé. Petrarch echoed Folquet's contemporary fame in the celebratory verse in his *Trionfi de amore* (canto 3). But of all the contemporary references to Folquet, Dante's evocation in *Paradiso 9* has the most enigmatic resonances for the ordering principles of our codex. Dante has Cunizza (ca. 1198–ca. 1280) introduce Folquet, calling him "questa luculenta e cara gioia / del nostro cielo" [this resplendent and precious jewel of our heaven] (ll. 37–38), just as Dante himself, a few lines later, will say of Folquet,

Ant ma
belif lam
oros penf
sa menf. ct
uefef uen
gitz emon
fin cor affi
re · per que
noi por nulf autre penftaber ·
nimais negus nomes dolz nip
lafenf · Ca donch uuifas cam m
aueisol conftire · Efina mors
aleuiam mon marture · Quim
pro mer igi mais trop lom do
na len · Cab feemblanf mariau
nat lonia men ·

En sai que tot quan fag es dre
tz ifienf · Fu quen puofch mais
famors miuol au atre · Q na e
feien ma donat tal uoler · Q ne
la non er iienenz mel no nenf ·
uenatz fier cauer man li sofpi
re · Tot sua uer si de leis cui o
fire · Non hai focors midaulo
rs nola ten · Ni dautra amor
non puofch auer talen ·

Bona dom na suif plaz flatz fu

frenf · Del ben que uf uoill q
uen soi del mal sufrire · Epois
tomalf nom porra dan tener ·
Ans mer feem blan quel par ca
en gal menf · pero suif plaz cr
dautra part me uire · Oftaz de
uof labentar el dolz rire · El bel
feem blan quem en follif monf
sen · puois partir mai de uos
mon eftien ·

Toz iorns mes plus bella cplus
plafenf · per queu uoill mal aif
oillf ab quenf re mire · Car atho
pro non porian uer · Et amon
dan uefon trop furpil menf · p
os danf no cf sinaif pos nom u
aire · Amz cf mos pros dom na
per queu malbire · Si maucier
que nouf eftata gen · Car io me
uf danf noftre · er efta men ·

Er cho domna nouf am saura m
enf · Q na uof soi fis er amos obi
traire · Vof rem per ore emi no
puofch auer · ff uf aug nofcer eibi
ami nozenf · pero me mal noui
auf mostar uidire · Mas el cf ga
rd podez mon cor de iuire · Q ue

Fig. 7. Initial *T* showing Folquet de Marseilles, bishop of Toulouse, or Raymond de la Torre, patriarch of Aquileia (Padua). New York, Pierpont Morgan Library, MS 819, f. 55.

L'altra letizia, che m'era già nota
   per cara cosa, mi si fece in vista
   qual fin balasso in che lo sol percuota.

(ll. 67–69)

[The other joy, which was already known to me as precious, became to
   my sight like a fine ruby on which the sun is striking.][25]

The choice of Cunizza as lead-in to Folquet reveals how Dante subtly builds
on the balance of spirituality and sensuality that we saw in Arnaut de Marueil,
although without maintaining Arnaut's equilibrium. With Paradise as the
venue, the spiritual cannot but dominate. Nonetheless, Dante sturdily links
troubadour poetry to the sensual: Cunizza was the mistress of the thirteenth-
century Italian troubadour Sordello, though now her light comes from another
troubadour, Folquet, seen as something of a guide and savior: "Cunizza fui
chiamata, e qui refulgo / perché mi vinse il lume d'esta stella" [I was called
Cunizza, and I am refulgent here because the light of this star overcame me] (ll.
32–33).

Cunizza's name and self-identity link her to an amorous past: "ma lieta-
mente a me medesma indulgo / la cagion di mia sorte, e non mi noia" [I gladly
pardon in myself the reason of my lot, and it does not grieve me] (ll. 34–35).
Folquet himself will maintain this thread by pointing out to Dante another
prominent denizen of the heaven of Venus: Rahab, the harlot from the Book of
Joshua (mentioned also at James 2:25 and Hebrews 11:31). Through Folquet,
Dante asserts that Rahab was the first Hebrew soul taken up into the heaven of
Venus after Christ's harrowing of hell. In medieval typology, as Erich Auer-
bach and others have pointed out, Joshua was a figure for Christ and Rahab was
representative of the Church.

Dante very deliberately gives a major historic and typological role to Folquet in *Paradiso 9*. He is not simply a poet and a warrior but, like Joshua, a
warrior-priest. By linking Folquet and Rahab, Folquet, rather than the papacy
with whom Dante was particularly at odds, represents the real type of savior for
the Church. So when Dante-Pilgrim addresses Folquet directly, he does so in
imagery taken directly from a major prophet, Isaiah.

"Dio vede tutto, e tuo veder s'inluia,"
   diss'io, "beato spirto, sì che nulla
   volgia di sé a te puot'esser fuia.

---

25. Texts, translations, and commentary from Dante Alighieri, *The Divine Comedy*, trans.,
with commentary, Charles S. Singleton (Princeton: Princeton University Press, 1975).

Dunque la voce tua, che 'l ciel trastulla
   sempre col canto di quei fuochi pii
   che di sei ali facen la coculla,
perché non satisface a' miei disii?
   Già non attendere'io tua dimanda,
   s'io m'intuassi, come tu t'inmii."

(ll. 73–81)

["God sees all, and into Him your vision sinks, blessed spirit," I said, "so that no wish may steal itself from you. Why then does your voice, which ever gladdens Heaven—together with the singing of those devout fires that makes themselves a cowl with the six wings—not satisfy my longings? Surely I should not wait for your request, were I in you, even as you are in me."]

The point here is not the pilgrim's question to Folquet—though it is yet another occasion for Dante to indicate his poetic, spiritual, and historical filiation with Folquet ("even as you are in me"). No, it is his description of the poet as both a six-winged seraphim and a monk whose cowl—but also whose bishop's miter—is formed by the upfolded wings of the seraphim. Isaiah 6:1–3 describes the seraphims standing above the enthroned Lord: "each one had six wings; with twain he covered his face, and with twain he covered his feet, and with twain he did fly."[26]

The main activity of the seraphim—just as Dante describes Folquet's "voice, which ever gladdens heaven"—is to celebrate the divinity by crying out "Holy, holy, holy, is the Lord of hosts: the whole earth is full of his glory" (Isaiah 6:3). The seraphim was both a category of archangel in the celestial hierarchy and a representative of ethical values, the virtues. Romanesque art sometimes placed seraphim above the cross in crucifixion scenes, and they also, as virtues, participated in the cortege of the elect, the *processio* and *conversio,* procession from and return to Christ, which was the Christian form of the Plotinian model for contemplation, the basis for attaining the "inner sight" that Plotinus describes as "seeing great Beauty" (*Ennead* 1.6.9).

---

26. Isaias Propheta: 6. in anno quo mortuus est rex Ozias, vidi Dominum sedentem super solium excelsum et elevatum et ea quae sub eo erant implebant templum / 2. seraphin stabant super illud, sex alae uni et sex alae alteri, duabus velabant faciem eius et duabus velabant pedes eius et duabus volabant / 3. et clamabant alter ad alterum et dicebant sanctus sanctus sanctus Dominus exercituum plena est omnis terra gloria eius (*Biblia Sacra iuxta vulgatam versionem,* vol. 2 (Stuttgart: Deutsche Bibelgesellschaft, 1983), 1102).

Now one of the more puzzling iconographical features of Morgan 819, beginning with two instances on the second folio (56) of the Folquet corpus, are a series of six-winged seraphim with three faces (see fig. 8). Besides the two occurrences on folio 56, there are three more in the Folquet section at folios 58v (fig. 9), 61v (fig. 10), and 64 (fig. 11). There are also four instances of the same symbol in the corpus of Gausbert de Puicibot that are proleptically reminiscent of Dante at the feet of Folquet in the heaven of Venus, for in this series, four iterations in all, the monk stands or kneels before the seraphim. Gausbert does not bear his name in this manuscript, only his ecclesiastical title, *lo monge de Pueisibot,* which conforms to his appearance in the pictures. The four instances begin with one at folio 211 (fig. 12), two on folio 212 (fig. 13), and, finally, one at folio 212v (fig. 14). Because the first instance of this symbol on folio 56 is keyed by a siglum to the word *amor* ("Pero conosch d'amor" [Therefore I know love]), modern scholars have interpreted the seraphim here as a symbol of the god of love.

That it occurs in the Folquet section and in the Monk of Pucibot corpus, however, suggests that Dante is the one who better understood the nature of the love represented by Folquet's songs when set against his life. That mediation is what the text and the pictures of the manuscript undertake in an allegory demonstrating not the rupture of worldly and spiritual love but their coexistence as a continuum of experience. This is not an either-or proposition, spiritual love versus Luciferian lust, but one continuous movement representing different stages in a person's affective and intellectual life.

In effect, the poles of physical and spiritual love constitute a *processio* and a *reversio* away from and returning to spiritual love. Folquet's portrayal as bishop at the head of his author corpus thus represents two different moments on the continuum: Folquet as troubadour leading inexorably to Folquet as bishop. His poetry, then, and the codex itself, demonstrates how the poetry of secular love chronicles the worldly part of this spiritual pilgrimage, thereby foreshadowing the higher meaning and self-discovery of love.

By joining these disparate parts of Folquet's life via picture and text and thus acting as an *ensenhamen* or teaching, Morgan 819 undertakes a definition of love as a continuum of the sort Plotinus expressed so well at *Ennead* 6.9.9.25 ff.

And the soul's innate love makes clear that the Good is there, and this is why Eros is coupled with the Psyches in pictures and stories. For since the soul is other than God but comes from him it is necessarily in love with him, and when it is there it has the heavenly love, but here love

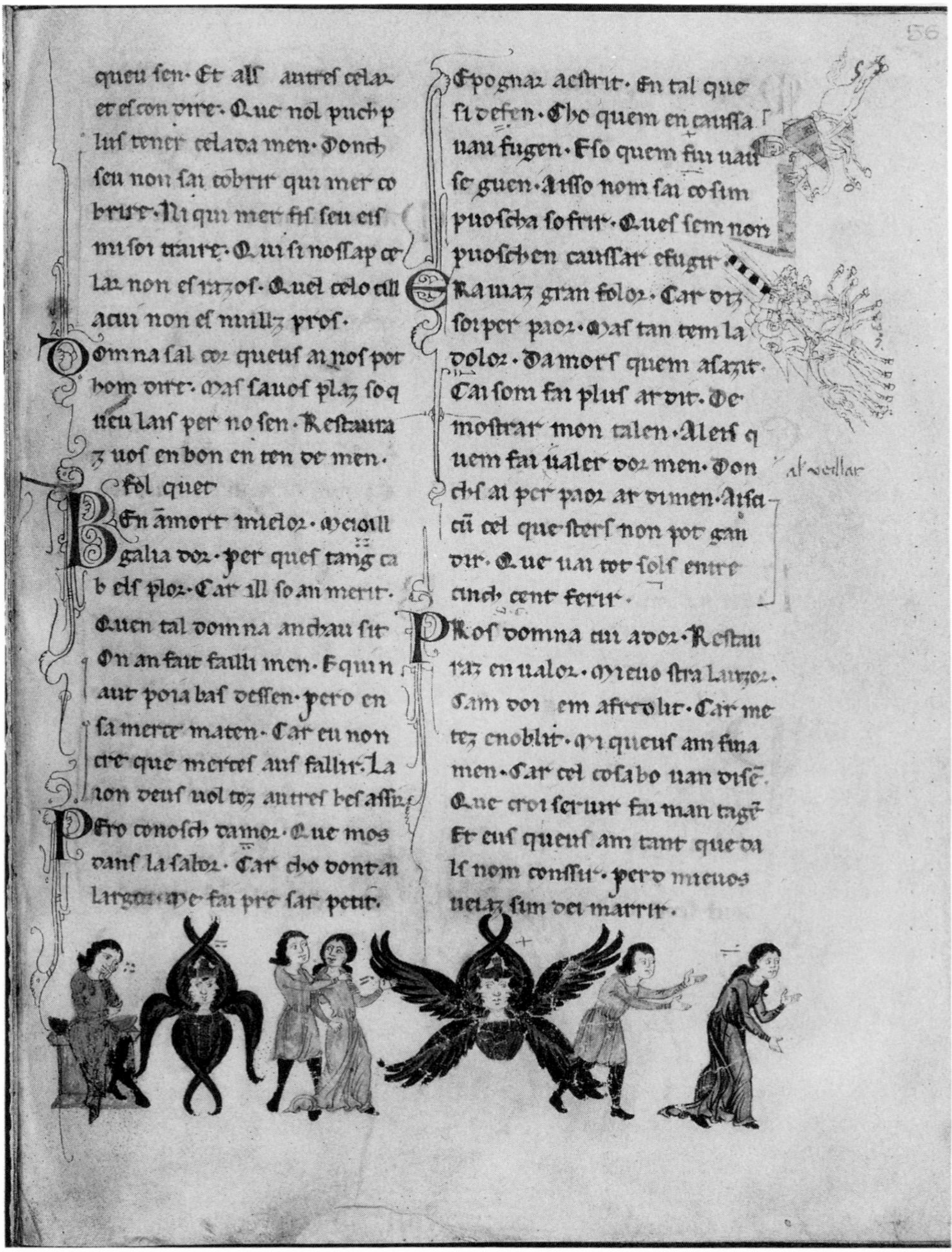

Fig. 8. *Bas-de-page* painting of seraphim with three faces. New York, Pierpont Morgan Library, MS 819, f. 56.

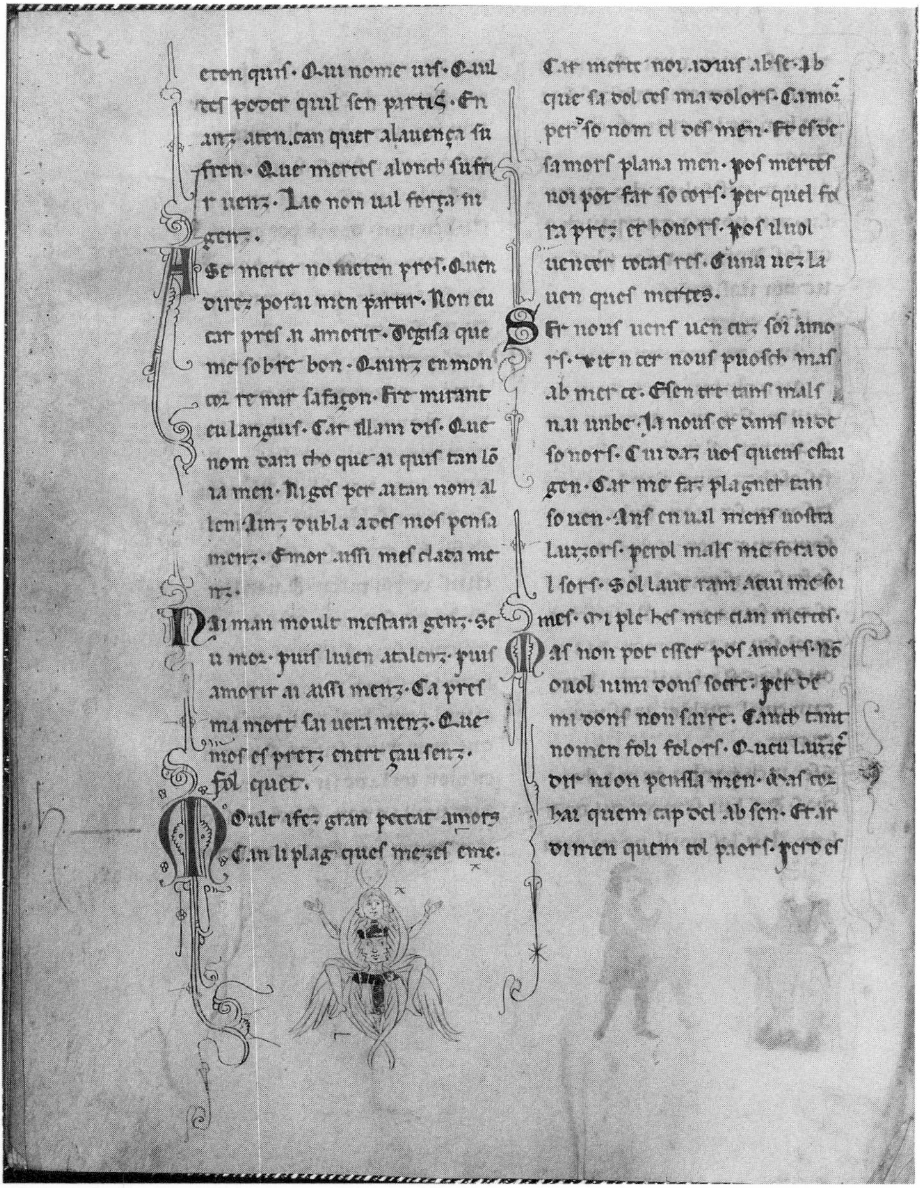

Fig. 9. *Bas-de-page* sketch of seraphim with three faces. New York, Pierpont Morgan Library, MS 819, f. 58v.

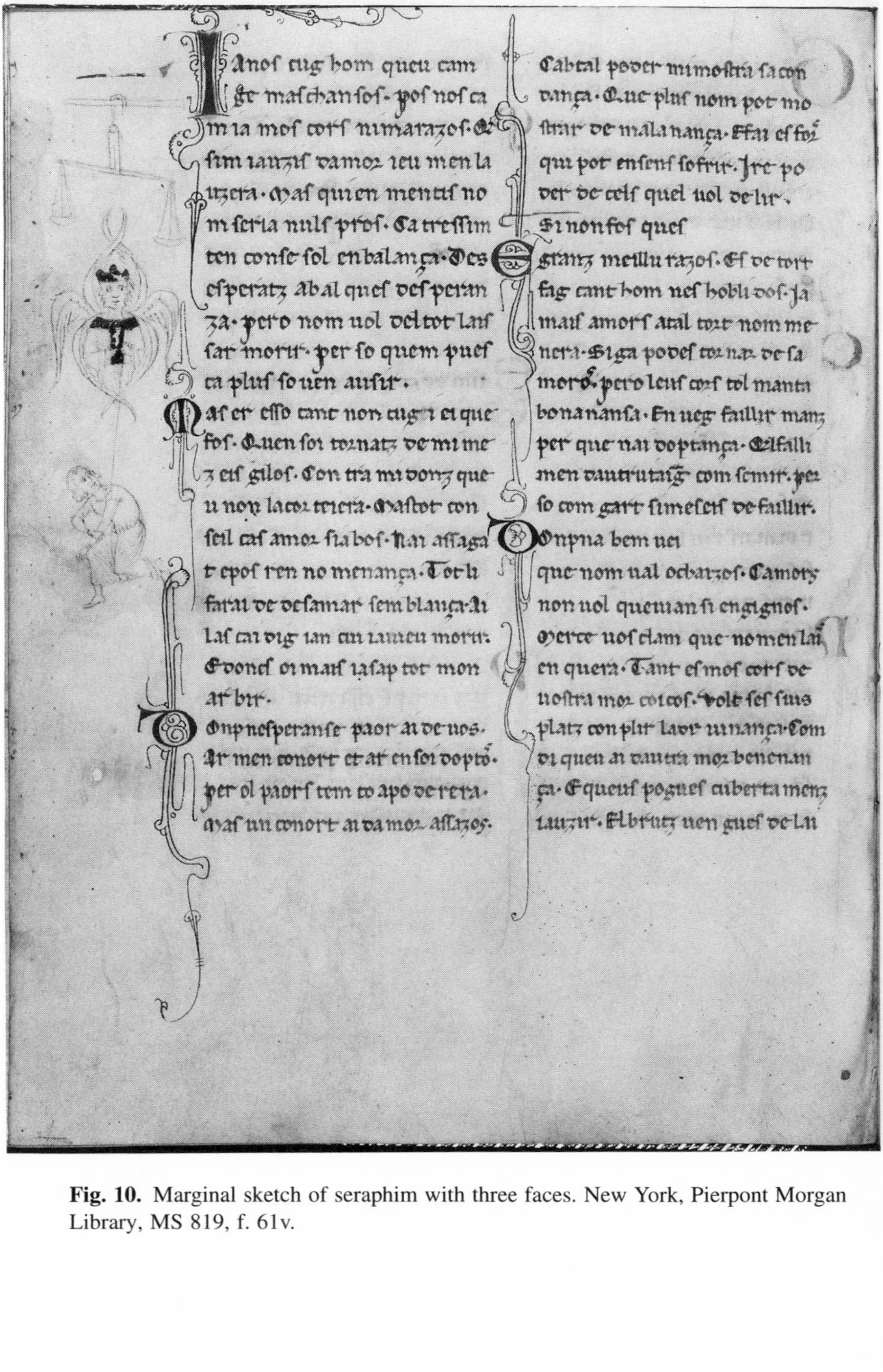

Fig. 10. Marginal sketch of seraphim with three faces. New York, Pierpont Morgan Library, MS 819, f. 61v.

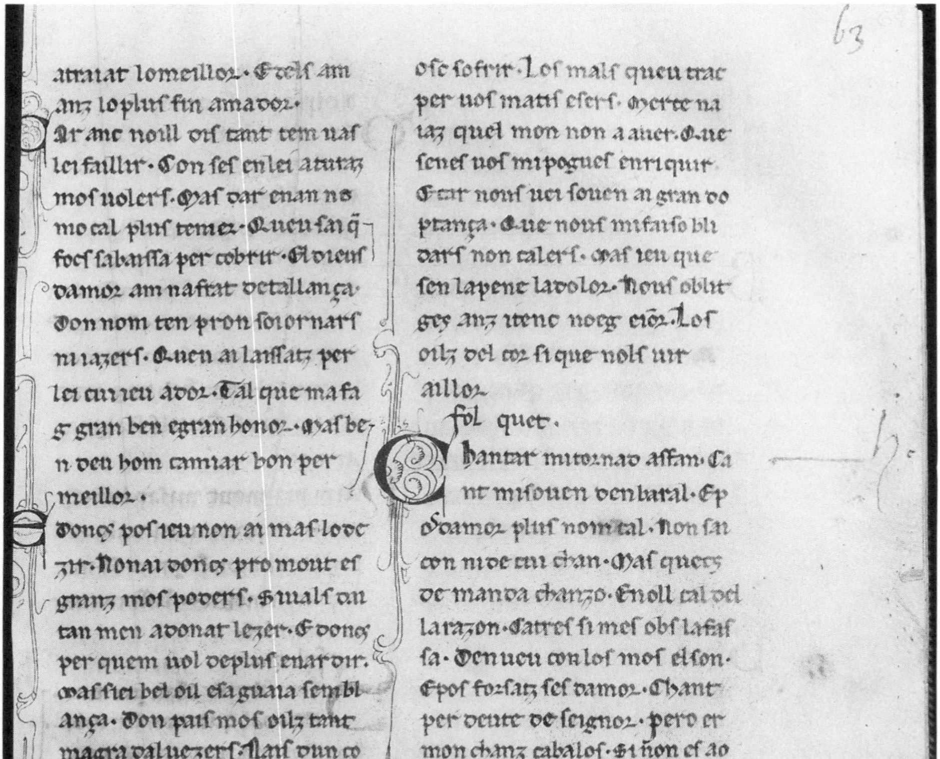

atrasat lomeillor· Ereis am
anz lo plus fin amador·
Ar me noill dis tant tem nas
lei faillir· Con ses en lei atutz
mos volers· Mas oar enam ns
mo cal plus temer· Quen sai q
foes sabussa per cobrir· El dieus
oamor am nastat oetallanca
Don nom ten proti soiornars
mi iazers· Quen ai laissatz per
lei cui ieu ador· Tal que ma fa
g gran ben egran honor· Mas be
n oeu hom camiar bon per
meillor·

Doncs pos ieu non ai mas love
zir· Nonai doncs pro mout es
granz mos poders· Si mais eu
tan men adonat lezer· E doncs
per quem uol deplus enar dir·
Mas fiei bel oil esa guaia sembl
ança· Don pais mos oilz tant
magra oaluezers· Mas dun co
nort tal que mon oefollor· Ca
oes mes uis quem uoilla oar
samor· Can uolu uas mi sofoi
lz ples de oonsor·

Doncs oonpna pos mais non p

ofe sofrir· Los mals queu trac
per uos mais eserf· Merte na
iaz quel mon non a auer· Ne
senes uos mi pogues enriquir·
Ecar nous uei souen ai gran do
ptança· Que nous mi fauso bli
oars non calers· Mas ieu que
sen la pene la oolor· Nous oblit
ges anz uene noeg eior· Los
oilz oel cor si que nols uir
aillor·

fol quet·

Chantar mitoznao assam· Ca
nt mi souen oen baral· Ep
Doamor plus nom tal· Non sai
con nioe cui chan· Mas quers
oe manoa chanzo· E noll cal oel
la razon· Catres si mes obs lafais
sa· Oen ueu con los mos elson·
Epos forsatz ses oamor· Chant
per oeute oe seignor· pero er
mon chanz cabalos· Si non es ao
ls ni bons·

Amador son oun semblan· Erie
cobe autre tal· Cab res ab oolor
moztal· Mer ma loz ioi on mais
an· Quen loc oefenestra son· Mas

Fig. 11. *Bas-de-page* sketch of seraphim with three faces. New York, Pierpont Morgan Library, MS 819, f. 64.

Fig. 12. Marginal painting of seraphim with three faces. New York, Pierpont Morgan Library, MS 819, f. 211.

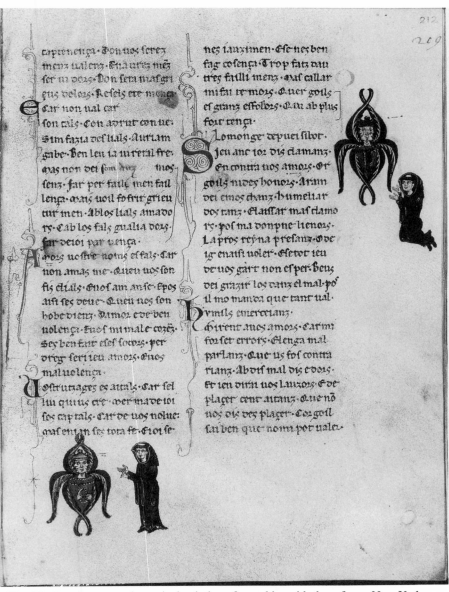

Fig. 13. *Bas-de-page* and marginal painting of seraphim with three faces. New York, Pierpont Morgan Library, MS 819, f. 212.

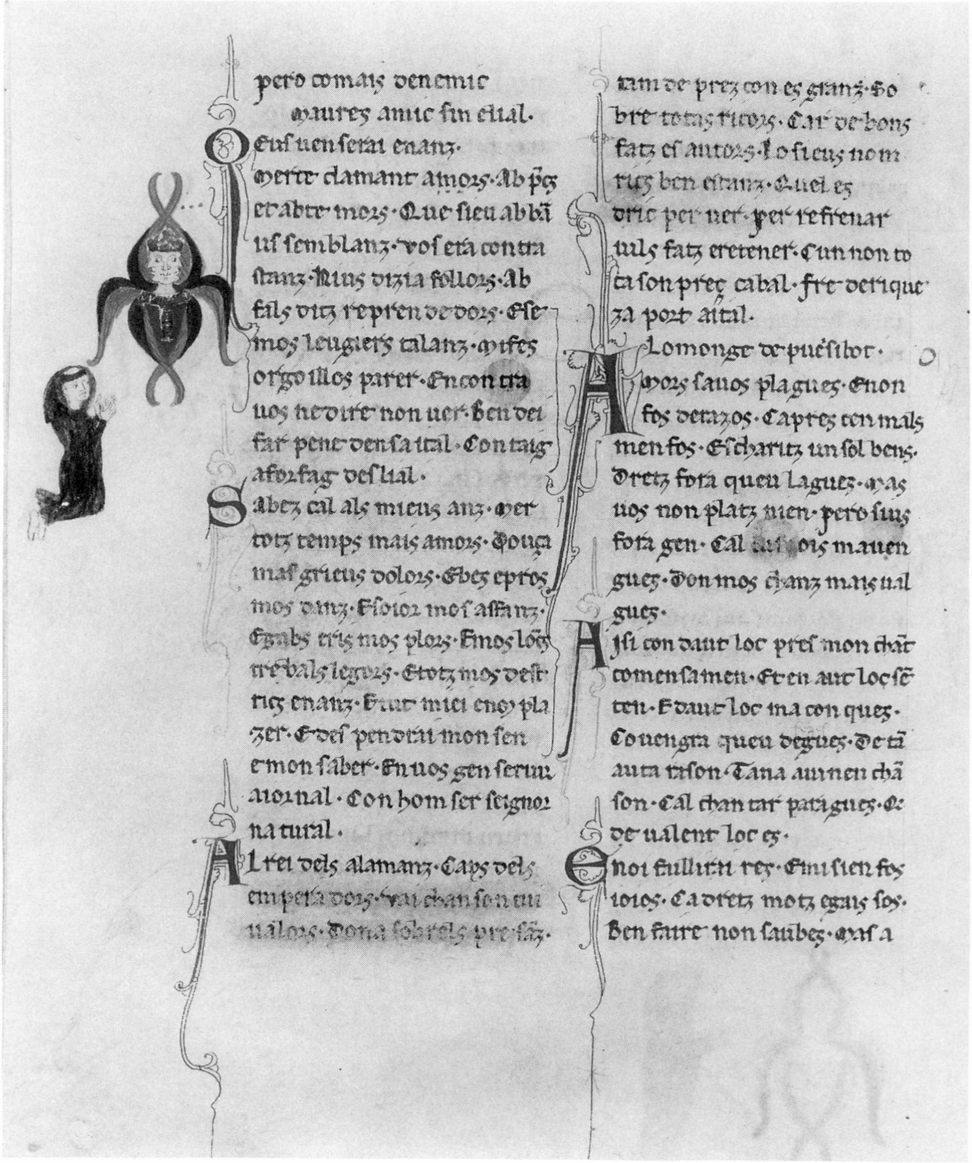

pero comais denemie
maures amie sin eual.
Deus uen seral enanz
uertz clamant amors ab pes
er abtr mors que sieu ab bã
uls semblanz vos eta contra
stanz mius vizia follors ab
sils ditz reprien dedors esce
mos leugiers talanz mifes
orgo illos parer en contra
uos hedire non uer ben det
far pene den sa ital contaig
aforsag deslial

Sabez cal als mieus anz mer
totz temps mais amors dou ga
mas grieus dolors ebez epros
mos danz Esdolor mos assanz
Erabs eris mos plors Enos loj
tre balz legors Etotz mos dest
titz enanz Erart miei enoy pla
zer E des pen deu mon sen
e mon saber En uos gen serun
aiornal con hom ser seignor
na tural

Al rei dels alamanz caps dels
enpera dors uai chanson tu
ualors dona sobrels pres saj

tam de prez con es granz so
bre totas ricors car de bons
fatz es autors los ieus nom
ritz ben estanz quel es
dric per uer per resñenar
tuls fatz eretenet cun non to
ta son pretz cabal frez de rique
za port aital

Lomonge de puesibor
mors sanos plagues Enon
fos detazos captres ten mals
men fos escharitz un sol bens
Dretz fora quen lagues eras
uos non platz uien pero sius
fora gen cal aui ois mauen
gues don mos chanz maugual
gues

Aisi con daur loc pres mon char
comen sa men Er en aut loc se
ten E daur loc ina con ques
Coueugra quen degues de ta
auta rt son Tana au nen chã
son cal chan tar patz gues de
de ualent loc es

Enoi eullirti rey Emu sten sos
ioios ca dretz motz egais sos
ben faire non saubez enas a

Fig. 14. Marginal painting of seraphim with three faces. New York, Pierpont Morgan Library, MS 819, f. 212v.

becomes vulgar; for the soul there is the heavenly Aphrodite, but here becomes the vulgar Aphrodite, a kind of whore. And every soul is Aphrodite. . . . The soul then in her natural state is in love with God and wants to be united with him; it is like the noble love of a girl for her noble father. But when the soul has come into the world of becoming and is deceived, so to say, by the blandishments of her suitors, she changes, bereft of her father, to a mortal love and is shamed; but again she comes to hate her shame here below, and purifies herself to the things of this world and sets herself on the way to her father and fares well. And if anyone does not know this experience, let him think of it in terms of loves here below . . . and that these earthly loves are mortal and harmful and loves only of images [εἰδώλων ἔρωτες].[27]

These thoughts suggest new ways of conceptualizing the palpable fascination with pictures keyed to verbal images in the poetry throughout Morgan 819, but particularly in Folquet's section. We find a striking example in the margin of folio 59b (see fig. 4), accompanying Folquet's *En chantan m'auen a membrar / cho qu'eu cug chantan oblidar* [Singing brings to mind what, in singing, I think I'll forget].

The key lines at the end of the first stanza are those illustrated in the margin in the full-figured picture of the poet bearing an image of his *domna* on his breast, exactly as stated in the poem: "Qu'ins el cor port, domna, vostre faichon / Que'm castia qu'eu no uir ma razon" [for in my heart I bear, lady, your image / which chides me for not changing my purpose] (ll. 12–14). By itself, the poem could very well illustrate the dialectic between materiality and spirituality, the body and the Good, that Plotinus discusses in *Ennead* 6.9.9.

There, Plotinus makes the point that the principle of the Good exists in the body, indivisible, "just as the light abides if the sun abides" *(Ennead* 6.9.9.7). The value of the image lies in its dialectical ambiguity—first representing the thing, and then pointing beyond itself to the authentic referent. Plotinus never condemns the image (εἰδώλων) as Plato does, but only the continuing love of the image after the authentic thing has been glimpsed or at least intuited. Folquet's *faisson* of the *domna* enacts that dialectic of discovery by castigating the poet for his obstinacy in refusing to turn his cognitive faculties (*razon*) from the image of the Good, that is, the poetic *domna,* to the Good itself that she figures.

---

27. Plotinus, *Enneads,* vol. 7, *Enneads VI.6–9,* trans. A. H. Armstrong, (Cambridge: Harvard University Press, 1988), 337.

The paradoxical opening of the song—"En chantan m'auen a membrar / cho qu'eu cug chantan oblidar"—has much less to do with memory and the inability to forget his love than with the nagging dialectic of artistic exemplarity. Since art forces one to be mindful (*membrar*) of what one would rather ignore, art is therefore the dialectical agent of the Good: "the soul's innate love makes clear that the Good is there, and this is why Eros is coupled with the Psyches in pictures and stories" (*Ennead* 6.9.9.25).

Now the manuscript brings out this link by staging a fuller version of the dialectic of exemplarity. Figure 4 shows us a hyperliteralization of the poetic text (which already literalizes the expression of carrying the image of the *domna* on one's heart) by the simple expedient of putting a picture of the lady on the poet's breast. This is, in one sense, a precocious version of the custom of wearing a locket with a likeness of the beloved over one's heart.

The manuscript picture focuses on the poetic image, doubling its descriptive power by literalizing it so that we really do *see* what it says. The picture forces us to look at the text, to gaze at it. Immediately, we see what we did not expect to see, namely, the impossibility of this image. Since it does not make sense to have a picture of the *domna* on the poet's breast—and we must see that the picture does stage its own improbability—that cannot be the correct image: we must look elsewhere, just as Plotinus asserts: "these earthly loves are mortal and harmful and loves only of images, and . . . they change because it was not what is really and truly loved nor our good nor what we seek" (*Ennead* 6.9.9.42 ff). And, as Folquet understands full well, it is always the represented image that obliges us to recognize our errant perception: the reader might say, "Your picture, lady, chides me for not changing my understanding."

While I am not suggesting that Giovanni Gaibana or one of his scribes had these passages of the *Enneads* in mind, I have elsewhere demonstrated the impact that Plotinus's philosophy did have on the development of picture and text in medieval manuscripts.[28] So far as Morgan 819 is concerned, the correlation of picture and poetic texts in so programmatic a fashion suggests that the whole manuscript has been designed according to a deliberate plan—especially at the key or nodal points I have discussed in this chapter. Much thought has been paid to principles of ordering. In particular, one can show that the three parts of the codex correlate closely with contemporary principles of rhetorical order as articulated in *artes rhetoricae* like Geoffroi de Vinsauf's *Poetria nova* (ca. 1210). Geoffrey's treatise was immensely popular in the Middle Ages and, according to Manly, was among those *poetriae* satirized by

---

28. "Textes mobiles, images motrices dans une civilisation manuscriptuaire," *Littérature* 99 (October 1995): 19–33; "Picture, Image, and Subjectivity in Medieval Culture," *MLN* 108 (September 1993): 617–37.

Chaucer in such passages as *The Franklin's Prologue* 709–28, while praised by Erasmus.[29] Geoffrey of Vinsauf was the subject of commentary already in the thirteenth century, as Marjorie Curry Woods demonstrated a decade ago.[30] Rita Copeland also points to the importance of the *Poetria nova* for exemplifying

> how the system of rhetoric is inscribed within the system of hermeutics. The *accessus* defines the subject and significance of the book ("artificiosa eloquentia") through a definition of the book's structure. The book's structure represents its subject . . .[31]

The *Poetria nova* deals with composing works by natural or artificial principles; the best kinds of beginnings in works; invention (the troubadours' *trobar*); how authors manipulate amplification and its opposite, abbreviation; and "difficult" versus "easy" readings (akin to the *trobar clus—clus* = "key," thus "difficult"—and *trobar leu—leu* = "light," thus "easy"). There is no doubt that the focus of Geoffrey's *Poetria nova* on the disposition or order of a work as a component of the work's comprehensive meaning (or impact) illustrates a consciousness of the importance of the book or of compositions organized as a whole.

To take one brief example, Geoffrey says that one can order a work according to the dictates of nature or of art. If by nature, the order will follow the natural sequence in which the contents came into being, that is, a chronological structure, such as that favored by so many modern anthologies of Old Occitan lyric beginning with Guilhem IX.[32] Ordering according to artistic principles recommends itself to Geoffrey as vastly superior to ordering according to natural principles, because it offers eight choices as opposed to nature's single means, that is, "when the order of discourse does not depart from the order of occurrence."[33] To order according to the principles of art means, first, choosing

---

29. In 1489, Erasmus writes: " You know your Cicero, your Quintilian, your Horace, your Geoffrey of Vinsauf, and you are certainly not unaware of the abundance of excellent advice on the art of poetry which they contain; whoever keeps their advice faithfully is bound to fulfill to perfection his function as a poet" (*The Correspondance of Erasmus,* trans. R. A. B. Mynors and D. F. S. Thompson, vol. 1 [Toronto: University of Toronto Press, 1974], 50). Quoted by Marjorie C. Woods, *An Early Commentary on the Poetria Nova of Geoffrey of Vinsauf* (New York : Garland, 1985), xvii.

30. Woods, *An Early Commentary on the Poetria Nova.*

31. Rita Copeland, *Rhetoric, Hermeneutics, and Translation in the Middle Ages: Academic Tradition and Vernacular Texts* (Cambridge: Cambridge University Press, 1991), 79.

32. This comes at the beginning of the second section of the *Poetria nova,* lines 87 ff. I follow Edmond Faral's edition, *Les arts potéques du XIIe et du XIIIe siècle* (Paris: Librairie Honoré Champon, 1962), 194–262.

33. Geoffrey of Vinsauf, *Poetria Nova,* trans. Margaret F. Nims (Toronto: Pontifical Institute of Mediaeval Studies, 1967), 18.

an ordering principle that shows the contents off to aesthetic and moral advantage and, second, beginning with an exemplum that sets the tone for the whole work. Such an exemplum tells the reader what to expect and how to read what follows.

From what we have seen of the structure of Morgan 819, it is not difficult to see that it follows the kind of artistic principles proposed by the *Poetria nova*. The codex begins with an exemplum that sets the manuscript's tone and that offers the rationale for art that one finds dominant in each section of the manuscript, as we saw in the poems of Folquet of Marselha and Arnaut de Marueil, the first two troubadours in the main part of the manuscript. Morgan 819 also resolutely places later material first, as Geoffrey counsels: "The poem travels the pathway of art if a more effective order presents first what was later in time, and defers the appearance of what was actually earlier."[34]

While the poems have a certain content that lends itself to the ordering treatment followed by the manuscript, it is precisely the manuscript's performative thrust that, through grouping and pictorial commentary, highlights and extends poetic content. This is the case with the exemplarity that we saw in Arnaut's *ensenhamen* with which Morgan 819 begins; it is even more so, for example, in the excerpt from the Romance of *Jaufre* presented on folios 10–12v (representing lines 7389–7672 of Lavaud and Nelli's edition of the *Jaufre*).

Synthetic or artistic principles underlie the body of the codex, which eschews chronological or natural order by beginning with Folquet and elaborating a structuring sequence favoring Plotinian-like contemplation. What Geoffrey of Vinsauf calls "art," I would call manuscript performance; and it, more than anything else (certainly more than content or genre per se), dictates the ordering of wildly disparate materials in Morgan 819. It certainly obliges us— as Plotinus asserts that the image always does—to read all the works in a different way from how we might read them in another context.

I urge that we reconsider the taxonomy by which we refer to classes of vernacular manuscripts. Referring to all of the Old Occitan codices together as *chansonniers* can be misleading and certainly does not encourage us either to study them as a whole carefully—as distinct from specific aspects of them—or to describe them as accurately as we might. Morgan 819 should not, I think, be called a *chansonnier,* if we mean by that term a miscellaneous collection of Old Occitan lyrics. I think that we would achieve more accuracy and insight by considering it as perhaps representative of a heretofore unrecognized class of

---

34. Ibid., 18–19.

thirteenth-century manuscripts that programmatically do for vernacular literature what the pandect did for Scripture in the sixth to the tenth centuries. Such
manuscripts need not be quite so ecclesiastically oriented as Morgan 819, but,
like it, they may be found to project a strong sense of *ensenhamen,* that is, laws
or rules for living.

A Book Made for a Queen: The Shaping of a Late Medieval Anthology Manuscript (B.N. fr. 24429)

Sylvia Huot

The manuscript fr. 24429 of the Bibliothèque Nationale, Paris, contains an anthology of historical, moral, and devotional texts, originally preceded by the hagiographic compilation now preserved as MS 588 of the Bibliothèque Ste-Geneviève.[1] The contents of the manuscript as it now stands are listed in the appendix to this chapter. The manuscript is of Parisian origin.[2] Each text is headed with a miniature, and certain narrative texts contain internal miniatures as well. The historical texts with which the anthology opens are of some help in dating the collection. Its first piece, a chronological table entitled *Le Nombre des anz,* provides space for entries from the year 1 to the year 1338; the last event recorded is the flooding of Paris in 1296. The lists of emperors and popes at the end of the *Aages du monde* reach only to the mid–thirteenth century, ending with Friedrich II (d. 1250) and Urban IV (d. 1264), respectively; the list

Work toward developing this chapter was supported by a grant from the George A. and Eliza Gardner Howard Foundation and by a summer research grant from Northern Illinois University, which I gratefully acknowledge.

1. The Ste-Geneviève manuscript ends with a table of contents for MS fr. 24429, introduced with the following rubric: "Ci aprés encommance .i. livre ou quel il a contenues moult de merveilles" [After this there begins a book in which are contained many marvels] (fol. 181v).

2. This assessment was confirmed by François Avril of the Bibliothèque Nationale in a private consultation. The illuminations are described as "linked to the Artesian region or its environs" in the exposition catalog *Manuscrits à peinture en France du XIIIe au XIVe siècle* (Paris: Bibliothèque Nationale, 1955), 33. The language of the manuscript, however, shows no trace of Artesian or Picard dialect, and the illuminations are similar in style to those in other Parisian manuscripts.

of French kings, however, extends through Philippe IV, who reigned from 1285 to 1314. These entries along with codicological evidence allow the manuscript to be placed in the closing years of the thirteenth century or the early years of the fourteenth.[3] From the crowned woman appearing in several of the miniatures,[4] one can further surmise that the manuscript was prepared for a queen, although there are no details that allow for a specific identification. Possible candidates from the period 1296–1338 could include Marie de Brabant, widow of Philippe III; Blanche, widowed queen of Navarre; Jeanne, wife of Philippe IV and queen of both France and Navarre; or Blanche, daughter of St. Louis and widow of the Infant of Castille. In the lack of a solid identification, I will refer to the book's original owner simply as "the queen."

In content as well as organization and decoration, MS fr. 24429 is typical of late medieval vernacular anthologies of didactic material. It forms an interesting basis for a case study precisely because it illustrates medieval reading practices so well. The texts introduce the lay reader to the techniques of meditative reading that were originally developed in ecclesiastical milieux but entered the vernacular tradition through the growing production of vernacular texts and translations for the edification of the laity. Furthermore, the manuscript is more than just a standard workshop production; in certain textual and iconographic details it is tailored to a specific reader, the unnamed queen for whom it was made. Both the conventional features of the anthology and its personalized details will be outlined in the following survey of its contents and highlighted through comparison of two kinds: with other manuscripts containing the same texts, and with the late thirteenth-century MS Arsenal 3142, a similar type of anthology that was almost certainly made for Marie de Brabant and that thus allows some insight into the kind of book that would be prepared for the entertainment and edification of a French queen.

The meditative nature of reading and its link to devotional practices are clearly articulated in a text known as *Li Livres des enfans Israël,* itself book 2 of *Del aignelet rosti,* here cited from its appearance in another fourteenth-century devotional anthology (Bibl. Nat. fr. 1802).

---

3. One could argue for a date of 1296 based on the fact that Louis IX, canonized in 1297, is not referred to as a saint. It may also be significant that the founding of the Templars is noted in the list of kings, but not their dissolution, which took place in 1312. Such omissions could, however, result from a lack of concern with detail or from an incomplete source text.

4. The queen appears in miniatures illustrating the *Pater noster* (fol. 49r), the *Meditacion* (fols. 58v, 60v), and the *Ensaingnement* (fol. 132v); in addition, the figure of Charity heading the *Vers d'Aumosne* is portrayed as a queen (fol. 45v), allowing identification with the patron. See figs. 1–3.

Trois manieres sont d'esperituel exercite: c'est leçons, meditations, et
oroisons. Ces trois sont si conjointes que l'une ne puet valoir sans l'autre.
Car leçons sans meditation tourne a negligence et a ociosité. Meditations
sans leçon mainne en erreur. Et meditations sans oroison engendre van-
ité. Et oroison sans meditation est sans lumiere et sans fervour. Pour ce
convient premiers le cuer enfourmer par leçon, et fermer par meditation,
et puis refourmer par oroison. (fol. 201v)

[There are three kinds of spiritual exercise: namely, reading, meditation,
and prayer. These three are so interconnected that one cannot be of value
without the other. For reading without meditation becomes negligence
and idleness. Meditation without reading leads to error. And meditation
without prayer engenders vanity. And prayer without meditation is without light or fervor. Therefore one must first inform the heart through
reading, fortify it through meditation, and then reform it through prayer.]

The importance of the book in devotional practices is further stressed in the
prologue to another text in the same manuscript, the *Mireoir de l'ame,* which
explains that the two paths to memory—sight and hearing, *veoir* and *oïr*—
correspond to two ways of receiving knowledge, namely, writing and speech;[5]
and that of these, the most reliable is writing.

Car quant l'en a oublié aucune chose que l'en a oïe, l'en revient tout iors
a memoire et a remembrance par escrit de la chose que l'en a oïe et
oubliee. Et pour ce convient il metre moult de choses en escripture, et
meesmement translater de latin en françois, pour ce que chascune chose
soit miex seue et plus communement. (BN fr. 1802, fol. 60r)

[For when one has forgotten something that one heard, one always comes
to remember it through the written record of the thing that one heard and
forgot. And therefore it is necessary to write many things down, and
likewise to do translations from Latin into French, so that everything
may be better and more widely known.]

---

5. The *Mireoir de l'ame* differs slightly from the *Bestiaire d'amour* of Richard de Fournival,
where the two paths to memory are identified not as *parole* and *écriture* but as *parole* and *peinture.*
On Fournival's formulation, see Mary Carruthers, *The Book of Memory* (Cambridge: Cambridge
University Press, 1990), 224; and my *From Song to Book* (Ithaca: Cornell University Press, 1987),
138–41, 164–73.

The importance of learning and remembering through the written text has a direct bearing on the salvation of the soul.

> Ausi nus ne peut connoistre les joies de paradis se il ne connoist les paines d'enfer. Et ces .ii. choses ne peut l'en connoistre fors par oïr dire et par escripture. Mes escripture est plus certaine que oïr dire. (Ibid.)

> [Also no one can know the joys of Paradise without knowing the pains of hell. And one can know these two things only through hearsay or through writing. But writing is more certain than hearsay.]

Although neither of the above texts appears in MS fr. 24429, both statements apply very well to its contents. The manuscript provides the queen with reading material to be used in meditation and private devotion, including specific instructions for techniques of meditative prayer. It contains numerous translations from the Latin, making available for her private study texts that could otherwise come to her only through the oral exposition of a reader capable of providing a running translation.[6] And it provides her very explicitly with a fund of knowledge that will guide her in this life and inform her about the joys and terrors of the next.

Some of the texts in the queen's book are themselves compilations or florilegia of teachings from classical, biblical, and patristic sources, grouped according to general themes or topics. Most notable among these are the *Auctorités* and the *Moralités,* a translation of the *Moralium dogma* that circulated widely during the later Middle Ages. Such compilations, miniature anthologies unto themselves, were particularly useful pedagogically as repositories of edifying materials. As the compiler states at the close of the *Moralités:*

> Et qui les voudra oïr, il les porra plus legierement ci prendre, que se il les aloit querant par pluseurs livres ou il sont espandu. Et plus bele chose est a .i. homme d'avoir une chose a main que aler querant ça et la pluseurs choses qu'il n'en peust ramener ensamble. (BN fr. 24429, fol. 45r)

> [And whoever wants to hear them [moral teachings], can get them more easily here, than if he had to go seeking them in the many books where

---

6. An example of this kind of mediated reading appears in the opening section of the mid-fourteenth-century *Roman de Perceforest,* in which the count of Hainaut has a court clerk read aloud a Latin chronicle, translating it as he goes. While the episode, which purports to explain the origins of the *Perceforest* itself, is undoubtedly fictional, the behavior of the count and his clerk probably reflects actual practices of the time.

they are distributed. And it is a better thing for a man to have a thing in hand than to go seeking all over for many different things that he can't put together.]

The structure of such texts, in which teachings from various authors are arranged by topic, reinforces a meditative and associative approach to reading: the reader dwells on a given theme, following it from author to author, building up a better and more detailed understanding of the topic before finally moving on to the next one. Thus the lay reader is trained, his or her habits shaped, in accordance with the practices of medieval clerics and scholars. Other texts in the queen's book introduce the reader to interpretive and exegetical techniques. The *Estoire Joseph,* for example, includes an exposition of Joseph as an allegory of Christ, while the various sermons explicate biblical passages.

The commentary on the *Pater noster* illustrates very well the meditative and expansive reading processes fostered by the anthology as a whole, as well as the vital link between reading, meditation, and prayer. The text is headed with an image of the queen kneeling before the enthroned Christ, an initial visual image of herself in a devotional mode. It begins with a line-by-line translation of the prayer, in which each verse is given first in red ink in Latin, then in black ink in a literal French translation. The text to be expounded having been presented, there follows a discourse on its holiness and its importance in Christian devotion. The exposition is offered so that the worshiper will understand the prayer she makes to God.

Et por ce que nous volons que vous sachiez que vos dites et que vos demandez a dieu, quant vos dites la pater nostre, si vos dirons en romans ce que la letre nos ensaingne. (fol. 49r)

[And because we want you to know what you are saying and what you are asking of God when you say the Our Father, we will tell you in the vernacular what the text teaches us.]

Following this the prayer is repeated once again with slightly expanded translation and then a third time with much more extensive commentary on each verse, including the citation of numerous relevant biblical passages. The Latin verses are always written in red ink, so that they are distinguished from the French translation and commentary written in black. Finally, at the end, in explication of the word *Amen,* the prayer is given one more time in French. This time the word *voirement,* "truly," is inserted in front of each verse in illustration of the affirmative role of the word *Amen.* As was stated in the *Livres des enfans Israël,* prayer without meditation is meaningless, and meditation without reading leads one astray. Here, then, the queen is provided with a text that is specifically written in French so that she can read it herself and that provides her with a textual context in which to understand the words of the Our Father. The fruits of her reading will be an enriched experience of prayer, with the possibility of meditating fully on each line that she utters.

The nature of this repetitive reading can be illustrated by examining the exposition of a single verse: "Pater noster qui es in celis sanctificetur nomen tuum." The first time through it is simply translated: "Nostre pere qui es es ciex, santefiez soit li tiens nons" [our father who art in heaven, hallowed be thy name] (fol. 49r). The second time through adds little that is new.

> *Pater nostre qui es in celis sanctificetur nomen tuum.* Nostre pere qui es es ciex, santefiez soit li tiens nons. Ces choses prions et demandons a nostre seingneur quant nous disons la pastre nostre. La premiere est que nous prions que saintefiez soit li siens nons, la ou nous disons: *Pater nostre qui es in celis sanctificetur nomen tuum.* (fol. 49v)

> [*Pater nostre qui es in celis sanctificetur nomen tuum.* Our father who art in Heaven, hallowed be thy name. These things we pray and ask of our Lord when we say the Our Father. The first is that we pray that his name be hallowed, there where we say, *Pater noster qui es in celis, sanctificetur nomen tuum.*]

The third time round, after quoting the Latin verse yet again, we are given a full page of commentary. There is a discussion of why God is addressed as Father, and how his name is sanctified through the love of the faithful. It is explained at length that his name is already completely sanctified in and of itself and that we pray for it to be sanctified in us also. The following brief excerpt gives the flavor of the commentary.

> Sires diex, saintefiez soit li tiens nons es cuers aus paiens et es cuers aus juis, et mesmement es cuers a cels que tu as porveu a sauver, et t'aimment si com il doivent. Et soit saintefiez li tiens nons aus mauves hommes es cuers, que il deguerpissent les pechiez en coi il gissent, et qu'il t'aimment si com il te croient voir seingneur. Et soit saintefiez li tiens nons es bons crestiens qui te croient et aimment, que il plus fermement te croient, et plus hardiement te puissent amer. (fol. 50r)

[Lord God, hallowed be thy name in the hearts of the pagans and in the hearts of the Jews, and likewise in the hearts of those that you have seen fit to save, and who love you as they should. And hallowed be thy name in the hearts of evil men, that they may turn away from the sins in which they lie. And may they love you as they believe you to be their true lord. And hallowed be thy name in good Christians who love and believe in you, that they may believe in you more firmly and love you more boldly.]

Following the exposition, in commentary on the word *Amen,* is the final affirmation of the prayer: "Sires diex, voirement soit saintefiez li tiens nons. Voirement nos aviengne li tiens regnes" [Lord God, truly, hallowed be thy name. Truly, may thy kingdom come] (fol. 51r).

In this way the *Pater noster* becomes a device for organizing an exposition of the Christian faith. By the time one has read through the entire text, having gone through the prayer four times, one is likely to have its terms well fixed in memory. And the prayer itself, thus memorized, further allows the reader to fix in his or her memory the various doctrinal points addressed under each of its verses. The text is a good example of meditative reading: by dwelling on a familiar text and going through it again and again, casting an ever wider net of associations from each of its lines, the reader eventually is led to a contemplation of many different points. These points, in turn, will provide the substance for informed meditation during prayer.

The *Vers d'aumosne* is a slightly different example of how a key text or image can be used to organize a moralistic treatise that draws together a variety of other texts.[7] The text is headed with a miniature that shows a woman who is wearing a crown and halo and distributing alms to the poor (see fig. 1). The halo identifies the figure as an allegorical abstraction, while the crown indicates the nobility of the virtue. At the same time, however, the crown suggests an identification of the allegorical figure with the queen for whom the manuscript was made: she is encouraged to imagine herself, in effect, as a living embodiment of charity. The text opens with an enumeration of the eleven qualities of almsgiving, each of which is then explicated by means of biblical citations. This exposition is followed by a statement of the five characteristics that must

---

7. Despite its title, the text is in prose. The "verse" in question is presumably the opening statement of the qualities of almsgiving, which, though laid out as prose, can be articulated as a rhyme of sorts: "Aumosne anestoie / et monteplie / et garde et coronne et combat et vaint / et acompaingne et aferme et prie et estaint / et rachate et enlumine et enseingnorist et oint" [Almsgiving purifies and multiplies and guards and crowns and combats and conquers and accompanies and affirms and prays and extinguishes and redeems and illumines and rules and annoints] (fol. 45v).

Fig. 1. Paris, Bibl. Nat. fr. 24429, fol. 45v (detail). Opening miniature for the *Vers d'aumosne*. (Photograph courtesy Bibliothèque Nationale.)

be present in all almsgiving: that one must give regularly, of money or goods obtained legally, for the love of God rather than for vainglory, to the poor and not the rich, and according to one's abilities to give. These points are correlated to the five fingers of the hand, and again each is explained through biblical or patristic citations. The image of the hand reappears in the closing statement: "Cil tent ses mains en vain a dieu et prie, qui selonc son pooir ne les tent vers le povre" [He reaches his hands in vain to God in prayer, who does not reach his hands out to the poor] (fol. 46r).

Thus the hand is a mnemonic device for remembering scriptural and patristic exhortations about almsgiving and is also the very symbol of charity: it is the means by which charity is dispensed to the poor and sought from God.[8] The

8. On the use of the hand and other familiar objects as mnemonic and organizational devices in didactic treatises, see Horst Wenzel, "An fünf Fingern abzulesen: Schriftlichkeit und Mnemo-

illustration, in which a queenly figure gives to the poor with her own hands, effects the immediate application of this lesson to the intended reader of the manuscript. As she reads, the queen is invited to visualize herself as the subject of the little florilegium on charity, to associate the qualities of almsgiving with her own fingers, and to imagine her own hands in both the distribution of alms and the supplication for divine favor. The text and its presentation in the personalized book not only provide a mnemonic system for an extensively intertextual set of teachings about charity but also project these teachings into the person of the reader, indeed onto her very body.

The most striking instance of the book as a vehicle for visual meditation is the text rubricated *Meditacions*. Here the queen's spiritual adviser—such is the fiction of the prologue—provides her with a system for meditative prayer. The opening miniature shows her kneeling before a clerical figure, presumably her confessor: thus he can be identified with the admonishing voice of the text that follows, while she is identified as the one to whom it is addressed. The prologue begins with the popular maxim "Qui bien aimme a tart oublie" [one who loves forgets slowly] (fol. 58v). This phrase is common in the courtly repertoire, but here it is applied to the great spiritual love that the narrator feels for his advisee, addressed only as "fille" [daughter]. Having expressed his love and desire to serve her, he acknowledges that she has asked for advice concerning his techniques of private prayer and meditation. To this end he has prepared instructions in a form that she can use in private study and devotion: "En ai ici que que soit escrit et en romanz por ce que par toi meismes le puisses lire quant il te plera" [I have written it all here in the vernacular so that you can read it yourself whenever you want to] (ibid.).

The method turns out to be a meditation on the fifteen joys of the Virgin. The narrator explains that "par ces .xv. ioies ai en continuel memoire pres de tot le cours de l'evangile" [through these fifteen joys I have in continuous memory nearly the entire gospel story] (ibid.). The fifteen joys are enumerated; each is headed with a miniature and given a short exposition. The narrator then explains that as he dwells on any one of the joys, he is inspired to prayer, and in his prayer he invokes the aid of the Virgin by recalling each of these events in turn. The queen will now be able to do likewise: once again a series of key images serves as a means of organizing and remembering doctrine and provides a vehicle for expansive meditation on this doctrine. The series of pictures and their accompanying explanatory texts will aid the queen in committing the

technik in den Predigten Bertholds von Regensburg," in *Von Aufbruch und Utopie: Perspektiven einer neuen Gesellschaftsgeschichte des Mittelalters,* ed. Bea Lundt and Helma Reimöller (Cologne, Weimar, and Vienna: Böhlau Verlag, 1992), 235–47.

narrative frame to memory, especially given the familiarity of the events and of their standard iconographic representation. The book itself is an integral part of the process. It is in the space of the book that the queen as reader and worshiper encounters the events of sacred history and the person of the Blessed Virgin. The miniature accompanying a special prayer inserted into the middle of the fifteen joys illustrates this point very clearly. Here the queen kneels before the Virgin and child; between them is the open book (see fig. 2). It is almost as though the Virgin has materialized out of the book in which she is represented; certainly the book is portrayed as a medium of communication. This scene of the reader and the Virgin meeting by means of the book is re-created every time the queen herself picks up the book and, gazing on the pictures of herself in prayer, uses it as a means of achieving a contemplative union with the Virgin or with God.

The relevance of the book to its royal owner is not limited to the *Pater Noster, Vers d'aumosne, Meditacions,* and *Ensaingnement*—the four texts in which she is illustrated as audience, as worshiper, and as the embodiment of Christian charity. Several texts also provide models of virtuous and saintly women, who might act as role models for a female reader: aside from the Blessed Virgin and the various female saints included in the hagiographic compilation with which the book originally opened, we encounter St. Anne (in the *Conception Nostre Dame*), Mary Magdelene (in the *Moralité des .iii. Maries et l'amor que la Magdalene ot*), and St. Thaise, whose story closes the collection. An important motif running through the anthology is the relation-ship of the pious woman and her spiritual adviser: Mary Magdelene is devoted to Christ; Thaise is converted by a monk. And the queen is portrayed both visually and textually in relation to the various real or implied authors whose voices speak through the texts. We have seen that the *Meditacions* is cast as instructions from her confessor. Likewise the *Moralités,* as it appears in MS fr. 24429, carries a dedication to a female reader: "Bele chiere amie, sachiez vos que por vos et por vostre trés grant honeur, et por vostre grant preu, ai je fet ce livre" [Fair, dear friend, know that for you and for your very great honor, and for your great worthiness, I have made this book] (fol. 34). We know, of course, that the texts were not actually composed for the owner of this manuscript, for they appear in other manuscripts as well. But the defining framework of one particular reader's spiritual and intellectual life, made explicit through illustra-tions and minor textual adaptations, establishes a context within which certain themes and motifs stand out and contribute to the coherence of the collection.

A brief comparison with other manuscripts containing the same texts is informative. The *Moralités,* for example, is addressed to a male reader in the

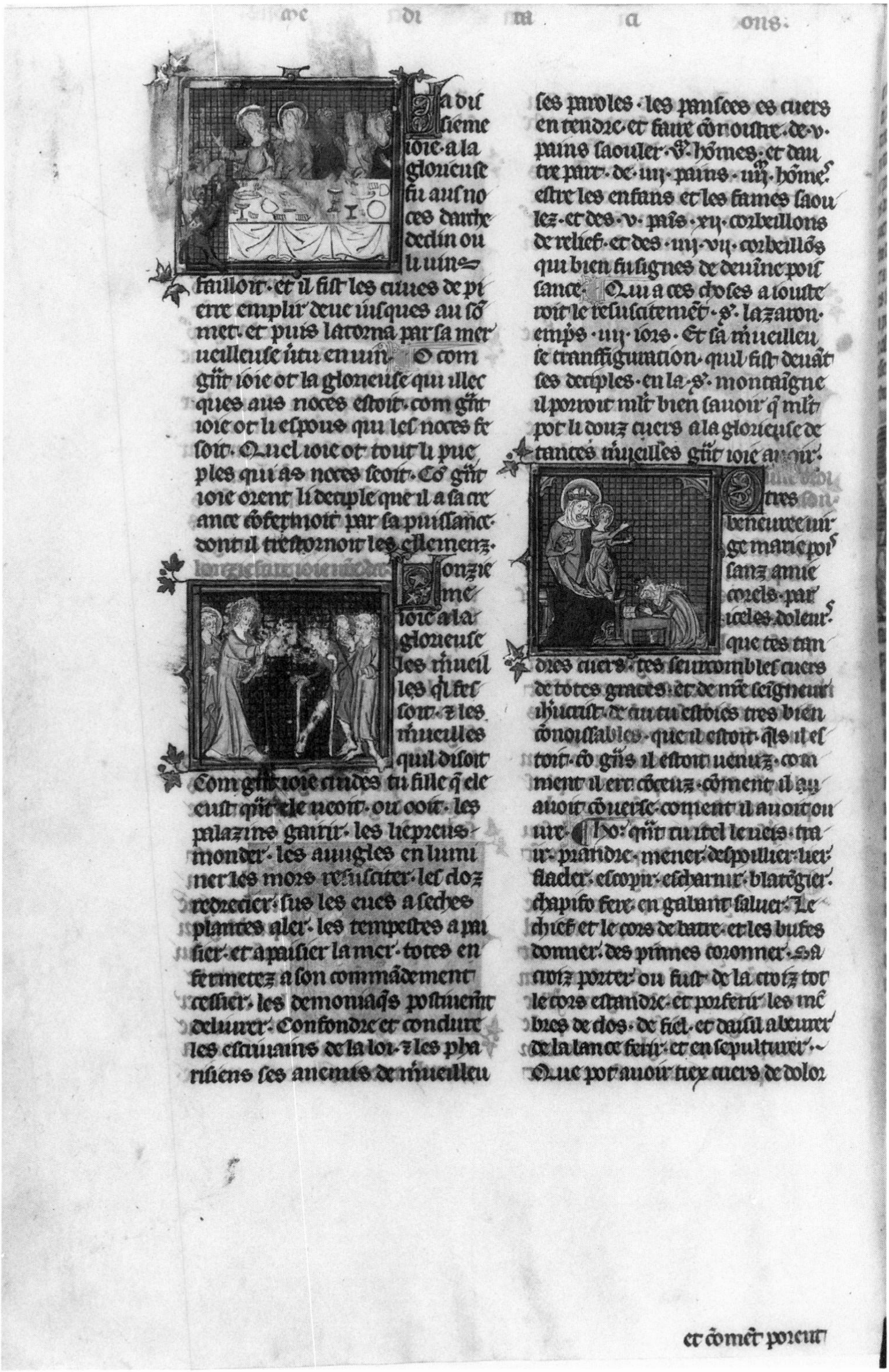

Fig. 2. Paris, Bibl. Nat. fr. 24429, fol. 60v. Illustrations from the *Meditacions,* representing (1) the tenth and eleventh joys of the Virgin and (2) the queen in prayer before the Virgin and Child. (Photograph courtesy Bibliothèque Nationale.)

Fig. 3. Paris, Bibl. Nat. fr. 24429, fol. 132v (detail). Opening miniature for the *Ensaingnement.* (Photograph courtesy Bibliothèque Nationale.)

many other manuscripts that contain it. Even in the MS Vaticana Reg. Lat. 1682, which contains almost exactly the same texts as MS fr. 24429 and is obviously closely related, the *Moralités* is dedicated to a "beaus chiers amis" (fol. 35v).[9] Similarly, the *Ensaingnement,* illustrated in fr. 24429 with an image of the queen receiving teachings from a male cleric (see fig. 3), is illustrated in the Vatican manuscript with the image of a cleric instructing a knight (see fig. 4). The *Meditacion* does retain its address to a female reader and thereby also the miniature showing a woman with her confessor; but, as one might expect, the woman in the miniature is not crowned. In the MS British Library, Egerton 745, prepared for a count of St. Pol—most likely Jean de Châtillon (d. 1344) or

9. For a detailed description of MS Vat. Reg. 1682, see Ernest Langlois. "Notices des manuscrits français et provençaux de Rome antérieurs au XVIe siècle," *Notices et extraits* 33, no. 1 (1889): 195–208.

Fig. 4. Biblioteca Apostolica Vaticana, Vat. Lat. 1682, fol. 124r (detail). Opening miniature for the *Ensaingnement.* (Photograph courtesy Vatican Library.)

his son Gui (d. 1360)—the instructions for prayer and meditation likewise retain their address to a female reader, albeit without the opening section of the prologue.[10] But the prayer to the Virgin, detached from the account of the joys and treated as a separate entry, is illustrated with an image of the count in devotion before the Virgin and Child; he can be identified by his arms, which appear again in the decoration of the initial with which the prayer opens (fol. 33r).[11] When the *Meditacion* appears in the MS Bibl. Nat. fr. 25462, it is addressed to a male reader: "Moi samble, biaus fils, que j'aie vers toi vraie dilection" [it seems to me, fair son, that I have a true love for you] (fol. 135r).[12]

10. See Paul Meyer, "Notice du MS Egerton 745 du Musée Britannique," *Romania* 39 (1910): 532–69. Meyer discusses the question of patronage on 537–38.

11. The miniature is reproduced in Meyer, "MS Egerton 745," facing 537.

12. MS fr. 25462 does not use the title *Meditacion* but introduces the text with the following

In all of these cases, one can see that the manuscript is carefully crafted to provide a space within which its intended reader can receive instruction and even encounter divine presences. Through the combined effects of miniatures and minor textual adaptations, the authoritative voice of the moral compilations and texts of spiritual guidance addresses itself directly to a particular kind of reader, a gendered, stereotypical figure of learning or devotion with whom the book's owner can identify. The first-person voice of the prayers, in turn, finds its embodiment in the person of the reader who, imitating the visual image of devotion, makes the text the basis of his or her own prayerful meditation.

Certain characteristics of MS fr. 24429 can be highlighted, finally, through comparison with a manuscript made at around the same time for Marie de Brabant, Bibl. de l'Arsenal MS 3142.[13] That the manuscript was prepared for Marie can be assumed from the half-page miniature that heads the opening text, *Cleomadés*. The miniature shows Adenet le Roi receiving the commission to compose *Cleomadés* from Marie de Brabant and Blanche, daughter of St. Louis; Marie's brother, Jean II de Brabant, also appears in the scene.[14] Marie is the central figure and also the largest, leaving little doubt that she, and not one of the other figures present, was the intended owner of the book. In addition to the collected works of Adenet le Roi and Jean Bodel's *Chanson des Saisnes,* the Arsenal manuscript contains an assortment of edifying material, including a collection of Marian poetry, the *dits* of Baudouin de Condé, the *Miserere* and *Charité* of the Reclus de Moliens, the *Fables* of Marie de France, the *Livre de philosophie et de moralité* of Alard de Cambrai, and various other didactic and devotional texts.

Like MS fr. 24429, then, MS 3142 presents a mixture of feudal history—albeit in fictionalized form—along with texts of moral and spiritual guidance. In both manuscripts one finds texts that draw on the imagery of feudal institutions and daily life—such as marriage, relations between lord and vassal, and the popular carol—for use as the basis of moral and spiritual allegory. This

---

rubric: "Chi commenche la maniere d'ourer ensi com uns sains abbés ouroit en devotion a Nostre Dame en ramembranche des .xv. joies que ele eut de son glorieus fill Jhesuxpist" [Here begins the manner of praying as a holy abbot prayed in devotion to Our Lady, in remembrance of the fifteen joys that she had from her glorious son Jesus Christ] (fol. 135r).

13. On the Arsenal manuscript, see Albert Henry, *Biographie d'Adenet / La Tradition manuscrite,* vol. 1 of *Les Oeuvres d'Adenet le Roi* (Bruges: De Tempel, 1951), 95–100. The Arsenal manuscript can be dated to the late thirteenth century and is illustrated in the same style as MS fr. 24429. I have discussed the contents and organization of MS 3142 in *From Song to Book,* 39–45.

14. This miniature is reproduced in Henry, *Biographie d'Adenet,* pl. 1 with description on pp. 96–97.

technique not only serves to cast religious and moral instruction in terms relevant to the lives of aristocratic readers but also encourages these readers to reflect on their own lives as images of a higher reality. The Old French *Eructavit,* in both manuscripts, explicates the Incarnation in the guise of a royal wedding. In MS fr. 24429, the poem entitled *Vertuz* presents the doctrine of sin and salvation in terms of a feudal lord wronged by one of his men; a similar image, more elaborately worked out as narrative with commentary, is the basis for the *Dit des .iiii. serurs* in MS 3142.[15] The *Moralité sur ces .vi. vers,* also in MS 3142, presents a reading of a simple dance song as a moral allegory warning against the temptations of the flesh. And the *Fables* of Marie de France present a series of simple tales based on the stereotypical behavior of animals and humans and used as the illustration of moral points. Through such texts as these, the lay reader is introduced to techniques of moralization and allegorization that he or she can then apply to other texts or even to real-life situations.

The use of mnemonic images and frames for moral and devotional instruction is also common to both manuscripts. We saw, for example, the use of the fifteen joys of the Virgin in the *Meditacion* as a device for meditation and prayer. Many of the Marian poems of MS 3142 are similarly organized around mnemonic patterns: the alphabet, the tales of the Old Testament, or the well-known words of the Ave Maria. The *dits* of Baudouin de Condé can be seen in this light as well. Each presents a commentary on social comportment or, less commonly, religious sentiment. In most cases the poem is constructed around a central image that serves as underlying metaphor—the dragon as an image of slander, the fur-lined cloak as an image of personal honor—and the image is illustrated in the miniature that heads the *dit.* Once again the reader is presented first with a visual image, then with a text that explicates that image—a presentation that engages both the visual imagination and the intellect in the process of moral instruction.

The image of Marie de Brabant that emerges from MS 3142 is that of literary patron. The figure of the author is an important iconographic motif throughout the codex. The codex opens with the elaborate illustration of Marie as patron of Adenet le Roi, and other depictions of Adenet as author appear at later points. In addition, the manuscript features author portraits of Marie de France, Alard de Cambrai, the Reclus de Moliens, and Jean Bodel, as well as the various named and unnamed authors of the Marian poems, most of which

---

15. See Arthur Långfors, "Notice des manuscrits 535 de Metz et 10.047 des nouvelles acquisitions françaises de la Bibliothèque Nationale, suivie de cinq poèmes français sur la parabole des quatre filles de Dieu," *Notices et extraits* 42:213–48.

are headed with the image of a cleric holding a scroll or kneeling before the Virgin.[16] A negative image of the royal patron appears at the end of the manuscript, where the final entry, the *Proverbes Seneke le philosophe,* is headed with an image of Seneca's suicide observed by Nero. The overall effect of this long series of author figures is to suggest that each of them is offering his or her text to Marie de Brabant, just as Adenet did at the beginning of the manuscript. And—unlike Nero, the archetypal evil ruler—Marie will receive these works in goodwill and profit from them. The manuscript as a whole implicitly casts her in the role of the educated monarch and posits a continuum linking the many ancient and medieval authors who successfully or unsuccessfully offered their wisdom to the aristocracy. This fundamental idea is stated explicitly and applied directly to Marie de Brabant in the prologue to a calendar that was prepared for her use, the *Kalendarium regine,* a copy of which survives in Bibl. Nat. lat. 15171. Here the author cites Vegetius on the ancient custom of preparing books for the edification of princes and cites Plato on the blessings of a learned ruler. He touches on Alexandar, Julius Caesar, and Charlemagne as examples of wise kings who fostered arts and letters, and then he announces the dedication to Marie of his own book, a calendar equipped with astronomical and meteorological teachings (fol. 88r–v). In this way Marie and her court writer are inscribed in a tradition of collaboration between scholars and noble patrons that extends back to antiquity and is integral to the well-being of the realm and to the advancement of civilization.

The presence of the patron and intended reader is slightly different in our two manuscripts prepared for French queens. MS 3142 uses heraldic emblems to identify the queen to whom it is offered, while the queen in MS fr. 24429 is unidentified. Both manuscripts contain a mixture of historical, moral, and devotional material. In the Arsenal manuscript, however, the queen's role is primarily that of noble patron of letters, while in MS fr. 24429 she is presented as a figure of piety. There is of course no contradiction between these two roles, and it is entirely possible that both books were prepared for Marie de Brabant.

Despite their differences, the two manuscripts made for a queen exemplify many of the same practices. In both cases, an assortment of texts—the majority of which were not composed for the patron in question—is shaped into a collection aimed at a specific reader. The personalization of the manuscript is not absolute and does not touch on every aspect of the book or on every text within it; it is more subtle than that, residing in details and intermittent re-

---

16. Only one poem, an anonymous *Salus de Nostre Dame,* in which the opening words of each stanza provide the Latin text of the Ave Maria, is headed with a miniature showing a woman in prayer before the Virgin, perhaps in reference to the female owner of the manuscript (fol. 299v).

minders. Nonetheless each book does address itself to its queenly reader, presenting her with an idealized image of herself; and this framework does impose a certain unity on the anthology, causing particular textual motifs to stand out. Each book makes use of techniques of allegorization and visual imaging that provide the lay reader with a means of accessing and remembering complex moral teachings and religious doctrines; each provides a wealth of material for meditative reading and recollection. As such, neither manuscript is particularly unusual. Rather, they stand as eloquent and sumptuous testimony to medieval reading practices, reflecting the extent to which both the expected use of texts and the personality of a noble patron could affect the material presentation of vernacular literature.

APPENDIX: PARIS, BIBL. NAT. FR. 24429

The manuscript originally began with a compilation of prose saints' vitae now MS 588 of the Bibliothèque Sainte-Geneviève, Paris. The first fifteen texts listed below are in prose; those that follow are in verse.

1. *Ici commance le nombre des anz et des aages des sainz et apostoiles et des empereeurs de Romme, et des roys de France, et de la nativité nostre Seingneur, jusques a nostre tens d'orendroit* (A time line from the year 1 to the year 1338; fols. 2r–17v)

2. *Les aages du monde*
   Inc.: "Se tu vues savoir les tens des aages . . ." (fol. 18r)
   Exp.: ". . . Et puis Urbains, qui nez fu de Troies en Champaingne." (fol. 25r)

3. *Ci commance li livres des pierres precieuses que on apele lapidaire*[17]
   Inc.: "Evaus fu un riches foys . . ." (fol. 25r)
   Exp.: ". . . Maintes les portent qui ne sevent que c'est, fors qu'il en sont asne du porter." (fol. 28r)

4. *Auctoritez*[18]
   Inc.: "Or oiez que nostre Sires dit en l'evangile . . ." (fol. 28v)
   Exp.: ". . . Mes contre luxure n'a mestier combatre, mes foïr." (fol. 34r)

5. *Moralitez*[19]

---

17. See Paul Meyer, "Les Plus Anciens Lapidaires français," *Romania* 38 (1909): 47, 57, 267.
18. See Meyer, "MS Egerton 745," 551.
19. See ibid., 555.

Inc.: "Talent m'espris que je raconte ce des philosophes . . ." (fol. 34r)

Exp.: ". . . Ainçois doit l'en metre us et painne a faire ce que il commandent." (fol. 45v)

6. *Ce sont les vers d'aumosne*[20]

    Inc.: "Aumosne anestoie et monteplie . . ." (fol. 45v)

    Exp.: ". . . qui selonc son pooir ne les tent vers le povre." (fol. 46r)

7. No rubric; instructions for confession

    Inc.: "A celui qui a sainte confession aproche doit dire li prestres . . ." (fol. 46r)

    Exp.: ". . . et si doit jeuner touz les vendredis." (fol. 49r)

8. *L'exposition de la pater noster*

    Inc.: "Pater noster qui es in celis . . ." (fol. 49r)

    Exp.: ". . . et le bien qui est gloire pardurable. Amen." (fol. 51r)

9. *Ici commance .i. sermon monseingneur Saint Pols*

    Inc.: "Christus factus est pro nobis obediens patri usque ad mortem . . ." (fol. 51r)

    Exp.: ". . . a la quele nous veille mener celui qui regne et regnera sanz fin. Amen." (fol. 53v)

10. *Ici commance .i. sermon Saint Gringoire pape*[21]

    Inc.: "Nous avons oï en la leçon de la saint Evangile la voiz nostre Seingneur . . ." (fol. 53v)

    Exp.: ". . . Et cil le vos otroit a cui honeur et gloire est, par toz les siecles des siecles. Amen." (fol. 54v)

11. *Le secont sermon Saint Gringoire*

    Inc.: "Seingneurs, tant devons creimbre li jor . . ." (fol. 54v)

    Exp.: ". . . et avec le Saint Esperit par toz les siecles des siecles. Amen." (fol. 55r)

12. *Le tiers sermon Saint Gringoire*

    Inc.: "Seingneurs freres, nous avons [oï] ce que li apostres dit . . ." (fol. 55r)

    Exp.: ". . . que nos nous puissons eschaper." (fol. 56v)

13. *Ici laidange couvoitise*[22]

    Inc.: "Nus ne puet aler . . ." (fol. 56v)

    Exp.: ". . . ou la saouletez est du ventre." (fol. 57r)

---

20. See ibid., 544.

21. On this and the following two sermons, see ibid., 543–44. Meyer reports having found no trace of these sermons in Gregory's corpus.

22. See ibid., 541.

14. *Ici commance le sermon mon seingneur Saint Beneoit ou commance-
    ment de sa ruile*[23]
    Inc.: "Escoute filz les comandemenz de ton mestre . . ." (fol. 57r)
    Exp.: ". . . Les officines ou l'en doit totes ces choses faire et tenir sont
    les cloistres des abaies et des bones congregations." (fol. 58r)
15. *Ci sont meditacions*[24]
    Inc.: "On dit en reprovier que qui bien ainme a tart oublie . . ." (fol.
    58v)
    Exp.: ". . . A garir de luxure couvient confession, jeunes, et oroisons."
    (fol. 63r)
16. *Ce sont les vers de la mort*[25]
    Inc.: "Mors qui m'as mis muer en mue . . ." (fol. 63r)
    Exp.: ". . . J'aim miex mes pois et ma poree." (fol. 66v)
17. *Du bon ange et du mauves*[26]
    Inc.: "Seingneurs, de par dieu vos semon . . ." (fol. 66v)
    Exp.: ". . . Qu'il seront quites de legier." (fol. 69v)
18. *Ici commancent les .vii. vertuz*
    Inc.: "Vous qui creance en dieu avez . . ." (fol. 69v)
    Exp.: ". . . Qui racine sont de tot mal." (fol. 69v)
19. *Ici sont les .vii. principaus vices*
    Inc.: "Le premerain nommer vos veil . . ." (fol. 69v)
    Exp.: ". . . Fors seul itant com fet aura." (fol. 73r)

23. Langlois refers to this text as the prologue of the Rule of St. Benedict ("Notice des manuscrits français et provençaux," 199). Meyer identifies it as a translation of the Rule of St. Benedict ("MS Egerton 745," 541–42).

24. See Langlois, "Notices des manuscrits français et provençaux," 200; Meyer, "MS Egerton 745," 542–43. The text in the Vatican manuscript lacks the descriptions of the individual joys. The text found in MS fr. 24429 is a conflation of entries 5–8 in the Egerton manuscript. The Egerton manuscript lacks the first part of the prologue appearing in MS fr. 24429, as well as the explanation of how to use the joys in meditation. The prayer inserted into the middle of the fifteen joys in MS fr. 24429 appears in the Egerton manuscript following the discussion of virtues and vices with which the text in fr. 24429 closes. In MS Bibl. Nat. fr. 25462, the prologue is essentially the same as in MS fr. 24429, aside from the change in dedication to a male reader, but the fifteen joys are slightly different; the prayer is included in the description of the eleventh joy, here identified as the Virgin's patience throughout the Passion; the explanation of how to use the joys in meditation is lacking.

25. The text can be attributed to Hélinand de Froidement. See Langlois, "Notices des manuscrits français et provençaux," 200; Meyer, "Notice du MS de l'Arsenal 5201," *Romania* 16 (1887): 64.

26. The poem describes the fate of the soul after death. It has been edited by Hartmut Kleineidam, in *Li Ver de Couloigne: Du bon ange et du mauvés,* Beiträge zur romanische Philologie des Mittelalters 3 (Munich: Hüber, 1968).

20. *Ici commance la conception Nostre Dame*[27]

Inc.: "Ou non dieu qui nous doint sa grace . . ." (fol. 73r)

Exp.: ". . . Amen amen chascun en die." (fol. 83v)

21. *Ici commance la moralité des .ii[i]. Maries et l'amor que la Magdalene ot et mostra de Nostre Seingneur ihesucrist*[28]

Inc.: "Puis que chanter me semont . . ." (fol. 83v)

Exp.: ". . . Bessiez la teste tuit enclin." (fol. 94v)

22. *Ici commance l'estoire de Joseph, comment ses freres le vendirent en Egypte*[29]

Inc.: "D'une ancienne estoire . . ." (fol. 94v)

Exp.: ". . . Pardevant la seue face. Amen." (fol. 105r)

23. *Ici commance Chaton*[30]

Inc.: "Seingnors vos qui metez voz cures . . ." (fol. 105r)

Exp.: ". . . Qui ne velt qu'autre face a li." (fol. 110v)

24. *Ici commance le romans de l'amor que nostre Sire ot a homme*[31]

Inc.: "Bien est amez qui amors aimme . . ." (fol. 110v)

Exp.: ". . . Uns et trebles en unité. Amen." (fol. 115v)

25. *Vertuz*[32]

Inc.: "Questionner vos veil d'un jugement . . ." (fol. 115v)

Exp.: ". . . Qui por avoir font de dieu livroisons. / Explicit li tretiez des vertuz." (fol. 117r)

---

27. This text, treated as a single unit in the manuscript, is in reality a pastiche of several texts that are often combined in the manuscript tradition. One finds here Wace's *Conception Nostre Dame* (fols. 73r–79r); a transitional passage leading to the text that follows (fol. 79r–v); the *Histoire des Trois Maries,* sometimes attributed to Wace (fols. 79v–80v); and the *Assomption Nostre Dame,* also sometimes attributed to Wace (fols. 80v–83v). See Meyer, "Légendes hagiographiques en françois," *Histoire Littéraire de la France* 33 (1906): 363–66; Meyer, "Notice du MS de l'Arsenal 5201," 53–56; Mario Eusebio, "Il manoscritto Ottoboniano Lat. 1473 della Biblioteca Vaticana," *Romania* 92 (1971): 380–87.

28. The title rubric as well as the entry in the table of contents at the close of MS Ste-Geneviève 588 read, "moralité des .ii. Maries," but an internal rubric reads, "C'est des .iii. Maries" (fol. 87v). The text is rubricated "Les mortalitez [*sic*] des .iii. Maries et l'amor que diex Nostre Seigneur mostra a la Magdalene" in MS Vat. Reg. 1682 (fol. 69r).

29. See Paul Meyer, "Légendes hagiographiques en françois," *Histoire Littéraire de la France* 33 (1906): 359. The poem has been edited by Ernst Sass, in *L'Estoire Joseph,* Gesellschaft für Romanische Literatur 12 (Dresden: Gesellschaft für romanische Literatur; Halle: Max Niemeyer, 1906).

30. Published by J. Ulrich, in "Die Übersetzung der Distichen des Pseudo-Cato von Jean de Paris," *Romanische Forschungen* 15 (1903–4): 41–69.

31. Edited by Félix Lecoy, in "*De l'amor que Dex a a home:* Poème religieux du XIIIe siècle," *Romania* 81 (1960): 199–240.

32. This is actually vv. 721–976 of the *Roman des romans,* ed. I. C. Lecompte, Elliott Monographs 14 (Princeton: Princeton University Press, 1923; reprint, New York: Kraus, 1965).

26. *Ici commance Eructavit*[33]
   Inc.: "La chançon que David fist . . ." (fol. 117v)
   Exp.: ". . . A lui loer et beneir. Amen." (fol. 130v)

27. *Ici commancent les .ix. manieres des painnes d'enfer*
   Inc.: "Qui liroit en la vie Job . . ." (fol. 130v)
   Exp.: ". . . Ce que tu consirres si donne." (fol. 131v)

28. *Ce sont les .x. commandemenz*[34]
   Inc.: "Aillors nos dit la sainte page . . ." (fol. 132r)
   Exp.: ". . . Per infinita seculorum secula. Amen." (fol. 132v)

29. *Ici commance un ensaingnement*
   Inc.: "Qui velt estre beneurez . . ." (fol. 132v)
   Exp.: ". . . Que nous le puisson fere. Amen." (fol. 133v)

30. *Ici commancent les painnes et les tormenz d'enfer que Saint Michiel l'archange moustra a Saint Pol l'apostre avant que il receust mort*[35]
   Inc.: "Seingneurs, or escoutez qui dameldieu amez . . ." (fol. 133v)
   Exp.: ". . . En pardurable vie en son saintisme fie. Amen." (fol. 140v)

31. *Ici commance la vie ma dame Sainte Thaise, c'uns sainz hermites qui avoit non Pannuces fist retraire de folie*
   Inc.: "Qui dieu donne droit sen certes moult puet haïr . . ." (fol. 140v)
   Exp.: ". . . Merci aiez de moi, ne me lessiez perir. Amen." (fol. 161v)

33. Edited by T. Atkinson Jenkins, *Eructavit: An Old French Metrical Paraphrase of Psalm XLIV*, Gesellschaft für Romanische Literatur 20 (Dresden: Gesellschaft für romanische Literatur; Halle: Max Niemeyer, 1909).

34. The ten commandments presented here correspond only in part to those of the Bible, covering the following points: to love God, to love one's neighbor, not to kill, not to envy, not to tell lies, not to commit usury, not to commit adultery, to honor one's parents, to treat others as one would wish to be treated oneself, not to covet.

35. Paul Meyer publishes an excerpt of thirteen quatrains from this poem in "Notice sur la *Bible des sept états du monde* de Geufroi de Paris," *Notices et extraits* 39, no. 1 (1909): 305–7. In "*La Descente de Saint Paul en enfer:* Poème français composé en Angleterre," *Romania* 24 (1895): 360, Meyer argues that the text in MS fr. 24429 is unrelated to the *Visio Sancti Pauli* and its various French redactions.

A Carolingian Schoolbook?
The Manuscript Tradition of Alcuin's
De fide and Related Treatises

E. Ann Matter

This chapter is an exploration of the possibility that what may seem to us a "miscellaneous" collection of treatises in medieval manuscripts had an internal logic that takes some effort to understand. My example is a series of works that, while appearing to the modern reader as a miscellaneous collection of different genres, nevertheless occur together in a startling number of early medieval manuscripts of the writings of Alcuin of York. These texts include trinitarian theology (*De fide Sanctae Trinitatis* and *De Trinitate ad Fredegisum quaestiones XXVIII*), Christian anthropology (*De anima*), a litany (*Adesto),* an elegiac poem (*Qui mare*), and a paraphrasing commentary on the Nicene Creed (*Credimus*).[1]

The relationship between manuscript witnesses for Alcuin's works and their printed versions is an interesting subject in its own right. The editions of Alcuin from which we still must work are reprintings of the 1617 Paris edition of André Duchesne (Quercetanus) and the 1777 Regensburg edition of Foster Froben (Frobenius). Froben's edition is the standard text of Alcuin's works, as it appears in volumes 100 and 101 of J. P. Migne's *Patrologia Latina (PL).*[2] Even a cursory evaluation of Alcuin's printed editions shows how manuscript

---

1. Migne, *PL,* 101:13–54, 57–64, 639–47, 55–56, 647–48, and 56–58, respectively.

2. I am grateful to Burton Van Name Edwards for his unpublished study of the *De fide* manuscript tradition. For the history of the printed editions of Alcuin, see Wilber Samuel Howell, *The Rhetoric of Alcuin and Charlemagne* (Princeton: Princeton University Press, 1941), 8–22. Frobenius's edition is reprinted by J. P. Migne in *PL,* vols. 100–101.

witnesses have been changed and rearranged for the sake of "modern" points of view about which texts belong together. Consider, for example, the transformation of Alcuin's "dialogues" from manuscript to print.

Alcuin certainly wrote a number of known question-and-answer texts, and he perhaps authored a good many more. The most sophisticated of these bear the marks of the Ciceronian and Augustinian dialogues so well known to medieval readers: characterization, dispute over conflicting ideas, and what Peter von Moos has described as "the art of instruction by dialogue."[3] Five of these treatises have been grouped together since Froben's edition, in a collection known as the *Opera didascalica:* they are reprinted in the *PL* in this form and are being critically edited by Martin Irwin for the Corpus Christianorum Continuatio Medievalis (CCCM) series published by Brepols in Turnhout, Belgium. These five treatises are *Grammatica, De orthographia, Dialogus de rhetorica et virtutibus, De dialectica,* and *Pippini regalis et nobilissimi juvenis disputatio cum Albino scholastico;* in the *PL* they appear with a sixth treatise, *De cursu et saltu lunae ac bisexto.*[4]

However, the manuscript witnesses and their presentation suggest that neither Alcuin nor the medieval scribes who copied his works thought of them as a coherent group labeled *Opera didascalica.* No known manuscript transmits all of these works together, although three manuscripts from the Bayerische Staatsbibliothek in Munich, Clm 13084 and 14377 (both ninth/tenth century from St. Emmeram) and Clm 6407 (ninth century from Freising), contain both the *Dialogus de rhetorica et virtutibus* (termed a *disputatio* by the manuscripts) and the *De dialectica.* Two of these manuscripts include a series of seventeen schematic diagrams (dealing, for instance, with the parts of rhetoric; the parts of philosophy; the parts of an oration; and the parts of prudence, justice, temperance, and fortitude), which are reprinted by Migne.[5] But the idea of a collection of Alcuin's dialogues on the trivium and related subjects by Alcuin clearly dates only to the eighteenth century.

The collection of treatises I mentioned at the beginning of this chapter has also been reclassified by Froben, but in the opposite way; that is, they have been separated from one another rather than grouped together artificially. The

---

3. Peter von Moos, "Monologue, Dialogue, and 'Disputatio' in the Twelfth Century" (paper presented at the Twenty-Third Congress on Medieval Studies, Kalamazoo, Michigan, 1988), 1. For an analysis of the differences between Platonic and Ciceronian dialogue, see K. J. Wilson, *Incomplete Fictions: The Formation of English Renaissance Dialogue* (Washington, DC: Catholic University of America Press, 1985), 23–45. For Alcuin's dialogues, see E. Ann Matter, "Alcuin's Question-and-Answer Texts," *Rivista di storia della filosofia* 4 (1990): 645–56.

4. *PL,* 101:849–1002.

5. Munich, Clm 13084, f. 47; Clm 6407, f. 38 (*PL,* 101:949–50).

disruption is neither drastic nor total: *PL* 101 keeps together the two trinitarian treatises (*De fide* and the *Quaestiones* to Fredegisius) as well as the short *Adesto* and *Credimus* that appear between them, under the category "Pars Tertia: Opuscula Dogmatica";[6] but the *De anima* and the short poem *Qui mare* are found instead among the works in "Pars Quarta: Opera Liturgica et Moralia."[7] Let us examine these treatises as they appear in medieval manuscripts.

This particular set of works by Alcuin is generously witnessed in the extant manuscripts, almost embarrassingly so. The appendix at the end of this chapter by no means lists all of the manuscripts of these works. It includes information about only the forty-five most important manuscripts, that is, those of the ninth and tenth centuries and those from the eleventh, twelfth, and thirteenth centuries from major collections that may testify to the history of the textual transmission. These are the manuscripts our team of Alcuin editors (Celia Chazelle of Trenton State University, John Cavadini of the University of Notre Dame, and myself) is using for a critical edition of five out of six of these treatises. (The sixth, *De anima,* is being edited by Paul Szarmach, director of the Medieval Institute at Western Michigan University, Kalamazoo, Michigan). All six treatises are scheduled to appear together in the CCCM series.

It is not very often that a team of editors has as many as forty-five manuscripts that need to be considered for a ninth-century treatise. The vast majority of the manuscripts (thirty-six out of forty-five) date from the ninth or tenth century, and the majority of these (twenty-two) can be firmly dated to the ninth century. Obviously, in the two centuries after its composition, the treatise *De fide* was extremely popular. *De fide* was most often found with the collection of works I briefly described at the beginning of this paper: the *Adesto,* the *Credimus,* the *Quaestiones ad Fredegesium,* the *De anima,* and the *Qui mare.* Thirteen of these manuscripts contain all six of these treatises, and eight more contain at least five of the six.

The entire collection is found overwhelmingly in the earlier manuscripts— those of the ninth and tenth centuries. As is demonstrated in the appendix, these manuscripts come from all corners of Europe: from various regions of France, that is, Carcassonne (London, B.L. Harley 4980), Orléans (Paris, B.N. lat. 2341), Limoges (Paris, B.N. lat. 2826), the monasteries of northern France (the Valenciennes and Verdun manuscripts), and Burgundy (Munich, Clm 28140); from the South German monasteries of St. Emmeram, Tegernsee, and Reichenau; from Helmstedt and Weissenburg and the Cathedral School of

---

6. *PL,* 101:13–64.
7. *PL,* 101:639–48.

Arno of Salzburg (manuscripts from Munich and Wolfenbüttel); from Switzer-
land (St. Gall); and from both northern and southern Italy (manuscripts from
Verona and the Monte Cassino manuscript in Rome's Biblioteca Casanatense).
One cannot say that the ninth- and tenth-century manuscripts always presented
the treatises together, since *De fide* is found in different collections, usually
other theological collections, in early manuscripts now in Angers, Autun,
Avranches, Ivrea, and Zurich. But in general, I think it is fair to claim that *De
fide* was most often part of this particular collection of treatises until the
eleventh or twelfth centuries, when it tended to be copied along with other
combinations of theological works.

A question with serious repercussions for theories of literature is whether
this arrangement was the intention of the author. Several manuscripts might
give us some clue. Two of these are closest to Alcuin in date and provenance:
Paris, B.N. lat. 2341 (from Orléans, second quarter of the ninth century), and
Paris, B.N. lat. 2826 (from St. Martial of Limoges, first quarter of the ninth
century); but neither comes very close to being a manuscript of Alcuin, who
died in 804. The third is a ninth-century Munich manuscript, Clm 15813,
which Bischoff has identified as being in the "Arn-Stil," that is, one of the
manuscripts that can be identified with Bishop Arno of Salzburg, one of Alcuin's favorite pupils. Arno brought many treatises home to Austria with him
and caused other copies, including this one, to be made in the scriptorium at
Salzburg.[8] So, even if the intention of Alcuin cannot (and probably should not)
be determined with any precision from these manuscripts, we can assert with
some assurance that Alcuin's pupils and their followers, including Arno of
Salzburg, tended to preserve (and therefore read) the *De fide* in the company of
several other treatises.

Once our editorial team reached this conclusion, it became obvious that we
needed to rethink the shape of the CCCM volumes devoted to the works of
Alcuin. Originally, John Cavadini had been approached by the editors at
Brepols with a request to undertake a critical edition of *De fide* along with other
theological works by Alcuin, notably the anti-Adoptionist treatises, which,
along with *De fide,* Cavadini is now in the process of translating for the Fathers
of the Church series, and on which he has published an important monograph.[9]
Certainly, *De fide* should be seen in the light of the Adoptionist controversy,
since its section on the person of Christ (book 3, the longest and most compli-

---

8. Bernhard Bischoff, *Die südostdeutschen Schreibschulen und Bibliotheken in der Ka-
rolingerzeit,* 2 vols. (Wiesbaden: O. Harrassowitz, 1960–80), 2:61–65, 152.

9. John C. Cavadini, *The Last Christology of the West* (Philadelphia: University of Pennsylvania Press, 1993).

cated part of the treatise) includes refutations of Adoptionist theology, or at least what Alcuin understood as Adoptionist theology. Alcuin argues, for example, that Christ was born of the Holy Spirit and the Virgin Mary (chaps. 3, 11, and 14) and that the Son is equal and in no way less than the Father (chap. 7); and he offers a careful discussion of what did happen at the baptism of Jesus (chap. 17).

Despite these thematic links between *De fide* and Alcuin's anti-Adoptionist writings, it is nevertheless evident that medieval readers of *De fide* did not tend to categorize it with the works of Alcuin against Felix and Elipandus but placed it instead in a collection that includes a number of what could be understood as instructional materials: litanies, a treatise on the soul, and, notably, a question-and-answer text. It seems that we would be missing an unusual opportunity to study medieval theology in its own context, rather than according to modern criteria, if we allowed *De fide* to be published with a group of anti-Adoptionist writings, separated from works in whose company it was transmitted in the first two centuries of its existence.

Consequently, we strongly urged Brepols that *De fide* be published together with the other works brought together in these manuscripts: *De Trinitate ad Fredegesium, De anima, Adesto, Qui mare,* and *Credimus.* We requested that Paul Szarmach's editing of *De anima* be included in the same volume as the other five works of the *De fide* collection. After some negotiation between editors and publishers, our request was granted.

This means that eventually a single volume of the Corpus Christianorum Continuatio Medievalis will present a collection of treatises by Alcuin arranged in an explicitly Carolingian order. The volume will probably bear a composite title, such as *Alcuini De fide, De Trinitate ad Fredegesium quaestiones, De anima,* the shorter works being subsumed under the major (in the sense of longer) ones. It has been the intention of this chapter to show how a collection of this sort would make good sense historically. As soon as the collection is in print, new avenues of interpreting this collection of Alcuin's writings can begin to be explored. Scholars of the twenty-first century will then study Alcuin's writings as part of a new, more theoretical, and more acutely contextualized approach in medieval studies.

This collection will, first of all, throw new light on the medieval understanding of theology—practical and theoretical, as far as this can be reconstructed. We will be able to recognize what connections in Carolingian theology were taken for granted, connections that are no longer part of our horizon of expectations. The collection will also bring together various aspects of theological investigation: dogmatics, moral theology, worship, and credal formulations. It will include original writings, restatement of the Fathers (especially Augustine), a letter to a friend, poetry, commentary (on the Nicene Creed), and an official contribution to imperial theology. That a treatise on the Trinity is followed by short liturgical works, a series of question-and-answer texts in the style of the Carolingian schoolroom, and a meditation on the reflection of the Trinity in the human soul suggests that this group of texts may have been a deliberate attempt at reformatting and reshaping the trinitarian mystery, most likely for teaching future Christian monks and priests.[10]

The political importance of this collection is evident in the full title of the longest treatise of the series, which always occurs at the beginning: *De fide sanctae et individuae Trinitatis ad gloriosum imperatorem Carolum Magnum Deo devotum.* The dedication to Charlemagne is not incidental, for many of Alcuin's educational treatises were shaped for and in the context of the imperial court. Although this series of texts was preserved by scribes for monastic and cathedral schools, it may have been originally intended for the theological education of the nobility. In this way, the collection may be more than just a schoolbook; it may represent a previously unexamined witness to the Carolingian theological enterprise, nothing short of the official Carolingian textbook of theology.

Such an assertion would have to be argued from intentionality, while the simpler claim, that this compendium was read as a schoolbook of theology, seems easily apparent. The manuscript testimony has been available all these centuries. It only takes the type of critical question asked by this volume to see that an apparently arbitrary miscellany can be recognized as a miscellany with an intention.

---

10. I am grateful to Kent Emery for this suggestion about the relationship of *De anima* to the other treatises in the collection.

MS/Date	De fide Sanctae Trinitatis	Adesto	Credimus	De Trinitate ad Fredegesium quaestiones XXVIII	De anima	Qui mare
Angers B.M. 279 (St. Aubin, ix)	1					
Autun B.M. 36 (ix–x)	1					
Avranches B.M. 109 (Mont-St.-Michel, x)	1					
Brussels, B.R. 1373 (St. Laurent, Liege, xii)	1	2	3	4	5	
Freiburg i. Br. Univ. 147 (x–xi)	1					
Ghent B.M. 581 (St. Maximin, Trier, xii)	1		2	2		
Göttingen, Univ. B. theol. 99 (ix–x)	1					
Ivrea, B. capit. 16 (x)	1					
Laon, B.M. 445 (ix–x)	1					
Leiden, Univ. B.P.L. 173 (x)	1	3	2	4	5	
London, B.L. Harley 4980 (Carcassone, ix)	1	3	2	4	5	6
London, B.L. Royal 6.A.xii (xi)	1			4	2	3
Madrid, B.N. 373 (Brindisi, x)	1					
Metz, B.M. 494 (St. Arnulf, xi)	1					
Milan, Ambr. S.17 sup. (x)	1	2	3	4	5	
Monte Cassino, Badia 3KK (890)	1			2	3	
Montpellier, Ec. Med. H.141 (xi)	1	4	2		3	5
Munich, Clm 14510 (St. Emmeram, Regensburg, ix)	1	2	3	4	5	6
Munich, Clm 14614 (St. Emmeram, ix)	1	2	3	4	5	6
Munich, Clm 15813 (Salzburg, ix)	1	2	3	4	5	6
Munich, Clm 18372 (Tegernsee, ix)	1	2	3	4	5	6
Munich, Clm 28140 (Burgundy?, 825–50)	1	3	2	4	5	6

Paris, B.N. lat. 2341 (Orléans, 825–50)	1	3	2	4	5	6
Paris, B.N. lat. 2390 (Moissac, xii)	1	2	3	4	5	6
Paris, B.N. lat. 2826 (St. Martial, Limoges, 800–825)	1	2	3	4	5	
Paris, B.N. lat 2849 (ix)	1	2	3	4	5	
Paris, B.N. lat. 2849a (x)	1			2		
Paris, B.N. lat. 2850 (St. Nazarius, Carcassone, xiii)	1	2	3	4	5	6
Paris, B.N. lat. 16362 (Sorbonne, xii)	1			2	3	6
Rome, B. Cas. 641 (Monte Cassino, 811–12)	1	2		4	5	3
St. Gall, Stiftsb. 272 (ix)	1				2	6
St. Gall, Stiftsb. 276 (ix)	1	2	3		5	6
Saint Michel, B.M. (x)	1	2	3	4		
Salisbury, Cath. 165 (xii)	1		2	3	4	
Troyes, B.M. 1165 (ix/x)	1			2	3	
Troyes, B.M. 1528 (ix)	1			2		
Valenciennes, B.M. 195 (St. Amand, ix)	1	2	3	4	5	
Vatican, Vat. lat. 650 (x)	1	2	3	4	5	
Vatican, Reg. lat. 231 (France, 820–30)	1	2	3	4	5	6
Verdun, B.M. 67 (St. Vito, xi)	1	2	3	4	5	
Verona, B. capit. LXVII (x)	1	2	3	4	5	6
Wolfenbüttel, Herz. Bib. 1147 (Helmstedt, ix)	1			2	3	
Wolfenbüttel, Herz. Bib. 4177 (Weissenburg, ix)	1			2	3	
Würzburg, Univ. M.P.th.f.58 (830–50)	1					
Zurich, Zentralb. Rh. 102 (Reichenau, x)	1				2	

A Cataloger's View

Barbara A. Shailor

To address the topic of miscellaneous manuscripts, I would like to begin by proposing that *miscellaneous* may not be an appropriate term for describing structurally or textually complex codices. Rather, it is possible to suggest that the physical format of a volume, the selection of texts, and the audience for whom the manuscript was intended can all reveal, on closer examination, that "miscellaneous" manuscripts are not as mixed or diverse as they may first appear. Often they have an internal coherence and a physical structure that is not initially evident either to the modern cataloger or to a scholar selectively editing one of several texts in a codex.

This chapter will attempt to formulate multiple answers to the question, from the viewpoint of a cataloger, what, if anything, is a miscellaneous manuscript? And this is not to suggest that this analysis will be all encompassing or will propose a definitive nomenclature. Rather, it is a selective look at four Beinecke manuscripts that are representative types of "miscellaneous" manuscripts.[1] All four manuscripts were produced and used in the fifteenth century and are not compilations of later owners or book dealers. There are two from institutional (i.e., monastic) contexts and two from personal collections. To-

The author would like to thank Dr. Consuelo W. Dutschke, who read and critiqued an early draft of this chapter, and Robert Babcock, Curator of Early Books and Manuscripts in the Beinecke Library, Yale University, who shared his insights on miscellaneous manuscripts, especially on the format of Marston MS 48.

1. In B. A. Shailor, *Catalogue of Medieval and Renaissance Manuscripts in the Beinecke Library, Yale University,* Medieval and Renaissance Texts and Studies (Binghamton, NY), vol. 1, MSS 1–250 (1984); vol. 2, MSS 251–500 (1987); vol. 3, Marston Manuscripts (1992).

gether they suggest a range or a spectrum of possibilities for a discussion of late medieval miscellaneous manuscripts.

Beinecke MS 377 is a small, compact, and attractively packaged volume produced in the second half of the fifteenth century, probably in Cologne.[2] Covered in dark brown calf and decorated with round and lozenge-shaped tools within diamonds and triangular areas, it bears the remains of hardware of a single fastening on the upper board. Turk's head knot placemarks appear on the fore edge to help the user locate the main text components within the manuscript.[3]

Even a cursory examination of the volume indicates that this is a composite manuscript formed from "booklets" or units of similar format that were individually produced and then bound together. The physical format of the volume and the uniformity of appearance of the discrete booklets suggest that, although there are four booklets and twelve distinct texts included in the single volume,[4] the manuscript exhibits coherence of physical format throughout.

Throughout the manuscript the outer and inner conjugate leaves of each quire are of parchment and the remainder are of paper. Figure 1 reproduces folio 1r, the first leaf in the first booklet. The script is carefully executed, as are the rubrics and delicate initials in blue, red, purple, and green. The similarity between this opening parchment leaf and that of the first leaf of the third booklet (f. 47r) is immediately apparent (see fig. 2). Although the latter is written by different scribes and on paper with different watermarks from those appearing in part 1, the overall format of both folios, the style of script, and the design of the decoration are alike. Part 2 (not illustrated here) is consistent, though once again with minor variations. When one turns to the fourth and final booklet, containing a series of six short sermons, there occurs the most modest presentation for the four parts: a smaller, plainer, blue initial with less ambitious red penwork extending down the inner margin. In general, however, the layout for the four parts looks alike: the bounding lines for the text are frame ruled in the same manner and the dimensions and proportions of the written

---

2. See B. A. Shailor, *Catalogue,* 2:234–37, for the complete catalog entry.

3. It is not clear precisely when the codex was configured in its present format, since the binding has been restored; it is likely, however, that the present components were bound together in the late fifteenth century or possibly in the sixteenth.

4. The four booklets and their contents can be schematically arranged as follows: booklet 1, ff. 1r–32v, William of St. Thierry, *Epistola ad fratres de monte Dei;* booklet 2, ff. 35r–46v, Bernard of Clairvaux and Bernard of Cluny [?], *Sermones;* booklet 3, ff. 47r–82v, Bernard of Clairvaux, *De gradibus humilitatis et superbiae* and Jean, l'Homme de Dieu, *Tractatus de ordine vitae et morum institutione;* booklet 4, ff. 83r–99v, Bernard of Clairvaux, Nicholas of Clairvaux, *Sermones,* etc.

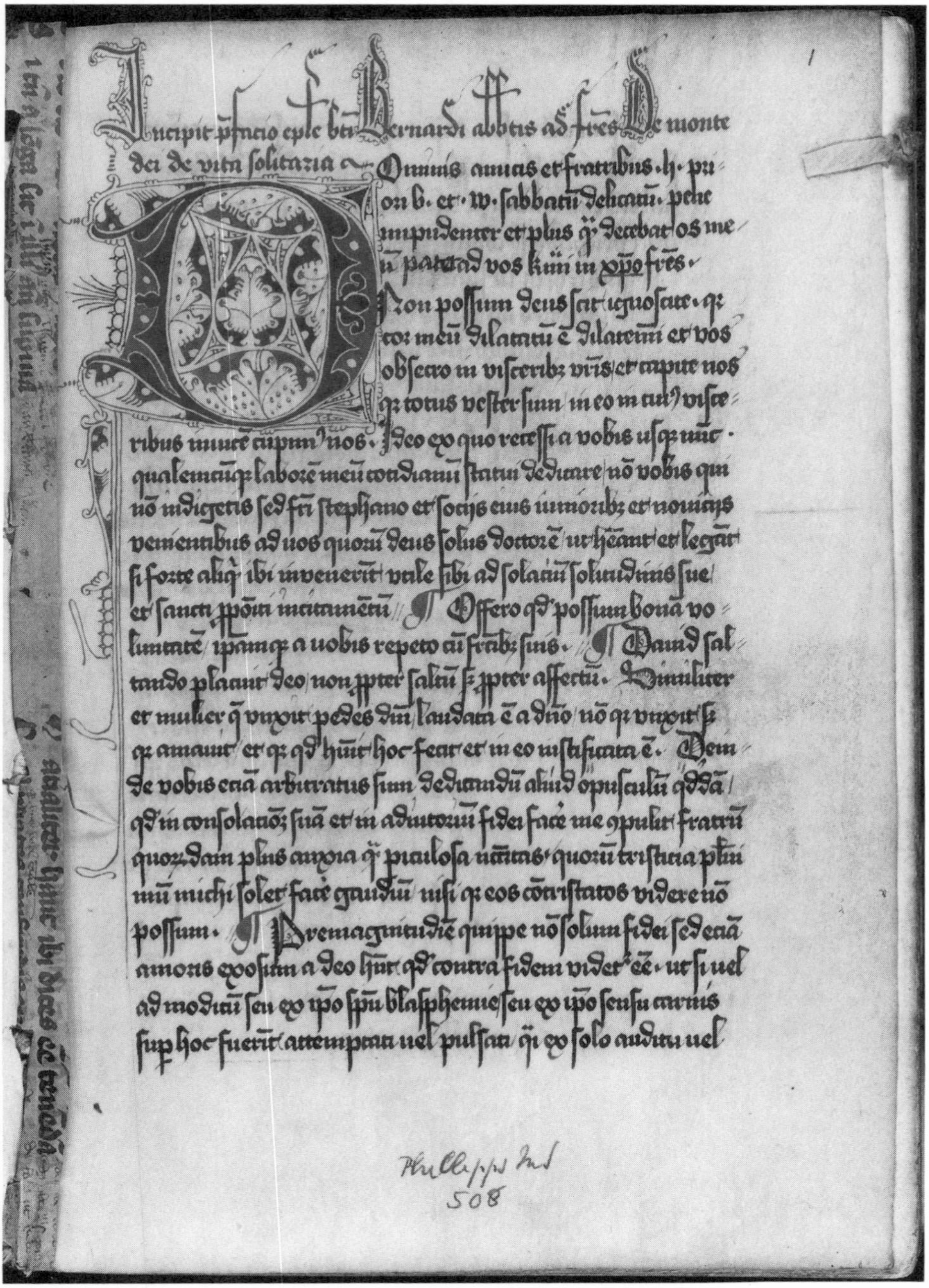

Fig. 1. Yale University, Beinecke Rare Book and Manuscript Library, MS 377, f. 1r

Incipit retractatio beati bernardi in librum de duodecim
gradibus humilitatis

In hoc opusculo cum illud de euangelio quod dominus ait
dicit vltimum iudicij se nescire ad aliquam finam confir-
mandam atque roborandam preferre in medium ipmude quod
dam apposui quod in euangelio scriptum non esse postea
deprehendi Nam cum textus? Habeat neque neque fili-
sat? ego deceptus magis quam fallere volens litte-
quippe immemor sed non sensibus/nec ipse iniquam fili? hois sat Vnde etiam tota ordiens sequente disptu
tatione eo eo quod non veraciter posui verum conatus
sum approbare assertionem Sed quia tale errore meu
multo postquam a me isde libellus editus/ a pluribus iam tra
scriptus fuit deprehendi cum non potui per tot iam libellos sparsu
persequi me iam noticiam credidi effugere ad professionis venire
Sed Alio quoque in loco quodam de seraphin opidx posui quod nunquam nunquam legi Vbi sane lector meus attendit quod ipmude quali-
puto dixeri volens videlicet non aliud quam putari quod certum red
dere de scripturis non valui Titulus quoque ipse qui de gradibus?
humilitatis inscribitur pro eo forsitan quod non humilitatis sed superbie
pocius sicut distinguit describitque videtur gradus calumpnia pa
tietur Sed hoc a minus intelligentibus vel actentibus eiusdem
tytuli racione quam tamen in fine opusculi ipse breuiter intimare
curam Sequitur duodecim gradus humilitatis

Duodecim? gradus? humilitatis est corde et opere humilitate
ostendere Vndecim? vt pauca et rationabilia loquatur
Decimus? si non sit facilis et promptus ad risum Nonus? e taciturn
tas ad interrogationem Octauus? tenere quod communis habet monasterij regu
la Septimus? est credere et pronunciare se omnibus viliorem Sextus
est ad omnia indignum seu inutile se confiteri et credere Quintus
confessio peccatorum Quartus obedientia in duris et asperis penam am
plecti Tercius omni obedientia se subdere maiori Secundus ipsam non amare

space are also similar. Parts 2, 3, and 4 use paper with closely related watermarks.[5]

Textually, the individual works within can be assigned by the modern-day cataloger to William of St. Thierry, Bernard of Cluny, Bernard of Clairvaux, Nicholas of Clairvaux, and others. But for the fifteenth-century institution that produced the volume the internal coherence is made apparent by a contemporary table of contents written on the front flyleaf.

Epistola beati Bernardi abbatis ad fratres de monte dei.
Sermo Beati Bernardi de annunciacione dominica.
Sermo eiusdem de villico iniquitatis.
Item tractatus de duodecim gradibus humilitatis.
Tractatus de uite [et] ordine et morum honestate.
Sermo eiusdem de septem panibus.
Sermo de beata virgine.
De obitu patris humberti.

Here the majority of the sermons, letters, and tractates were attributed to Bernard of Clairvaux, as is evident from the use of the Latin words *item* and *eiusdem*.[6] Whether or not the booklets in this volume were copied to be bound together in this particular sequence in a single codex is an intriguing question not only for this volume but for many others composed of fascicles. What is obvious about the codex is the harmonious consistency of format, contents, and medieval attribution of authorship, all of which would have been appreciated by the audience by whom it was owned and read: a fifteenth-century order of Augustinian canonesses in Cologne.[7]

The physical appearance of the second "institutional manuscript" is less aesthetically pleasing than the volume from Cologne and may perhaps be more representative of a miscellaneous manuscript from a monastic context. Marston MS 140 is a compilation of multiple texts in four distinct parts that appear, at least at first glance, not closely related thematically, but that have been neatly bound together, presumably shortly after they were copied.[8]

The codex has a sturdy monastic binding, with a kermes pink cover and the remains of one fastening, the catch on the lower board. There are traces of

---

5. Briquet Lettre Y 9182–84.

6. The same attributions occur in the rubrics for each text.

7. Inscription written above table of contents on front flyleaf: "Liber monasterij Sancti [name effaced] ordinis sancti Augustini canonissarum regularum in Colonia."

8. See B. A. Shailor, *Catalogue*, 3:269–75, for the complete catalog entry.

damage, presumably from a chain attachment, at the head of the lower board. Internal evidence suggests that at least part 1 was written around 1441;[9] paleographically speaking, all four parts could have been produced in the mid–fifteenth century or slightly later. A list of saints in a calendar, also in part 1 (ff. 3r–9r), supports ownership by an institution with Benedictine interests and a possible connection to Salzburg. Part 4 is signed by a scribe in Carinthia in southern Austria.[10]

This volume may perhaps be viewed as a "medieval almanac." The following quotation from a recent article in the *Los Angeles Times* about the *Old Farmer's Almanac*—now in its 201st year—provides a possible lens of interpretation: "at the heart of the Almanac, ever since Robert B. Thomas sold the first edition in Boston for six pence . . . , are the weather forecasts and the astronomical and astrological data that tell about the movement of the tides, the moon and the forces that, many believe, dictate everything from the best time to plant your corn to the optimum moment to castrate your bull or have surgery. In all this, there is the unspoken, somehow comforting message that our lives are subject to repeated patterns and a universal order."

What texts contained in the volume support this interpretation? From a cataloger's perspective, the codex begins as a conglomeration of short texts. Part 1, a mere thirteen leaves, contains virtually everything a religious institution might want to know about the calendar. For example, on folios 3r–9r occurs a calendar with extensive computational information, including columns for the cycles of conjunctions and oppositions of the sun and moon (each subdivided for the Golden Numbers, the hour, the minute, and the distinction of day or night); the calendar also includes the numerical calendar day, the dominical letter, the Roman calendar day, the quantity of the day (in hours and minutes), sunrise and sunset (each with hours and minutes), and an outer column with the indication of the bad-luck days (according to the "Egyptian" system of two days per month) and the name of the signs of the zodiac. The *claves terminorum* are signaled either in the margins or in the space for the saints. After three additional complementary texts occur the directions and charts reproduced in figure 3. On folio 10v is a diagram and explanation for determining the Golden Number and the *claves terminorum,* followed by a second diagram and explanation for determining the dominical letter. On the facing recto (f. 11r) is a diagram and explanation for determining the interval in

---

9. Folios 12v–13v contain a table for the years 1441–62, with phases of the moon on certain days, specifying the length or the conjunction or opposition.

10. The colophon on f. 268r reads: "Deo gramaczi / Finitum per me Georium diechercz [?] De falle Ivnensj [?] partibus karinthie."

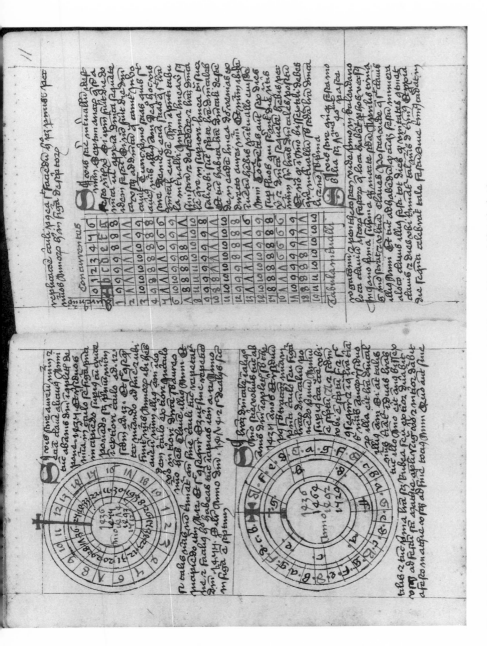

Fig. 3. Yale University, Beinecke Rare Book and Manuscript Library, Marston MS 140, f. 10v

days between the last Sunday of December and the first day of January. At the bottom of the leaf is an explanation for determining the five movable feasts of Septuagesima Sunday, Quadragesima Sunday, Easter, summer ember days and Pentecost, by means of the *claves.* These texts, in turn, are followed by a table for the years 1441–64, with phases of the moon on certain days, specifying the length of the conjunction or opposition. All of these texts and much more occur on the thirteen leaves constituting part 1.

Part 2, the longest chunk and most cohesive segment of the volume (ff. 14r– 138v), contains extensive pieces of the *Legenda aurea* of Jacobus de Voragine.[11] Given the calendrical character of part 1, the following part is complementary since the chapters are arranged according to the year, beginning with extracts *de tempore* followed by those *de sanctis.*

Part 3 (ff. 139r–73v) contains an anonymous letter to John Huss written in 1439 after the Council of Constance; it is followed by thirty-five articles on the erroneous dogmatic teaching of the Greek Church, written in the circle of the papal court during the endeavor to reconcile the Greek and Roman Churches at the Council of Ferrara and Florence in 1437–39. Part 4 (ff. 174r–269v), which consists primarily of two Latin-German vocabularies, one for nouns and one for verbs, also includes, added as afterthoughts, short notes on drunkenness, the virtues of the mass, and a brief passage giving instructions on copying (which is both poorly composed, in bad Latin, and carelessly written).

With respect to physical format, there is little to admire in this composite codex. The script is serviceable but not elegant, the page layout varies from text to text, and the decoration is crude and sparse throughout. Despite its homely appearance, the volume must have been an extremely valuable reference work in the monastery, where it was chained for easy access. Members of the religious community that owned it could determine and verify dates of vital importance with respect to the liturgical calendar, locate appropriate passages drawn from the *Legenda aurea,* consult the most recent tracts about the nature of erroneous dogma, and consult its Latin-German dictionaries. This bound

---

11. The arrangement of the extracts from the *Legenda aurea* is as follows, with numbers referring to Roman numerals in T. Graesse's edition (Leipzig, 1846): 1 De adventu domini; 6 De nativitate domini; 13 De circumcisione domini; 14 De epiphania domini; 31 De septuagesima; 32 De sexagesima; 33 De quinquagesima; 34 De quadragesima; 35 De jejunio quatuor temporum; 53 De passione domini; 54 De resurrectione domini; 70 De letania majori et minori; 72 De adscensione domini; 73 De sancto spiritu; 37 De purificatione beatae Mariae virginis; 51 De annuntiatione dominica; 99 De sancto Jacobo majore; 131 De natiuitate beatae Mariae virginis; 145 De sancto Michaele archangelo; 162 De omnibus sanctis; 163 De commemoratione animarum; 182 De dedicacione ecclesiae; 86 De natiuitate sancti Johannis baptistae.

volume must have served well as a manual of *auctoritas* for the institution that produced, used, and preserved it.

If we move into the realm of miscellaneous manuscripts compiled and often produced by individuals for their personal use, the subject must be viewed somewhat differently, for one is considering the intentions and interests of their owners. Scholars must ask, on the one hand, what the form and contents of a volume reveal about the particular interests of that person and, on the other hand, how the volume fits contextually within a specific cultural milieu. Two examples from the Beinecke collection illustrate the issue.

Marston MS 48 was actually called "Humanistic Commonplace Book" by its previous owner, Thomas E. Marston.[12] In physical format, it is significantly different from the two preceding examples; with respect to its use, it presumably fulfilled a special need for the unidentified Italian humanist who produced and owned it. Regrettably, the volume is no longer in its early binding, so it is difficult to reconstruct its former external appearance. Even so, its tall and narrow proportions (290×107 mm) suggest a portable format not seen in the codices produced for institutional purposes; one can easily envision its Renaissance owner sticking the manuscript into the deep fold of his garment and then pulling it out for consultation. The physical composition of the volume is also unusual in that quires are constructed of very large and bulky gatherings of paper. Of the four remaining quires, the first consists of fifty-two leaves, the second and fourth of seventy leaves, and the third of fifty-eight. It is likely that each gathering was once a discrete booklet and perhaps served the purpose of a modern-day paper pad or spiral-bound notebook in which a scholar would take notes; it is also possible to speculate that in the third quarter of the fifteenth century, when the texts were copied, the booklets may have sat on the shelf or been carried around as discrete entities, only to be bound in a later period.[13] In addition, the first quire is dated 1464 in the upper margin of the first leaf. Since one of the final leaves in the second quire is dated 1457, the booklets are not currently arranged in the order in which they were written.

Whereas the first composite codex considered above (MS 377) was apparently produced in booklet format with the intention that it would be bound into a codex, the notebook structure of this Renaissance manuscript implies a different reason for the method of production. Its design suggests that the owner was keeping these notes in a format intended for convenient personal use. Paper, not parchment, was used throughout. Little attention was devoted to

---

12. See B. A. Shailor, *Catalogue*, 3:83–93, for the complete catalog entry.

13. The patterns of dirt and stains on the first and last leaves of each notebook support the theory that each had a separate existence before being compiled into a single volume.

such codicological niceties as prickings, rulings, or anything other than the plainest decoration consisting of initials, paragraph marks, or headings highlighted in red or ocher. Given its modest appearance, the volume was certainly not conceived as a commercial product to be sold.

And what of the contents? The main fifteenth-century humanistic hand entered almost exclusively extracts and paraphrases from classical and Renaissance texts.

Notebook 1 (ff. 1–52) is totally devoted to quotations from Columella's treatise *On Agriculture* and Pliny the Elder's *Natural History;* all the extracts were copied according to the order of the text.

The passages in notebook 2 are somewhat more wide-ranging, though one can discern an interest in later Latin authors, especially in biographers and historians. Among those writers included are Valerius Maximus, Diogenes Laertius (in the Latin translation of Ambrogio Traversari), Josephus (in the Latin translation of Rufinus), Suetonius, Justinus, and Aulus Gellius. Notebook 3 appears to have a less thematic structure; the fifty-eight leaves contain quotations and paraphrases from Plautus, Cicero, Vegetius, Seneca, Plutarch, Walter Burley, and Pliny the Younger. The third notebook concludes as well with a booklist of ninety titles, mainly humanistic, many of which are followed by an evaluation in florins.

Between notebooks 3 and 4 there seems to be a lacuna, for the text on folio 181r begins in medias res with extracts from books 9 and 10 of Servius's commentary on Virgil (the Roman numeral IX is entered at the top of f. 181r; see fig. 4). The Servius extracts are then followed by portions of Quintilian and of George Trebizond's *Rhetorica.* The final forty-five pages of this seventy-leaf gathering contain many Latin and Italian texts, including much unidentified vernacular poetry written by later owners, the earliest of whom made additions probably at the end of the fifteenth century or the beginning of the sixteenth. It is clear that the final forty-five leaves had been left blank by the original owner, who ceased making entries on folio 204v.

This Renaissance manuscript, composed of notebooks containing the systematically arranged entries of its owner, probably served as a valuable source of relevant quotations and notes. Although the criteria used for inclusion in these notebooks may not always be readily discernible by the modern-day cataloger, this "miscellaneous" collection bears evidence of much use by its compiler, who frequently entered *nota* signs and pointing hands to mark passages of special interest. One also wonders how many other similar notebooks were made and used by the humanistic scholar who wrote in these.

The final Beinecke manuscript has been called the Wagstaff Miscellany, in

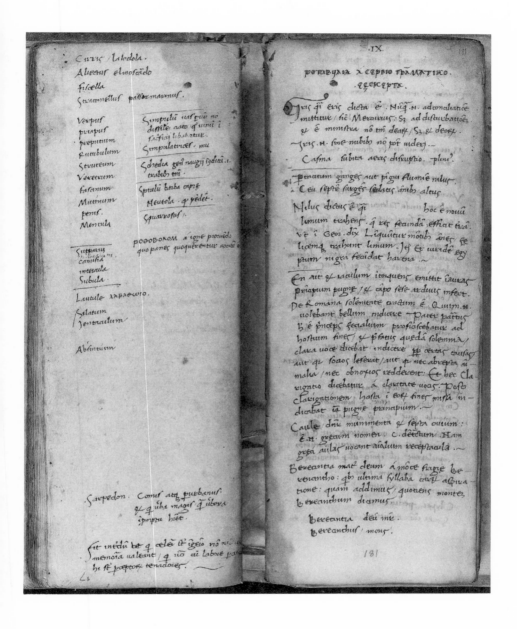

Fig. 4. Yale University, Beinecke Rare Book and Manuscript Library, Marston MS 48, ff. 180v–81r

honor of its former owner, David Wagstaff. It is the rattiest looking of the
codices under discussion and the most complex codicologically and textually
speaking. Whereas Marston MS 48 exhibits some degree of intellectual and
literary coherence, this volume is more encyclopedic in nature and function.[14]

Beinecke MS 163 is large in size, with many leaves measuring three
hundred-by-two hundred millimeters. Composed of 193 leaves of parchment
of uneven quality, its collation is irregular: individual gatherings range from
four to ten leaves. The page layout changes from text to text, with most leaves
being only frame ruled to delineate the written space; some leaves are unruled.
There was little consideration for the consistency of overall presentation of the
volume beyond the approximate size and proportions of the leaves. The elaborate binding, which was designed to protect the book, is now extremely well
worn. The codex is covered with tawed skin, originally pink in color, but only
traces of the color remain. The envelope flap to cover the fore edge has been
partially cut away.

The contents of the volume are fascinating: it has everything a fifteenth-
century member of the English gentry might want or need to know of a
scientific, legal, or medical nature, with much more inserted wherever space
would permit. Treatises on hunting and hawking are intermingled with a parlia-
mentary text and wine recipes. Medical advice (for people and horses), prog-
nostications, and poetry all are incorporated within.

The first item, the *Historia septem sapientum Romae* occupies the first two
quires and is signed by its owner John Whittokysmede (1410–82), a member
of Parliament for constituencies in Somerset and Wiltshire. Unlike the preceding volume, after this point most of the beginnings and conclusions of texts do
not correspond so neatly with the quire structure; and instead of a single
individual using the same style of writing (as in Marston MS 48), here there
appear to be two main scribes. In one instance, even, the scribe writing the
Confession on folios 179r–83v begins in Anglicana formata only to lapse into a
more cursive grade as the text proceeds. Many other hands have added abundant notes and texts in the margins and blank spaces throughout the codex.

The texts and the page formats used for each text vary widely. For example,
on folio 55v several of the many medical recipes for horses were added in a
later hand in English; on the facing recto, actually the beginning of a bifolium
stuck into the gathering, is the neat and orderly beginning of a long collection
of 185 cooking recipes (f. 56r). A sharp break in the physical format and
structure of the codex also occurs at folios 101–3, where the *Tractatus mirab-*

---

14. See B. A. Shailor, *Catalogue,* 1:216–23, for the complete catalog entry.

ilis aquarum is immediately followed by miscellaneous medical recipes in English (ff. 101v–2v). The last leaf of the gathering (f. 102) has been trimmed away, revealing beneath it the beginning of a treatise on astronomy, which is often found in collections of scientific writings (see fig. 5). The conclusion of this work on astronomy, carefully written and attractively decorated with pen-flourished initials throughout (ff. 103r–12v), is followed by an unidentified poem in Latin on a leaf of the central bifolium.

The volume meanders along in this seemingly random fashion, with more than thirty-five discrete texts bound together; this number of items would be far greater if one were to separate out and distinguish among various notes, verses, charms, and individual recipes. After identifying and describing each text and segment of this codex, the cataloger can truly appreciate the prodigious effort required to locate exemplars for each of the texts within and the effort involved in copying them.

The volume ends with what may originally have been a separate booklet once composed of ten leaves, written in an uneven Anglicana script, perhaps a century earlier than the rest of the manuscript. The leaves are smaller in size, and there is a three-column format to accommodate the text, which lists emperors, kings, and archbishops and their sees. This portion of the codex seems to have been inserted as an afterthought, perhaps as an expedient way to preserve a disbound quire.

The entire volume, as the leaves reproduced in figure 5 suggest, shows signs of wear and heavy use; some recipes include marginal notations regarding their efficacy. Although one might question the literary quality of the texts contained within, its practical and didactic value for its owner is readily apparent and provides a conceptual framework for understanding the codex.

For the cataloger of medieval and Renaissance manuscripts, the so-called miscellaneous manuscripts encompass a broad range of types, from a handsomely produced collection of sermons and treatises to the careful notes of a Renaissance humanist. In each case, however, there is an underlying principle of organization that helps the modern-day cataloger and scholar to explain both the physical format and the contents of the volume. The historical context for a volume (rarely discussed within a catalog entry) provides invaluable insight into the function of each volume within the culture that produced it.

If I had it to do all over again at the Beinecke collection or if I were starting in on another collection, I would try to describe more explicitly and consistently the relationship between the structure of the codex and its texts; I would speculate on the apparent principle or principles of organization and would place each volume more firmly in its cultural milieu. The end result would, I

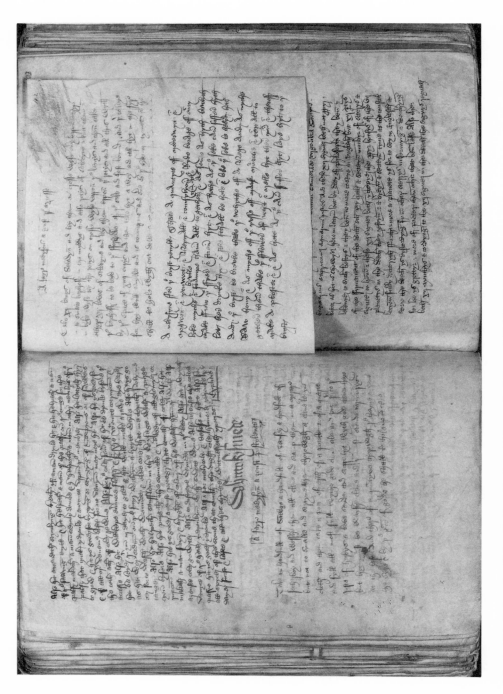

Fig. 5. Yale University, Beinecke Rare Book and Manuscript Library, MS 163, ff. 101v–2r

believe, be the recognition that miscellaneous manuscripts were seldom "miscellaneous" for the audiences or individuals that produced, read, and used them. To label them as such today (without a more specific nomenclature or taxonomy) hinders our efforts to understand the manuscripts and their cultural context.

Retractations

James J. O'Donnell

As its introduction makes clear, this book is a self-exemplifying artifact. It is a codex miscellany devoted to the study of the codex miscellany. To a specialist in late antique texts like myself, accustomed to dismissing the miscellaneity of manuscript contents to get at the one or two items of ancient descent that are of real and pressing interest, it is refreshing and intriguing to be held up in my headlong rush and forced to problematize what I have been eager to dismiss.

That eagerness to dismiss is endemic in the category. "Miscellaneity" as a defining characteristic of manuscript collections is a palpably false unity that covers what we *perceive* to be disorder. It is a Borgesian category: that class of manuscripts that belongs to no class of manuscript. The exercise of attending the remarkably collegial and animated colloquium where the chapters in this book first had life breathed into them, and now the rereading of the printed texts, has the effect of bringing that definition into the foreground of our consciousness and so of destroying, or at least sharply limiting, it. The failures to classify that are brought together in these studies are implicit criticisms of our ability to classify, and in seeking the principles of order that animate these books, we find instructive revision to our instinctive habits of classification.

It is also important to recognize that at least one fundamental change has come over the making of books since these manuscript collections were put together, and it needs to be borne in mind as a constituent element of the incomprehension that separates us from medieval bookmakers. I do not refer precisely to the introduction of print but to the ensuing industrialization of bookmaking. Once books became a mass-market product, it was inevitable that adjustment of the contents to the new, much larger market and its tastes would ensue. One important quality of the machine-made book is transparency of purpose and lucidity of organization. To sell a book, you must make clear to your buyer what the book is. In Hollywood terms, this means that "high concept" is better than "low concept."[1] In the conditions of the early history of the printed book, this meant a kind of distinguishing and packaging of the written product in discreet units or in collections whose coherence would be transparent to a broad public.

We inherit that expectation. When, then, we come to study medieval manuscripts, which we easily imagine as books quite like ours only lovingly hand-produced, what baffle us most readily are precisely those aspects of these books that take advantage of the comparative latitude they enjoyed by reason of not being directed to a larger market. Each chapter in this collection (and in this is the collection's own miscellaneity) addresses the individuality and idiosyncrasy of one or a few manuscripts, ranging in date over seven centuries and in location over most of the geographical spread of western Europe. But in so doing, the gradual, cumulative impact is to make us more sensitive to what the editors have called "the whole book," that is, the totality of the book *and its functions* in its medieval settings, redirected from our modern expectations to a broad range of medieval contexts.

In the case of E. Ann Matter's study, for example, we get to move behind modern expectations of the edition of a famous theologian's writings (the sort of text of Alcuin that Matter herself labors to produce and whose identity has been constructed at discrete times in the modern era)[2] to the bookmaking concerns of a period much closer to his own time. *Schoolbook* turns out to be a rewarding piece of taxonomy to apply: it gives us a context and a purpose quite different from that which we bring to these texts, but one that suddenly dissolves the miscellaneity into a quite satisfactory order. Similarly, Sylvia Huot's focused study of a single manuscript reveals a principle of order (Mar-

---

1. A proposed sitcom about three blondes who live with a chimp and a bodybuilder would be an example of high-concept thinking, while a sensitive, low-key drama about homely, middle-aged people who live in a nondescript house and muddle through life without drugs, firearms, or detectable opportunity for sexual arousal is very low concept indeed.

2. See L. Jardine, *Erasmus: Man of Letters* (Princeton, 1993), for the way the collected works of the Fathers offered a vehicle for a sixteenth-century publishing entrepreneur to shape and project a vision of the cultural organon of his own time; equally interesting is H. Weigel, *Nur was du nie gesehn wird ewig dauern: Carl Lachmann und die Entstehung der wissenschaftlichen Edition* (Freiburg im Breisgau, 1989), which shows Lachmann "inventing" Lessing by paying him the tribute of editing his collected works, a novelty at that time for so recent an author. In going through the newspapers of the eighteenth century and retrieving Lessing's critical essays, Lachmann was in fact creating a literary work that had never existed and, by bringing it together with Lessing's other works, was creating a new Lessing who had never really existed.

ian devotion) otherwise veiled from us by the rebarbativeness of that ideology to modern scholarly preconceptions.

In other ways, the studies presented here dissolve the perceived miscellaneity of their targets and in so doing eat away at our presumptions about what makes books. Stephen G. Nichols's chapter looks in a way backward rather than forward and reminds us that the codex itself as principle of organization is a contingent thing, implicitly comprehensive and inclusive by contrast to other ways of organizing texts. Our expectation that the exploitation of a medium of communication is simultaneous with its introduction is a false one, and the medieval trajectory of the codex book reminds us that the exploitation of the medium was elaborated in stately stages over most of a millennium.[3]

With Ralph Hanna III's discussion of the conditions of production we come to a pragmatic consideration of the alternatives to genre as organizing principles in a setting in which even the language of the manuscript is a variable consideration. The studies by Julia Boffey and A. S. G. Edwards form a triptych with Hanna's piece in a way. Boffey uses a modern editorial kind of question (tracing John Lydgate's "minor poems," a phrase already embodying a generic judgment of great importance) to show how the boundaries between the physical and the intellectual conditions of production are important but difficult to trace, with precisely the intellectual conditions the hardest to reconstruct. Edwards shows a late stage in manuscription collection, when the future is beginning to be discernible. The figure "Chaucer" begins to be an organizing feature in manuscripts, and his aggrandizement means emphasis on the large and important work, with then a deliberate attempt to orchestrate a place for the lesser works on a charted landscape. We are not quite yet at the stage I spoke of earlier, where we create the author by collecting and organizing the works, but one can just begin to see here the first intimations of such an inclination.

Two of the most tantalizing pieces in this collection offer a different reminder: that even our idea that a physical book should be a closed, fixed artifact is an artificial one derived from the economic and physical pragmatics of print culture. Siegfried Wenzel's study of sermon collections shows that the boundary between "collection" and "notebook" is far more fluid in these manuscripts than in modern books; by "notebook" I take him to mean something like an open-ended collection created and arranged for its usefulness to the owner/

---

3. Mary A. Rouse and Richard H. Rouse, *Authentic Witnesses: Approaches to Medieval Texts and Manuscripts* (Notre Dame, 1991), brings together technical studies of the last two decades that demonstrate many aspects of late medieval resourcefulness in exploiting the codex's possibilities; so also does the work of Paul Saenger, especially "Books of Hours and the Reading Habits of the Later Middle Ages," in R. Chartier, ed., *The Culture of Print* (Princeton, 1989), 141–73.

author, making sense purely in terms of the owner/author's needs (which change from time to time), and frozen in time as a definable, catalogable "book" only when the life goes out of it, when the owner/author ceases to use it. Such a book is like a house abandoned by its owner: we may enter it and find much of interest for our purposes, even take away a few treasures for ourselves, but often we will shake our head at the disarray, the odd arrangement of possessions, the curious gaps in collections—when, indeed, the house was perfectly livable only a short time before. To extend that metaphor, a sermon "collection" begins to be a bit more like a bed and breakfast establishment, inhabited by the owner and used in obvious ways, but still made open to a public clientele as well. The modern printed book, to extend the metaphor past the breaking point, is a discount chain motel, deliberately made lifeless in the interests of universal utility.

The fascinating Munich manuscript that Georg N. Knauer displays is just such a disorderly house of extraordinary interest. The translation of the *Batrachomyomachia* that he extracts from it is a pearl of great price, and Knauer's study has the merit of painstaking "archaeological" reconstruction of the site in which it is found, with profit for both our knowledge of the poem's translation history and our knowledge of Reuchlin and his rich intellectual milieu.

We return at the end of this collection of papers to miscellaneity in its most diverse form. Barbara A. Shailor, a distinguished cataloger of medieval manuscripts, reports, like a nineteenth-century explorer back from a remote continent, on specific challenges to taxonomy and interpretation that individual manuscripts and fragments pose. Read in the context of the other chapters in this book, her discussion shows clearly the power and the limits of the notion of miscellaneity, as well as the value to be found repeatedly in breaking through the crust of that notion and using it as a marker that puzzles of particular interest and difficulty lie beneath the surface.

I suggest that it is here also that the value of the approach taken in the colloquium and in this book becomes clear. "Miscellaneity" arises as a class of the unclassed, a scandal to our attempts to wrestle the past into an order and shape comfortable to ourselves. The value of these studies taken together is that they allow no settled pursuit of a single trajectory of interpretation or ideology. They repeatedly derail the reader's expectations—just as the manuscripts studied here have done—and represent by implication elements of diversity in medieval Latin and vernacular culture that are otherwise likely to be subdued into silence and order. If this book leaves those elements gabbling their multiple messages at us excitedly and reminds us that this diversity is the natural condition of humankind and human culture, then precisely in the disorderliness of this volume will its excellence be perceived. The reader who cherishes that cheerful raffishness in this volume will find that it is a book that has not yet had the life sucked out of it by the process of publication—one that lives robustly in the way its derailed expectations startle the reader into fresh perceptions of order.

Index